ART FOR ALL

ART FOR ALL

How to Buy
Fine Art for
Under $300

Alan S. Bamberger

Wallace-Homestead Book Company
Radnor, Pennsylvania

To my wife,

Louise,

and to our two wonderful sons,

Elliot and Nicholas

Published in Radnor, Pennsylvania 19089, by Wallace-Homestead,
a division of Chilton Book Company

Designed by Anthony Jacobson
Manufactured in the United States of America

Library of Congress Cataloging in Publication Data

Bamberger, Alan S.
Art for all : how to buy fine art for under $300 / Alan S.
Bamberger.
p. cm.
Includes index.
ISBN 0-87069-692-0
1. Art—Collectors and collecting—United States. 2. Art—
Economic aspects—United States. I. Title.
N5201.B36 1994
707'.5—dc20 94–5897
CIP

1 2 3 4 5 6 7 8 9 0 3 2 1 0 9 8 7 6 5 4

Contents

Part III: How to Find Affordable Art

Part IV: Specific Types of Affordable Art

Appendices

Acknowledgments

Plenty of artists, art experts, program directors and art business professionals took time out of their busy schedules in order to help me accurately convey the following affordable art information to you. Since much of the art that they represent is underappreciated at best, we not only had to introduce people to it, but in many instances, also had to figure out workable ways of locating, evaluating and sometimes even pricing it. I would especially like to thank the following people (in no particular order) for their invaluable contributions.

Harry Rinker (for the concept), Michael Bell, John Garzoli, the San Francisco Art Commission, the California Arts Council, Jeff Gunderson, the Ohio Arts Council, the South Carolina Arts Commission, Jayne Dark, the Iowa Arts Council, the Society of Western Artists, the Mid-America Arts Alliance, the National Watercolor Society, the San Francisco Museum of Modern Art Rental Gallery, Maurizio Martino, Maxine Rosston of the Achenbach Foundation, Harris Stewart, the San Francisco Public Library Art Department, Paul Hertzmann, Bonnie Grossman, Richard Kamler, Sally Denman, Kathleen Manning, John Hayes, Alan McCorkle, Jaye Johnson, Nick Lederer, Kendra Langer, Bob McLeod, the Academy of Art College in San Francisco, R.R. Bowker (a Reed Reference Publishing Company), Drew Steis of Art Calendar, Nancy Reddin, Very Special Arts, the National Institute of Arts and Disabilities, Joe Hosking, Chuck Rosenthal, San Francisco Open Studios, the Lighthouse for the Blind, Bob Colin, Bobbie Hess, Karen Klimak, Sophia Lane, Frances Granau, Bob Pritikin, Brettt Roncelli, Suzanne Lacke, Linda Cabellon-Dever, the National Endowment for the Arts, and all the artists who answered my classified ad in *Artweek*.

Introduction

These days, the words "affordable art" seem almost like a contradiction in terms. You walk into just about any art gallery anywhere, look at the prices of the art hanging on the walls or displayed on the pedestals and about the last word that comes to your mind is "affordable." The happy ending—and I'll tell you this at the beginning—is that not only does affordable art exist, but there's much more of it out there than most people realize.

I was not always aware that this was the case nor was I one to recommend paying as little as possible for works of fine art. The recent evolution of the art market has considerably altered my once conventional orientation, however. For example, the emphasis on art as a source of beauty, drama, pleasure and emotion has gradually given way to art as a source of investment, as an index of financial status or sophistication, or as a means of impressing one's friends. In other words, art collecting has become an increasingly mercenary pursuit.

Money has clouded the picture and become the prime consideration in far too many art business transactions. Dealers pump up prices of the art they sell and attempt to make those prices seem fair and reasonable to collectors. Artists get caught up in the gallery scene and contribute to the problem by finding the most expensive artists whose work seems comparable to theirs and attempting to charge those same prices. On the client end, collectors fall victim to believing that dollars equate with quality and that the more it costs, the better it must be. All this has led to art prices spiraling out of reach of the great majority of the population.

Some art dealers have the nerve to say that art is not for the masses anyway, but only for that small percentage of the population knowledgeable enough to understand, appreciate and, of course, afford it. These elitists probably have no idea that, in recent years, attendance at American art museums alone has approached eighty million visitors annually (attendance at all museums and related public institutions is well over six hundred million admissions annually)! This means that if what the dealers say is true, only a select few thousand of these many millions have any knowledge of or interest in collecting art, regardless of whether or not they can afford it.

While doing a television interview several years ago, a man phoned in to ask me about what he called the "Cheap Art Manifesto." When I asked him to explain, he told me that this was the idea of art being affordable and accessible to everyone. I was amused by his naïveté and replied that people compete to own the best art and the way that they compete is with dollars—the more a collector wants a Van Gogh, for instance, the more he must be willing to spend because plenty of other collectors want to own it, too. For that reason, I went on, the best quality art will always be out of financial reach of the average individual. Nothing more needed to be said as far as I was concerned. But as time passed, I got to thinking more and more about this "Cheap Art Manifesto." Why shouldn't everyone be able to afford art?

Much of the established art world believes that the only worthwhile art is art that costs a significant amount of money. Nothing else deserves even a second look beyond the possiblity that it may be momentarily entertaining. When the worthwhile art that I liked—or thought I liked because it was accepted by the art estabilshment—finally got so expensive that I could no longer afford it, I decided to look elsewhere and see whether affordably priced art can be worthwhile too.

At first, I believed that this would be a fruitless task and that, in the end, I would probably have to be satisfied with my collection as it stood. The results of my search turned out to be quite the opposite, however. I discovered that the so-called expensive, worthwhile art represents only a minute fraction of one percent of all the art in existence, much of which happens to be worthwhile, too. Now, not only do I have a wide variety of art to collect (and money left over after I buy it), but you or anyone else can experience the same degree of success once you understand and develop the skills necessary to recognize, locate and acquire affordable art.

If those in the business insist on pricing art out of reach of 99% of the population and, in so doing, deny them the pleasures of collecting, something has to be done. As you will see, this is a problem with a multitude of solutions—thousands upon thousands of works of art that you can afford regardless of your income. The "Cheap Art Manifesto" is about to be brought to life.

Before learning about this wonderful art, though, it is necessary to explore and understand a bit about art as a commodity and about how the conventional art business works. Far too many people have been indoctrinated into believing that patronizing the established art business is the one and only option for serious collectors. With appropriate background information, this pattern can be broken and new and different ideas about art and collecting be introduced and taken seriously. Changing your fundamental beliefs and attitudes about what the art business and art collecting are all about will open your eyes to the fantastic world of affordable art.

Part I

Looking at Art the Old Way

1 Art and the Art Business

When you talk about art that everyone can afford, you talk about a concept very foreign to the art business establishment. Few in that realm are interested in hearing anyone suggest that, as a collector, you may be able to leave \$5,000, \$10,000, \$20,000 and \$50,000 works of art behind, substitute \$300, \$100, \$50 or even \$20 pieces in their places and achieve not only the same collecting goals, but also the same levels of personal satisfaction that owning the expensive pieces provides.

To suggest that a painting costing less than \$300 can have anywhere near the significance or impact of a \$20,000 painting is a radical idea. The overwhelming majority of dealers who support high prices instantly reject this notion. To them, compared to a \$20,000 painting, a \$300 one is little more than junk and that's that. This may be true in their eyes, but is it true everywhere? There is, after all, a huge conflict of interest inherent in any such value judgment emanating directly from the art business establishment.

Webster's New World Dictionary defines the word "art" as "human ability to make things; creativeness." Turn this definition around and you have "art" being those things that are the products of human creativity. No reference is made to price, rarity, what art looks like, or any other special circumstances or characteristics that qualify something as art.

This means that there's an awful lot of art in the world. When you take a look around, though, the opposite seems to be true. The art that you consistently read or hear about or see for sale at galleries does not appear to exist in great quantities and, to make matters worse, unless you're wealthy, you can't afford it anyway.

This happens because many in the art business establishment obscure the idea of what art is collectible by controlling what you see, how much you see, how much it costs, and how you are informed about it. They define art differently than *Webster's* out of necessity, the necessity being that art dealing is a business and a business has to make money in order to survive.

This may seem perfectly logical—all businesses have to make money in order to survive—but by examining how the art business is set up, you begin to see the remarkable financial impact that structure has on prices.

No formal studies have been done in this area, but estimates suggest that each and every artist who is represented by a gallery is, to varying degrees, responsible for the livelihoods of as many as ten individuals. These people include gallery owners and staffs, art consultants, art book and periodical publishers, art writers and critics, staffs of art periodicals, art bookstores, museum staffs, advertising people, art show promoters, framers, manufacturers of artist supplies, and art supply stores. You can imagine how much money has to be generated by art sales in order to make the whole system work and what the people who patronize it have to believe about what they're getting for that money.

How Art Dealers Influence Collectors

Art dealers position themselves as experts, authorities, arbiters of taste, trend setters, or fashion spotters. Collectors, in turn, become convinced that they need dealers to dictate what types of art they are supposed to buy for their collections. This would be fine if all art and artists were represented equally, but they're not. The problem is that expensive art receives an incredibly disproportionate amount of attention. Even when art isn't expensive to begin with, after being selected and exhibited by mainstream galleries, it almost always ends up being so.

Many dealers depersonalize art by separating out the artists from marketing and sales presentations. Human aspects of art are minimized or, at worst, ignored altogether and replaced with investment-oriented information, statements about how famous artists are or who owns their art, hints that availability may be limited and talk that prices could go up at any time. Attention is diverted away from how and why art comes into being; personal meanings that art holds for artists or conveys to collectors become irrelevant. The result is that works of art are transformed from creative human endeavors into status symbols, commodities like stocks and bonds, fashion statements, rarities, and marks of sophistication. According to the dealers, of course, these things cost money. (The art/money relationship deserves special attention and will be the subject of the next chapter).

Art dealers promote the idea that good art is hard to find and that they're the only ones who know how to find it. Because they supposedly possess all this knowledge that you don't, you have to go along with them. In reality, they don't want you looking for art on your own because that cuts them out of the profit picture. Wonderful art is everywhere and plenty of people who are not in the art business know where to find it. The further good news is that they don't charge a penny for telling you where it is.

The art business promotes the idea that the process of creating art is expensive. Collectors assume that the time, effort, labor and overhead involved in producing art are substantial and that, therefore, it has to sell for a lot of money. This is true in some cases, but in most, it's not. You'd be surprised at how low the selling price can be while still allowing the artist to make money. Dealers don't tell you this, though, because they'd be hurting their own business if they did.

Get Back to Basics

As long as your views about art are based exclusively on what you hear from art dealers at art galleries, you're not going take affordable art seriously and you certainly won't feel good about buying it. You have to get back to basics and experience art at its most fundamental levels without all of this art business interference. Put aside your preconceived notions about money, rarity, sophistication, taste, how famous an artist is, who knows the most about art, what's right or wrong to buy, and what is involved in creating a work of art. Approach art collecting with an open mind, a willingness to learn and a sense of adventure. A vast and varied art community is waiting to welcome you with open arms.

For starters, imagine yourself sitting alone in a room and facing a piece of art—any piece of art. Imagine that you know absolutely nothing about this art and nothing about the artist who created it. Instead of trying to figure out how much it's worth, how your friends might react to it or what the experts might think, turn inward and get in touch with your own response.

What happens to you when you look at this art? How does the art make you feel? What do you think about when you look at this art? Pay attention to your own reactions and make this a completely personal experience. This is how you begin to determine whether any special bond exists between you and the art—not by looking around at others' reactions or listening to who says what.

No matter how much or how little it costs, or how famous or unknown the artist is, it's going to have an impact on you, a unique and special impact. The art will communicate to you, you will respond. No one else will respond in quite the way that you do.

Now imagine that the artist comes into the room and sits down with you. It's just you, the art and the artist. The artist describes this work of art and explains the ideas behind it. He talks about its meaning and significance. He talks about why he made it, how he made it, how long it took, what went through his mind while he was making it and what he thinks about it now that it's done. You ask whatever questions you have about him and his art until you are completely satisfied with his answers and fully understand how and why this art came into being.

This is the human way to look at art—the honest way. It's what art, art collecting and experiencing art are all about. You may never be able to interview each and every artist whose work you like, but you can certainly learn to focus your attentions on art people and away from money people.

Artists conceive, create and produce for themselves and their fellow human beings based on deep personal convictions, not financial considerations. Each and every work of art provides a glimpse into the being of the artist who creates it. Artists use their art to communicate to others the world as they see it.

In the end, though, you decide what you want in your art and when you see a piece that you think you might like, you decided whether or not it has what you're looking for. Don't expect others to tell you what only you can tell yourself. Even the artists can only go so far in helping you. The important questions are the ones you ask yourself and the final decisions are yours.

Here are the types of considerations that you should substitute for preconceived notions and art business dictates:

- What do I enjoy looking at?
- What makes me feel good?
- What kinds of art best express my feelings?
- What do I want to look at again and again in the coming years?
- What makes me see things from new and exciting perspectives?
- What arouses my emotions?
- What transports me to far away places?
- What expands my consciousness and ways of looking at reality?
- What makes me think about new ideas?
- What provides glimpses of how things were in the past, are in the present, or can be in the future?

The established art business seems almost out of place in all of this. In particular, what special significance do high prices have when it comes right down to you and the art? Will that $20,000 painting supply you with more of what you're looking for than the $300 one? Will it be more thought provoking, more meaningful, and if so, by how much and in whose eyes? The answers depend on your own personal requirements and have little relation to price.

Unfortunately, most people don't believe this. Honest, human ways of looking at art are the exception rather than the rule. The art business continues to prosper with those who can afford the prices patronizing established galleries and spending tons of money on expensive art. Those who can't, do nothing. Millions of potential collectors never even get started collecting because they don't think that they can afford anything good.

Insufficient understanding of the art/money relationship is at the core of all this. Before any changes can come about, people need to realize how art prices are set, how they're maintained and why they're set so high so often. A look behind the scenes at dollars and cents issues is necessary to move art buyers away from overpriced art and toward the discovery and exploration of new, exciting, engaging and, most importantly, affordable areas of collecting.

2

Art Prices Are Out of Control

To focus purely on art prices is to focus on the art market in a most unflattering light. The good part about this exercise, though, is that once it's over with and the dynamics of pricing art become better understood, you won't feel so confined by established art business dictates. In order to reach the overwhelmingly positive goal of collecting art without guilt, these negatives must first be dealt with.

The surprising aspect of art prices as they stand is that hardly anyone ever bothers to question them. Walking into a gallery, for example, and asking why a particular painting costs $10,000 is tantamount to insulting the dealer's integrity. At the very least, it's inappropriate art buying etiquette.

You're supposed to accept art prices as validating the art and be increasingly impressed by art the more expensive it is—whether you like it or not. If a painting only costs $5,000, for instance, supposedly it's not as good as if it costs $8,000. That's the way you've most likely been taught to think, but it's not necessarily the way things are. Inappropriate art buying etiquette or not, high art prices must continually be questioned and questioned hard.

To begin with, art is a confusing commodity. Of all material goods produced by man, art is probably the most difficult to understand in practical terms:

- It has no obvious function in society, as does a car or a washing machine, for example.
- No clear relationship exists between price and product.
- A vast variety of new art is constantly being created and added to the huge amount that's already out there.
- Anyone can call himself an artist.
- Anyone can call himself an art dealer.
- Anyone can call whatever he creates "art" and ask whatever price he feels like asking for it.

Now if the world were a perfect place, art buyers would know as much about art as they do about other consumer products, in spite of this bizarre set of circumstances. Complete disclosure would be the norm. Art would be bought, sold and traded in free-market settings, as are other consumer goods, and art prices would be set according to what those free markets would bear. You would be fully informed about the significance of whatever you were interested in buying, your questions would be answered and all selling prices would be justified by art-market data. You could then decide what to purchase based on accurate information in combination with your own personal tastes.

Unfortunately, that's not the way things are. The art business only appears to be a free-market system. True, every work of art you see for sale has a price attached to it and a story behind it. The art business seems to create order out of chaos by setting those prices and presenting the art, but this can be deceiving. The big giveaway is that art prices end up being awfully high and explanations end up being awfully fancy an awful lot of the time.

Why Art Is So Expensive

There are three good reasons why art genuinely deserves to be expensive. The first is that it takes a great deal of time, effort, labor, materials and overhead to produce. Casting a bronze sculpture, for example, cost hundreds of dollars at the very least, not including the time involved in creating the image in the first place. If a sculptor spends several months creating an image and then pays to have it cast, you can easily see why a minimum of $4,000 or $5,000 is a fair retail asking price for the finished piece. Likewise, if a painter spends hundreds of hours creating a highly detailed and complex painting, he should be paid at least $4,000 or $5,000 for his efforts. Artists deserve fair wages for their labor and overhead just like anyone else who works for a living.

The second reason concerns supply and demand. Van Gogh paintings, for instance, rarely come onto the market and when one does, plenty of extremely wealthy collectors are prepared, checkbooks in hand, to compete for it. These people might be more willing to joust or duel for the painting and forego the money aspects, but that's not the way the art business works. Paying lots of money is now and will forever remain the single best way to acquire art that is much shorter in supply than it is in demand.

The third reason, related to supply and demand, is that certain works of art are highly important, historically significant, technically superior, products of pure genius. The greatest works of art, just like the greatest talent or the finest products produced in any other field, always command top prices. Only a small percentage of all art falls into this "greatest" category—never quite enough to satisfy the demand for it.

A sad aspect of the art business is that, at times, the not so good reasons why art is expensive tend not only to outnumber but also to overshadow the goods ones. Only a small percentage of art is truly great, truly important, truly rare, truly labor and materials intensive, or in such demand that sellers deserve to charge exhorbitant prices for it.

The vast majority of art falls into the ordinary-to-good category, should be priced far, far less than superior art and according to whatever merits it has. That's not the way it happens, however. Sellers consistently prefer maximizing profits to presenting the facts and concoct or manufacture impressive-sounding explanations to make art seem more valuable than it actually is. They opt for this latter pricing strategy because, obviously, there's a lot more money in it. Here are several ways that they accomplish this:

Pure hype: Sellers recognize popular tastes or trends toward particular types of art and exploit them by using sophisticated marketing techniques. These include publishing glossy promotional brochures, putting on high-profile shows, getting laudatory articles placed in art trade publications, arranging media appearances, doing saturation advertising or mass mailings, or hiring public relations consultants to create auras or mystiques around artists and their art. Consequently, artists appear to be more important than they actually are, their art appears to be more significant than it actually is and high selling prices appear to be more justified than they actually are.

Hype masquerading as scholarship: Art dealers sometimes finance or publish impressive-looking books or exhibition catalogues about artists that they represent. These are designed to look like (and are often confused with) books or catalogues published by academic or scholarly institutions like museums, historical societies or universities. This strategy works for dealers because collectors tend to believe that books or catalogues legitimize art and are only written about important artists. And, of course, art by important artists can only be expensive.

Auction antics: Special interests inflate auction prices to give the impression of either a robust art market or segment of the art market. For example, a dealer with large holdings of a particular artist's work places a piece up at auction and has friends, acquaintances or business associates bid it up to a certain price. That figure is determined in advance and set significantly beyond any amount previously paid for anything else by the artist. The dealer then uses that sales result to justify raising prices on everything that he owns. Collectors accept the increases as realistic because they are only aware of the auction result itself and not of its contrived nature.

Coattail logic: A dealer links a work of art that he is selling to either a highly collectible type of art or art by a famous artist in order to justify a high asking price even though no such relationship exists. For example, a collector is told that a painting he is looking at is as good as a Picasso and that if it were a Picasso, it would cost a million dollars. Since it's not a Picasso, it's only $50,000. This strategy has the effect of making what looked like an expensive price to begin with suddenly look like a great bargain.

Manipulating supply and demand: Sometimes galleries, gallery chains, dealers or artist agents exclusively represent artists' art and position themselves as the sole resources for acquiring that art. They deliberately manipulate markets by limiting the quantities of art that are available for sale at any given moment, thereby creating atmospheres of scarcity. Potential buyers are told that certain pieces are either sold-out or in short supply and are encouraged to get in on the action before it's too late. These practices not only pressure collectors into buying, but also make high prices seem justified. In order to complete the illusion of thriving markets, controlling dealers, galleries or agents arbitrarily raise prices at regular intervals to give the appearance that the art is increasing in value.

Creating the illusion of greatness: The real estate people call this "location, location, location." An art dealer rents gallery space in an upscale business district, creates a beautiful interior with designer furnishings, hires a well-dressed and socially adept sales staff, and has the best food and drink at his art openings. In so doing, he creates the illusion that the quality of his art is related to the location and setting in which it is being sold and is, therefore, superior and deserving of high prices. The real reason for high prices—overhead.

Employing sophisticated display techniques: Galleries use the best wall coverings, the best track lighting, the best frames, the best floor coverings and whatever else is necessary to highlight their art. Properly displayed and lit, almost anything can look like a world-class masterwork. And, of course, world-class masterworks cost money.

Using the mass media: The world's major auction houses, in particular, are the culprits here. Their public relations departments regularly release exceptional and record-setting prices to the news media. The public gets the idea from repeated stories that art performs well financially over time and is deserving of high prices. This broad-based coattail effect impacts virtually all art prices in the upward direction.

Art as Investment

No art price discussion is complete without addressing the fact that numerous art dealers, either overtly or subtly, convey the impression that art makes a good investment. Why do they do this? Because art is a lot easier to sell and a lot easier to price expensively when the people who buy it believe that it increases in value over time.

Art as investment is one of the most powerful misconceptions (and selling tools) advanced by the art business and, perhaps, the greatest stumbling block to people allowing themselves far more freedom of choice in their purchases than they currently do. Attention to money overshadows that placed on the merits of the art itself and, consequently, buyers compromise their personal tastes in favor of possible financial gain. At worst, art is debased to the point where collectors refuse to buy it, no matter how much they like it, unless they believe that it will be worth more in five or ten or fifteen years.

What you are probably not aware of is that a lot less art increases in value over time than you think—a fact that dealers do not often discuss. The great, rare, significant and important art tends to fare the best. Everything else tends to go nowhere and when it does, it's usually down. Finding a $4,000 painting that will be worth $2,000 in ten years is a great deal easier than finding a $2,000 painting that will be worth $4,000 in ten years. This may be disturbing to investor-collectors, but it's absolutely true. In particular, high-priced art that is subject to hype, supply-and-demand manipulations, and other price-bolstering techniques like those you've been reading about, fares poorly once it leaves its controlled gallery settings.

Furthermore, all art, no matter how fairly represented or priced it is to begin with, is worth significantly less the instant you pay for it and walk it out the gallery door. This is due to the commissions that dealers charge to buy and sell art. Few collectors are aware of how large these are because they're built into selling prices and rarely discussed.

In extreme cases, galleries mark prices up 200% to 300% over cost and charge 40% to 60% to private parties who want to resell their art. Average dealer mark-ups range from 50% to 100% and resale commissions between 30% and 50%.

To get an idea of how this impacts your potential profits, paying commissions as low as 20% to buy and 20% to resell (uncommon in the art business) means that the art has to appreciate a full 50% above pre-commission cost before you see your first penny of profit! This takes years or even decades in the huge majority of cases. Compared to the 1% or 2% standard commission in securities transactions, you see how ridiculous it is to consider art in the same category of investment.

The Choice is Yours

The point of all this is not to scare you away from the established art business, but rather to increase your understanding of how it operates. Established galleries sell plenty of high-quality art at fair-market prices. Those of you who have the capital, love art, know what you're looking for and are not buying as an investment can go the established route and build fantastic collections. At least now you have a better idea of where you stand and what the long-range financial implications of your spending are likely to be.

On the other hand, maybe you love art, but don't have the money. Or maybe you have the money, but would rather spend it on something other than art. Or maybe you're beginning to see that high prices do not automatically equate with good art and that traditional art business transactions are not necessarily what they appear to be.

If so, you can step outside of the established mode and still feel good about it. Spending $10, $50, $100 or $200 for a work of art can be a pleasurable and rewarding experience rather than a meaningless, silly or embarrassing one. By substituting the words "pleasure art," "art I love," or "art that's fun" for "investment art," "expensive art," or "status art," you open yourself up to whole new worlds of collecting.

But even in this low-stakes realm, money considerations are not entirely irrelevant. Just a few decades ago, for example, people were replacing their Victorian-era art with the latest abstract and modern looks. Quality Victorian art was to be found not in the art galleries, but in the flea markets and secondhand shops. Only those few people who loved it were buying it and nobody was paying much for it.

And think about Van Gogh (1853–1890). He only sold one painting in his lifetime and for hardly any money. He was almost completely ignored by serious dealers and collectors.

The point of these two examples is that at any given moment, a great deal of art is either not taken seriously or overlooked altogether by those in the mainstream art world. Only with the passage of time do more and more people gradually begin to take notice. In money terms, what starts out selling for little or nothing because nobody wants it slowly begins to appreciate in value as increased recognition leads to increased demand and more formalized structure in the marketplace.

This phenomenon brings us right back to the conventional art business, a system that should never be entirely forsaken. Certain aspects are definitely worth saving. A lot of good has come of the art trade in recent years, particularly relating to research, connoisseurship, scholarship and the introduction of new and sophisticated ways of collecting.

True, these advances have been almost exclusively applied to collecting expensive art, but they're just as applicable to art in even the lowest price ranges. Knowing how to select and buy the way the experts do provides the foundation necessary for building a respectable, compelling and potentially valuable collection regardless of whether your budget is $200 or $20,000,000.

Part II

Looking at Art the New Way

3 Buy Like the Pros

No matter what type of art you're looking to collect, you have to adopt a workable strategy in order to understand, appreciate, locate and eventually own this art. Generally, in the case of the affordable art, you can't simply go down to the corner gallery and ask for it—they won't have it. In dealing with these unstructured, undeveloped markets and art that is not readily available, you need to borrow from the established art business and do exactly what the pros do when they want to explore new, unusual or unfamiliar art that they find attractive or intriguing. Their techniques and methods work for them every time and they can work for you too.

Starting Out

Experts universally agree that before you buy anything, you should know what you like, and once you start buying, you should buy what you like. No matter how great a piece of art sounds, who recommends it, how much it costs or what you read about it, you are the one who has to make the final decision about whether or not you really want to own it. You can do this effectively only after you know what's available, what your tastes are, and where your preferences lie.

The way to start out is simple—look first and buy later. When you read, see or hear about a type of art that seems appealing, prepare to explore it fully. This means finding out as much as possible about who creates and produces it, what its history is, who the better-known artists are, who sells it, why it's significant, who collects it, and how much of it there is. It also means continually monitoring your own personal reactions to what you look at in order to solidify and define your preferences—your favorite colors, mediums, subject matters, sizes, shapes, artists, time periods, and so on.

Never make the mistake of limiting your exposure to those few pieces that you initially come into contact with. By being thorough ahead of time, you avoid making snap judgments based on inadequate information, you gain an overview of the marketplace and you refine your tastes. You also get an idea of the wide variety of available art that you would enjoy owning and you come to realize how much of it is priced within your range. Simply stated, the more you know, the more money you can save.

Select Like the Pros

Anytime you zero in on a particular type of art, your end goal is to select specific pieces that genuinely thrill you—pieces that you would seriously consider buying. The key is in locating a wide variety of resources that sell this art. The more choices you have, the better you'll be able to make fine distinctions when buying and the better your chances of getting art you really love at prices you can live with.

Parts III and IV of this book get specific about how and where to find affordable art and introduce you to some of the variety that exists. Individual chapters recommend procedures for learning about and acquiring certain types of this art and direct you in your initial searches should you decide to follow up on any of them. That's a start, but you need more. Because much of this art is not bought, sold or collected on a formal basis, you have to do some legwork on your own to locate it—legwork that art galleries or art dealers normally do for you. The following directives are designed to help you with this process:

Describe what you're looking for. When you make first contact, no matter who it's with and whether by phone or letter, describe what you're looking for or think you're looking for. Find out whether they have what you want and note when they do.

Ask for names or lists. Always end initial conversations by asking for names of additional dealers, collectors, art teachers, museum curators, artists or anyone else who may be able to help you find what you want. Note and follow up on every lead you get. In the end, you'll have a good working list of potential resources.

Next comes the fun part:

Make on-site visits. Personally visit as many resources as possible and look at all the art that satisfies your basic criteria. When you are unable to visit, request that they send slides or photographs (most places will).

Don't make hasty decisions. Pay special attention to all works that you can see yourself owning. Select a number of pieces—more than you intend to buy—from a variety of resources. A common mistake that less experienced collectors make is to prematurely focus on one or two artworks, believe that these are the only ones that are right for them and that nothing else will ever satisfy. The more art you see, the more you realize the fallacy in this way of thinking.

Collect detailed information. Note essential details of each piece such as where you see it, who the artist is, how much it costs, its size, medium, and so on. Have sellers apply you with data about this art such as exhibit catalogues, artist statements, artist biographies, and photocopies of news articles or reviews that include the artists. When little or nothing printed is available (as is often the case with undercollected art), assemble as much verbal information as you can.

Get photographs. Whenever possible take photographs of interesting pieces home, study them at length and make up your mind at a relaxed pace. When photos are unavailable from sellers, either photograph the art yourself or see whether you can at least get photographs of similar looking pieces.

Evaluate Information Like the Pros

At this point, you have a stack of photographs and information sitting in front of you and you're probably wondering why all the fuss. You like all of this art and you don't see what the printed matter has to do with anything. If you're like most people, you'd probably rather pick your favorites from among the photographs right now and skip the background information.

You can certainly go this route, but let's assume that after comparing photographs you like several pieces equally well and you only want to buy one. Or suppose that you only have enough money to buy one. You can flip a coin if you want, but you have better options. Without much effort, you can learn how to spot the piece that's the best value, the one with the broadest appeal to collectors, the artist with the most potential, and the style that's the most innovative, progressive and significant.

If being able to make these distinctions appeals to you, put the photographs aside for the time being and begin doing what all experienced dealers and collectors do—read what you've been given by the sellers and learn about this art. Build a foundation which will enable you to understand what your selections are all about. Always look for the following information:

- Where, when, why and how particular styles or types of art originated.
- What the art's history is.
- How it has changed or evolved over time.
- Which artists are thought of as its originators.
- Who the better-known artists are and why.
- What collectors like the most and why.
- What the artists or the people who are selling it like the most and why.

No matter what type of art interests you, this information exists and you should be aware of it. In addition to extracting this data from what sellers give you, read whatever books or articles they recommend, speak with whatever authorities they tell you to contact, meet and speak with as many artists as possible, and visit the appropriate museums, galleries, libraries or other institutions. For balance, make sure you include outside experts who have no financial stake in what you buy.

This may sound like drudgery but it's not, especially when you love the art. It's a fascinating and wonderful adventure—or at least it should be. If you ever find the learning process getting tedious, it may be a sign that you've made a wrong choice and that you should be looking for art in other areas. The role that education plays in making your final decisions, in forming a good solid collection, and in purely enjoying what you own cannot be overestimated.

Experts from all facets of the art world continually analyze facts and evaluate data on their way to separating out the best from the rest. Here are some additional tips from the pros that will help you do the same:

Maintain your focus. Once you determine what specific types of art you like, stick with them. The more highly defined your preferences, the easier a time you'll have learning, selecting, evaluating and buying. The quality of your collection will suffer if you spread yourself too thin.

Look at the entire range of what you like. Explore as widely as possible within your chosen realm. Keep abreast of what's going on and who's doing it. Don't go exclusively with one or two artists or one or two sellers. You'll end up with a lopsided collection.

Choose specific artists. Learn about the artists whose work interests you. Have they exhibited at museums, corporations or other locations? Find out whether they've won any awards or participated in any competitions, no matter how small. Look for favorable reviews by art critics and favorable comments from art collectors, scholars, authorities and other respected members of the art community. The more of this you see, the better.

Listen to the authorities. Find out who knows the most about the art you like and take every opportunity to learn from them. Whenever possible, discuss specific artists and works of art—this is an invaluable exercise because it allows you to view art through experienced eyes. Find out which artists they consider good and why, which pieces they consider good and why. Have them show you how they compare and contrast individual works in order to recognize what's good or significant.

Further your education. If you really want to get serious, think about taking a basic art history or art appreciation course at a local museum, art institute, college or university.

Evaluate Art Like the Pros

Once you've got your background information squared away and you have a foundation of basic knowledge from which to operate, you can refocus on those specific pieces you think you'd like to own. Return to your photographs and review them or, better yet, revisit the sellers and see the art again in person. At every step of the way, ask whatever questions you have and keep asking until all have been answered to your satisfaction. Here are some recommendations from the pros on what to look for:

Look at the way the art is put together. See whether it exhibits characteristics like care, attention to detail, thoughtfulness, quality materials, and so on. You want art that is well-crafted and enduring, not sloppy or poorly made.

Look for a balance of concept and technique. An artist may have great ideas but be unable to realize them because he is technically incapable of doing so. This does not mean that his art has to possess the qualities of a Van Gogh or a Rembrandt, but rather that it's reasonably competently done. Professionally executed, finished works of art are what you should look for.

Look for signs of significance and originality. This doesn't mean that what you like has to be an evolutionary breakthrough in the history of art, but rather that it exhibits special qualities on at least some level. Find out whether the art has been done before and if so, for how long and by whom. Decide whether it adds new dimension to what already exists. You want art that's original, engaging, thought-provoking, and exciting. Have sellers and other authorities comment on these and other aspects, and have them back up their statements with facts.

Look for signs of success. Have sellers supply evidence that the art you like is being well-received by the segment of the art community that is the most familiar with it. This is especially important if you're just starting out or are unsure of what you're looking at. It also applies to all art, no matter how much or how little it sells for.

Look for signs of productivity. Artists who produce a lot of art and make concerted efforts to get it out before the public, either by themselves or through dealers, tend to be more serious and dedicated to surviving as artists—and more successful. Even if they give their art away or sell it for very little, this is still a good sign. Also keep in mind that whether or not an artist is alive, the larger the body of art that has been produced, the better the chances that it will be exhibited, promoted and seriously collected at some point in the future.

Examine an artist's total body of work. This doesn't mean that you have to see every single thing the artist has ever created, but rather that you get an overall view of where he has been at various stages in his career. You want to see signs of progress, growth and advancement on both the technical and conceptual levels. Watch out for similar themes being repeated over and over again or recent works which do not possess the intensity, attention to detail or technical acuity of earlier ones.

Find out what the artist does best. The art that an artist does best tends to be the art that collectors want most and, therefore, the art that becomes the most collectible. Artists and sellers will tell you what this art is. Experimental or atypical pieces may not be of the caliber or have the survivability of the better-known works.

Lastly and most importantly, start small and start slowly. When you're finally ready to buy, don't immediately go for the top of the line. Be conservative and try to spend the minimum amount of money possible to get what you like the best. Once you own it, see how you like it, see how it feels, see how it wears over time. In this way, you gradually solidify your tastes without taking any big risks. As you gain experience and confidence, you can work your way up to larger, more complex, less widely accepted, more progressive and controversial, or more expensive pieces if those are your intentions.

Follow these recommendations and you'll become knowledgeable about whatever type of art you like and develop the ability to discriminate between good, better and best, no matter what your budget. Don't believe for a moment that just because the art you like doesn't cost a lot of money that no scholarship, intelligence or connoisseurship has evolved or is in the process of evolving around it. Plenty of examples of what we consider today to be among the world's great works of art went virtually unnoticed and sold for hardly anything when they were first introduced to the public.

Now that you know a bit about selecting any kind of art for your collection, you need to know, in general terms, what affordable art is. Before you can go out looking for it, you have to define it. You need to understand it in the most basic sense so that when you come across it, you'll know how to recognize it. In addition, you won't overlook or ignore art that deserves to be taken seriously.

4 How to Recognize Affordable Art

Affordable art is everywhere and it's easy to recognize once you know how. It can be virtually anything as long as it satisfies four basic requirements—it's original, it's created by an artist, it's for sale, and it falls within a certain price range. These requirements may sound simple, but some explanation is necessary in order for you to understand how vast an amount of art falls into the affordable category. Broadening your definition of what art is increases your freedom of choice in the marketplace.

It's Original

The term "original" means that the art can be anything—and that means *anything*—as long as the artist had direct hands-on participation in the conception, creation and production of the art. Eliminate any preconceived ideas you may have about what qualifies as art.

Because of experiences they've had since childhood, many people have trouble accepting how amazing a variety of art, affordable or otherwise, actually exists. Every one of us is born with a blank slate regarding art, but what happens over time is that our parents, teachers, friends and acquaintances gradually crowd that slate with their opinions until hardly any room for free thinking is left.

Suppose, for example, that you're back in kindergarten and that your art class assignment on this day is to draw an apple. You eagerly take out your purple, green and black crayons and draw a green form shaped like a figure eight with black and purple lines coming out of it. You then make purple, black and green dots all over the back side of the paper and, finally, crush the whole thing up. For whatever reasons you have at that moment, this is an apple. What's more important is that it's your apple, you're proud of it and you think you did a great job making it.

When the art teacher comes by to critique your work, you find out differently. You are gently but firmly informed that you don't crush paper and that an apple is round and red with a place on top for the stem and maybe a leaf or two. You sadly accept this fact, throw away your apple, get a new sheet of paper and draw the art teacher's apple in its place.

The combined effect of this and similar experiences is that your definition of art becomes narrower and narrower and narrower. You are told that art should look a certain way, be made a certain way, mean certain things, be this size, this shape, these colors, have this texture and so forth. If it fails to satisfy any of these conditions, it's bad, incompetent, a bunch of scribbles, trash, junk, stupid and, of course, it's not art.

None of this is true. Art can be a bunch of shoe laces glued to a stick. It can be a piece of mud that's been formed into a face, an upside-down letter "A" carved into a piece of an old car tire, a picture of a dog made out of scraps of fabric, five hundred thumb prints on a sheet of paper—the possibilities are infinite.

When you're not sure whether what you're looking at is art, ask the person who claims to be the artist. Find out whether they thought it up and made it themselves. When that's not possible, ask the seller about the artist and how the art came into being. Keep an open mind, assemble all available printed and verbal information, evaluate it according to the criteria of the previous chapter and make your decisions just like the experts do. If it's not art, you'll know it.

The only confusing aspect of the requirement that the art be original is knowing how to distinguish between original art and fine art reproductions. Reproductions of original works of art are often marketed just like original art, and if you don't know what to look for, you can easily end up owning something that you did not set out to buy. The topic of reproductions versus originals will be fully addressed in the next chapter

It's Created by an Artist

The term "artist" refers to anyone capable of producing original art, and that means *anyone.* An artist can be of any age, any intellectual level, any socio-economic status, any educational background, any state of physical or mental health.

Unfortunately, people tend toward stereotypes in this area too and, by so doing, restrict their collecting options. Artists are thought of as people who drape themselves in smocks and live and work full-time in cluttered studios surrounded by stacks of paintings, drawings, or sculptures. They're seen as eccentric, temperamental, covered with paint splatters, strange dressers, people with unconventional ideas, people who are lost in their own thoughts, and so on.

Artists are not necessarily any of these things. Some may possess certain of these characteristics, but an artist can also be your next-door neighbor, the man who picks up your garbage, a teller at your bank, your doctor, the girl who mows your lawn or the police officer you see at the coffee shop every morning. Never dismiss an individual's art as not being serious or genuine because he or she does not seem like a "real artist" to you.

It's for Sale

The requirement that the art be "for sale" means more than that it simply has a price tag attached to it. It means that it can be for sale *anywhere* and for *any reason.*

Most people have had limited exposure to situations where art is for sale. They believe that conventional art galleries in commercial business districts like malls, town or city centers, shopping plazas or vacation areas are the best places or even the only places to buy art. Ask them where else art is for sale and they'll have no idea.

This "business district" or "vacation destination" art is certainly art, but it's a particular kind of art and not at all representative of the total range of art in existence. It's art that sells well in commercial settings. It can fool you, though, because there's a lot of it and what you see for sale can vary widely from one gallery to the next. You can visit one hundred different galleries, for instance, never see the same type of art twice, but at the same time never realize that, in a commercial sense, you're looking at the same art over and over again. You get the idea that you've seen everything when, in fact, you're barely scratching the surface.

Don't be misled into thinking that conventional galleries represent all the art there is and that no further exploration is necessary. The art they sell is generally pleasant, attractive, decorative, relatively free of controversy, and in line with current tastes and fashions. It tends to fall within standard price ranges that don't change much from gallery to gallery. Much of it is by familiar names or at least by names familiar to the people who buy it. It is the art that works the best within the context of the settings in which it is being sold and nothing more.

The truth is that art can be for sale on the street, at a flea market, at a church bazaar, at a cat show, at an artist's studio, at your next door neighbor's laundry room, out of the back of a station wagon, at a senior center, at a baseball game, wherever. It can be for sale because the artist wants everyone in town to own a piece of his work, because a voice from above ordered him to sell, because he needs the money to buy a van, because he's losing his storage space, because he's going off to Nepal for two years, whatever. Never dismiss art as not being serious or genuine because of circumstances surrounding its sale or where it is being sold. Evaluate it according to the guidelines of the previous chapter and you'll do just fine.

It Falls within a Certain Price Range

Since the subject of this book is affordable art, "a certain price range" will be defined as anywhere from a few dollars on up to about $300 or so.

Just about anyone can afford art at these prices, but the hard part is believing that it actually exists. Not only does it exist, but there is no price level below which an object or item is no longer considered to be art. Forget any preconceived ideas you may have about how much art should cost in order for it to qualify as art.

As previously stated, most people have only seen art for sale in conventional commercial gallery settings. This art tends to cost more than $200 to $300 and, if anything, those figures represent the very low end of the cost continuum. People come to believe, from their repeated gallery exposures, that all art prices start in the low to mid-hundreds of dollars and proceed rapidly upward from there. This is absolutely untrue.

The main reason why conventional gallery art is so expensive is that if the art cost any less it wouldn't be commercially viable. The high prices often have less to do with the art itself than with the profit margins that are necessary for these galleries to stay in business. An art gallery with any degree of overhead expenses would have great difficulty surviving, for instance, if its walls were covered with art costing between $10 and $150. That's why you never see this—not because there's no art available in the lower price ranges. It is available and there's plenty of it. To illustrate this point, each piece of art shown in this book costs less than $300; much of it is substantially less.

Remembering these four requirements will help keep your mind open and awaken you to new art collecting possibilities. Maximize your contacts with art, no matter what it is, who did it, where you see it for sale or how much it costs, and don't pass over or reject anything because of preconceived ideas. So much wonderful art already exists and so many capable artists continually produce more and more fantastic pieces every day that you do yourself a huge disservice by ignoring or dismissing any of it.

Before you begin to explore the affordable marketplace, though, several important cautions are in order. Certain segments of the art business are well aware that the word "affordable" has an unmistakable attractiveness about it and that with proper marketing, that word can be translated into big bucks. The next chapter is about art that is billed as affordable, but really isn't. What's more, a lot of it isn't even art.

5

Affordable Art or Smoke and Mirrors? What to Avoid

This chapter is not about what to collect—everything is OK to collect. It's about making sure that what you end up buying is what you believe you set out to buy. The types of art discussed here fail to satisfy either or both of two of the affordable art requirements—that it be original and that it's created by the artist who conceives it.

Limited Edition Prints that Are Copies of Originals

Once upon a time in the not-too-distant past, a man who owned a commercial printing company went to a fancy art opening at a local gallery. The gallery was showing paintings by a well-known artist. The man looked at one of the paintings, saw the selling price and was amazed at how expensive it was. He walked around the entire gallery, looked at all the other paintings and saw that they were equally expensive. He got to wondering whether other art galleries sold expensive paintings like this too.

The next day, he called various galleries to find out about their paintings. Every dealer he spoke with had expensive pieces for sale so, one by one, he visited these galleries to see what their paintings looked like. He saw all kinds of paintings and they all cost plenty of money. Then it hit him!

"Instead of printing travel brochures and selling them for next to nothing like I do now, I'll make nice big color prints of paintings like the ones that I've been looking at. They'll cost about the same to produce as the travel brochures, but I'll sell these prints for hundreds of dollars each. That sounds expensive, but compared to price tags on the paintings, they'll seem like bargains. I'll market them to people who like the paintings but can't afford them. They'll think they're getting great deals and I'll make tons of money!"

There was one slight problem, however. The man's prints were not original works of art like paintings are. They were copies or reproductions of paintings that were mechanically printed the same way as the illustrations in his travel brochures. They were not different than calendar prints, posters, magazine illustrations or any other mechanically reproduced images of art that were for sale everywhere and cost no more than a few dollars each. Paying hundreds of dollars a piece for his prints made no sense.

"I can get around that," he thought. "I'll call myself a fine art publisher instead of a commercial printer. I'll print my prints in small quantities that I'll call 'limited editions' and I'll have the artists responsible for the originals sign and number them. Instead of marketing them as copies or reproductions, I'll call them hand-signed and numbered limited edition lithographs. That's technically what they are, anyway, so I'm not misrepresenting anything. They'll sound important and people will think that they're original works of art just like paintings."

So he began producing his prints and advertising them in beautiful full-page color ads in art magazines. He designed his ads to look just like the ones that the art galleries used to sell their expensive original paintings. People saw his ads and, sure enough, thought that his prints were original works of art too. They also thought they were saving huge amounts of money compared to what the paintings cost so they bought without having the slightest idea of what they were getting. Meanwhile, the owner of the fine art publishing company made tons of money, never printed another travel brochure and lived happily ever after.

This may or may not be exactly how the limited edition reproduction or copy print business got it's start, but it's probably not too far from the truth. Today, it represents a substantial percentage of the art market with the larger publishing companies having operating budgets reaching well into the millions of dollars. Among the types of reproduction prints now being produced are offset lithographs, continuous tone lithographs, repligraphs, serigraphs, collotypes, multimedia prints, laser scanned lithographs, lithoserigraphs and more. And just as before, the great majority of people who buy these prints have no idea what they're getting.

Here are the facts: These limited editions are not original works of art. They are not made by the artists who conceive of and create the originals. They are reproductions or copies of original works of art printed by printing companies. You do not get original works of art when you buy them. You get signatures of artists on mechanically produced copies of original works of art.

Certain reproductive processes like those used to produce serigraphs involve a degree of handwork, but the handwork is that of publishing company employees, not the artists themselves. Advertisements claim that artists "oversee" or "closely cooperate" in the reproduction of their originals, but those that actually do are in the small minority. Their participation is rarely hands-on and it involves little more than checking to see whether colors and finished prints accurately reproduce the originals. The overwhelming majority of artists take little or no part in reproductive processes—all they do is sign and number the finished products.

Publishers use a variety of techniques to obscure this minimal artist involvement and the fact that the prints are copies and not originals. The most obvious two have already been mentioned—they print the copies in limited quantities and then have the artists sign and number them. This gives the copies the same basic look as original prints that are entirely conceived and created by artists.

To enhance the illusion, sophisticated marketing departments then create fancy names for these copies and combine those names with confusing or ambiguous words and phrases like hand signed, consecutively numbered, hand pulled, acid-free paper, no-fade inks, certificate of authenticity, 100% rag paper, limited edition art, subscription edition, commission offering, authentic, original, or produced in close cooperation with the artist. For example, an authentic original offset lithograph sounds important and accurately describes the great majority of limited edition prints, but it also accurately describes a picture on the front page of your daily newspaper!

To complete the illusion, copy prints are marketed and sold just like original art. They are advertised in art magazines just like originals. They are sold out of galleries just like originals. They are displayed on gallery walls beautifully framed, lighted and hung just like originals. They are expensively packaged and shipped just like originals. The gallery employees who sell them treat them just like originals. You will never see limited edition reproductions, for example, rolled into tubes, wrapped in plastic and sold out of boxes or cubicles like posters or other decorative prints, even though that's basically what they are!

The big publishing companies thoroughly accomplish their objective—laypersons have great difficulty telling the difference between originals and copies. They buy reproductions by the tens of thousands, all the while believing that they are getting original art.

As for the phrase "limited edition," it's totally abused. Any fine artist, museum curator, art scholar, art professor or other art expert will tell you that artist-produced limited editions normally consist of less than one hundred imprints and rarely exceed two hundred. Any number greater than that is considered more in the mass-produced category than the limited one. Publishing company copy prints are printed in editions of several hundred at the very least, many run into the thousands, the largest exceed 60,000! To put the upper end of these figures into its proper perspective, a book with sales in excess of 50,000 copies is considered a best seller. By the way, are you aware that limited edition copy prints that are offset lithographs are printed at rates of around 1,000 per hour? Does this sound like original art to you?

And now for the issue of affordability. A key selling point of limited edition prints is supposedly how affordable they are when compared to originals. "This painting would cost $25,000, but the limited edition print costs only $700" is the type of statement prospective buyers commonly hear. The truth is that the print is totally unrelated to the painting, hand signed and numbered or not. As has been repeatedly stated, the print is nothing more than a copy of the original with a signature and number on it that the artist takes several seconds to apply. You might as well compare a plastic scale model of a Mercedes-Benz to the real thing in order to try and justify a $700 selling price on the plastic model.

Looking at the affordability issue from another perspective, suppose that a fine art publishing company makes a limited edition print of the Mona Lisa. Granted, they can't get da Vinci to sign it, but let's say that the chief printer and a museum curator sign it and that all other aspects of production are identical to those of every signed and numbered limited edition print that the company has ever produced. Do you believe that the print's value has any relation to that of the priceless Mona Lisa? Of course not!

Perhaps the most outrageous aspect of the limited editions business is the huge difference between basic production costs and retail selling prices. The great majority of these prints cost no more than a few dollars each to produce—about the same as any decorative print or poster. Serigraphs are the one notable exception, but even the most expensive ones cost well under $100 each to produce. Yet these prints sell for hundreds and often thousands of dollars each. They're not affordable at all—for what they are, they're outrageously overpriced!

The people who buy these prints have no idea how inexpensive they are to produce. Even the great majority of retail dealers and galleries that sell them have no idea. They all believe that production costs are far higher, thereby justifying the retail prices.

And consider the total amount of money that sales of these prints generates. On the retail end, anywhere from tens of thousands to millions of dollars can turn on a single edition of a single print. And who gets all that money? Not the artists (except for the few who control the publishing and sale of their own editions). They get modest royalties for licensing or turning over their images to publishers. Much of the revenues go to printers, color separators, sales people, shippers, packers, dealers and other middle men. The really big bucks go to marketers, promoters, gallery chain operators and publishing company owners.

This is not art—it's big business! Big business has figured out how to sell common everyday decorative posters and poster-sized prints for hugely inflated prices. The uninformed public believes that these commercially produced copies are original works of art.

Keep in mind that limited edition copy prints are perfectly acceptable to buy and collect. If you love a particular image and this is the only way that you can get it, go ahead and buy it. Have no illusions, though, about what you get. If you want original works of art created by the artists who conceived them, avoid copy prints.

Until recently, recognizing limited edition copy prints was not that difficult. Since they were printed the same way as most commercial illustrations, all you had to do was look for dot matrix patterns—the same types of patterns you see when you look closely at newspaper or magazine illustrations. All you needed was a stronger magnifying glass. This still holds true for many, but certainly not all, copy prints because printing techniques are now far more sophisticated.

Some of today's dot matrix patterns are so fine that you need a handheld microscope to see them. Special textured papers can obscure matrix patterns. Printing techniques such as serigraphy and continuous tone lithography eliminate dot patterns altogether. In other words, simple tests no longer work across the board.

There is one identification technique, however, that has always worked and will continue to work for as long as copy prints are produced—asking the right question. If you ever have any doubts about whether you are getting an original or a copy, all you have to do is ask "Is this a copy or reproduction of an original work of art?" If the seller is not sure or is unable to give a satisfactory answer, have him check with the publisher. Better yet, ask them both and get their answers in writing. You might even double check with an outside expert such as an art professor or museum curator just to make sure.

Other Types of "Art" to Avoid

Variations on the limited edition copy print business pervade nearly all segments of the art trade. Although advertised and marketed as affordable art, it is in truth, overpriced and, in the great majority of cases, not art and not made by artists. For those of you who insist on owning originals, here are additional products to avoid:

Reproductions of famous works of art. Any type of art from any time period can be reproduced, including bronzes, paintings, prints, antiquities, metalwork, ceramics and porcelains. Contemporary recasts of Remington bronzes and reissues of Currier & Ives prints are two examples. These and other similar reproductions are occasionally marketed as limited, authorized, collector editions, precision crafted using the finest materials and techniques, unique, or special. Marketers attempt to establish connections between reproductions and the originals by focusing on the fame and importance of the original artists. The money issue is also prominent as price comparisons are frequently made with the originals in order to make the reproductions seem reasonable.

No matter how these are marketed, they are copies. They have no connection to the originals other than being visually similar. The original artists are not involved in their production, their value is only decorative and is not related to that of the originals. What's more, they are no different than the modestly priced reproductions you see for sale at gift shops and department stores everywhere. If you have any doubts about whether you are looking at an original or a reproduction, remember to ask if the piece is a copy or reproduction of an original work of art.

Textured reproductions of paintings. These are almost always copies of famous works of art, but they deserve special mention because of the ways in which they are produced and marketed. Many are printed on canvas and elaborately framed. To laypersons, they can look and sound pretty attractive when combined with clever marketing techniques.

Potential buyers are told that these paintings look exactly like the originals, that surfaces are textured just like the paint on the originals and that they won't be able to tell the difference between these and the originals. They may even be told that art experts are unable to tell the difference. Sellers convey the idea that owning these copies is just like owning the world's great art masterpieces.

These claims are nonsense. First of all, anyone who knows art can tell the difference in an instant. Second, these are mass-produced copies. Third, they may sound cheap when compared to the originals, but for what they are, they're grossly overpriced.

Museum reproductions. These have traditionally been available exclusively through non-profit museum gift shops, and revenues from their sales have been used to help finance museum operations. Recently, however, private enterprise has gotten into the act. Museum reproduction businesses have been popping up in shopping malls across the country and issuing fancy mail-order catalogues.

They sell the same basic items that the museums sell, but they market them entirely differently and charge higher prices. Sophisticated store displays make these copies look more important and more like art than the museum shops do. Catalogue photographs make them look like fine art masterworks. All items are elaborately described and, of course, the usual efforts are made to focus on quality production techniques, the rarity of the originals, connections between the copies and the originals, and to hint at their collectibility.

Once again, these are mass-produced copies, no matter how great they sound or are displayed. They have no connection to the originals in any way other than the visual. Not only are these items grossly overpriced for what they are, but the profits from their sales go into the pockets of private business people, not to museums. Museums may get modest licensing fees for authorizing reproductions, but that's not much compared to what they get when they produce and sell the items themselves.

If you want museum reproductions, buy them from museum stores or order them through museum catalogues like those published by The Metropolitan Museum of Art in New York, the Art Institute of Chicago or the Museum of Fine Arts in Boston. That way, you save money and support museums at the same time. If, however, you want original art, avoid these copies altogether no matter who sells them.

Limited edition copy prints with small amounts of handwork. Another recent arrival on the copy art scene are limited edition copy prints made as previously described but with the addition of small amounts of handwork. The prints are then signed and numbered. Marketers have a field day promoting these because, in a sense, each print is unique. Selling prices are higher than for regular limited edition copy prints, but they're still billed as affordable when compared to the cost of genuine originals.

These prints, like their copy print relatives, are little more than copies themselves. The substantial price increases over copy print costs are not justified by the time and labor involved in applying the few added brush strokes or other handwork. Dollar for dollar, these prints are even more overpriced than copy prints. If you have any doubts about what you are looking at, rephrase the question suggested before and ask: *Is this a copy or reproduction of an original work of art that has been retouched by an artist?*

Remarqued limited edition copy prints. This is also a print with handwork. Instead of altering images, though, artists add small sketches to their signatures and limitation numbers, usually in the bottom margins of the prints. The sketches are never much larger than a couple of square inches and rarely take longer than a few minutes to execute. Nevertheless, they increase per-print prices by at least $200 in the great majority of cases. And consider this: an artist who charges $200 for a two-square-inch sketch that takes five minutes to execute is making $40 per minute or $2,400 per hour.

Limited edition photographs reprinted from old images. Another recent entry into the copy print market are reprints of vintage photographic images. These are often enlarged from the originals and are sometimes signed, titled, numbered or accompanied by certificates of authenticity. The photographers who took the original photographs are sometimes famous, the original photographs themselves are usually valuable or collectible, the subject matters of the originals are often historical or significant. Copy photographs showing famous sports figures or panoramic views of cities taken decades ago are among the more popular subject matters currently being exhibited and sold.

Copy photographs can be made from any existing photographic images, including negatives, photographs and movie film. To make these copies sound important or original, marketers use ambiguous-sounding terms and phrases like original glass negatives, never before published, certificate of authenticity, archivally printed, hand titled, numbered, exclusive limited edition, or original prints. Selling prices can range well into the hundreds of dollars and, as with other limited edition copy prints, copy photographs are billed as affordable compared to what the originals cost.

The truth is that copy photographs are printed in the same exact way that you would have a print made from any old negative or photograph that you have lying around your house. All photo finishers, including the one at your corner drugstore, can make them. As with other copy prints, copy photographs have no relation to the original images other than their visual similarities. Neither do they have any connection to the original photographers, the values of the originals or the collectibility of the originals.

What are they worth? They're worth as much as they cost to print—as little as a dollar and hardly ever more than a few dollars except in cases where prints are extra large in size or are printed on special paper according to museum standards. Regardless of these variables, though, copy photograph production costs are always minimal compared to retail selling prices.

Copy photographs can sometimes make great additions to your collection, though, especially when originals are either in museums or are prohibitively expensive. Information about how to bypass dealers, save big dollars and get great copy photographs of just about any subject matter taken by just about any famous photographer can be found in Chapter 12.

You now have a basic foundation from which to operate in the world of affordable art and are ready for practical tips on how and where to find it. Because affordable art is not a big moneymaker, hardly anyone bothers to advertise it, hardly any high-profile galleries sell it and hardly anyone in the news media pays any attention to it. You cannot simply open your local Yellow Pages, look under the heading "Affordable Art" and find out where to get yours. Without much effort, however, you can find the affordable art that's right for you at the prices that you want to pay.

Part III
How to Find Affordable Art

6 Use Your Museums

This may sound hard to believe, but one of the best-kept secrets in the art business is museums. Unfortunately, the percentage of fine art owners who have any level of museum involvement beyond brief or infrequent visits is surprisingly small. This lack of participation is grounded in several widely held misconceptions.

One is that museums have little, if any, practical application to everyday art. People believe that the art on exhibit is so rare, important, old or valuable that it has no relation whatsoever to what art galleries sell or what individuals of average means can afford to buy. Museums are viewed as institutions for the wealthy, sophisticated, highly art-educated upper echelons of society.

People also keep their distance because they're self-consciousness about their lack of knowledge. They're reluctant to go beyond occasional visits because they believe that they can never possibly understand what art is all about. They are embarrassed to admit how little they know or to publicly discuss their tastes and preferences. Related to this is a fear that museums want to impose their tastes on others, that the museum represents what's right and everything else is wrong. Paradoxically, museums are almost seen as more of an obstacle to enjoying art than to appreciating it.

These and other popularly held misconceptions may seem to make sense on the surface, but none are based in fact. Museums are for everyone. They exhibit every kind of art imaginable, they cater to all segments of the community and they offer much more than most people can even begin to realize.

What Museums Are and How to Find Them

The image that you probably have when you think of a museum is that of a large building, usually granite, usually classically styled with marble-floored galleries, long hallways, high ceilings, high security, attendants everywhere and hushed people staring in awe at the world's great art masterpieces. This accurately describes only a very small percentage of museums.

Museums are places where all types of art are preserved, studied and exhibited, not just rare, priceless masterpieces. Furthermore, museums are not all cavernous granite buildings. Some are no larger than one-room cabins. They come in all sizes, shapes, architectural styles and they're everywhere. You find them in the biggest cities and the smallest towns.

In addition to pure art museums, there are many museums and museumlike establishments that display art as part of their overall focus. You can find circus art at circus museums, scouting art at scouting museums, mining art at mining museums, local and regional art at local and regional museums or historical societies, Hungarian immigrant art at Hungarian-American museums and cultural centers, African-American art at African-American art museums. You can find art by children, religious art, baseball art, Idaho art, or Kentucky art. Whatever art you like, chances are excellent that some museum, society or institution somewhere shows it.

Not only are art museums places where you go to see art, but they're also great places to meet people who know about art or share your interest in a particular kind of art or subject matter. Curators, art dealers, art students, art professors, art collectors and just plain art lovers are all people you might come into contact with at museums. The misconception is that these people are all wealthy art experts and that you know nothing; the truth is that the great majority of them are just like you.

And here's the important part: Art museums are places of learning. Once you know where to go, you can learn about the art you like, meet people who collect that art, learn how to locate it, and meet people who can offer appropriate advice.

Museum professionals are about the most unbiased people you can get to know and they have no stake in getting you to change your mind. They are not in the art business, they are not beholden to any special interests and, consequently, they'll fairly represent all aspects of whatever situation you present them with.

Most of the museums that show the types of art that average everyday people can afford are small, have modest operating budgets, and may only be open part time. They are not high-profile institutions like major national or international museums, so you have to make a bit of an effort to locate them.

One way you can do this is to check your local Yellow Pages or those of nearby major cities under the heading of "Museums." Telephone directories are a great resource and you can often find the names of museums that you had no idea even existed. Other good resources are weekly entertainment or calendar sections of local newspapers where museum-sponsored events and current exhibitions are often listed.

If you like a particular type of art and no museum in your area shows it, look in *American Art Directory* and *The Official Museum Directory*. Each lists thousands of museums and related institutions; both are published by R.R. Bowker (245 West 17th St., New York, NY 10011) and can be found or accessed through almost any university, museum or public library.

The Official Museum Directory lists all members of the American Association of Museums; the *American Art Directory* lists many American as well most major international museums. *The Official Museum Directory* is your best bet for locating smaller and more specialized museums, but the *American Art Directory* contains additional worthwhile information that will be discussed in later chapters. Both directories list museums by geographical location and cross-index them by category and subject. If you're interested in sports art, for example, the current edition of *The Official Museum Directory* lists approximately 50 American sports museums.

What Museums Offer

No matter what your financial status or level of art education, you can participate in a multitude of activities and functions offered by the great majority of museums everywhere. Basic memberships are open to anyone and rarely cost more than $50 per year.

The misconception is that people who belong to museums are wealthy art experts. The truth is that, for the most part, they're ordinary everyday people who happen to like art. Never feel intimidated about becoming a museum member. Membership is, without question, one of the best ways to learn about the art you want to collect.

Standard membership benefits often include invitations to museum openings, free admissions or discounted admissions to lectures and special programs, automatic subscriptions to museum newsletters or related publications and free museum admissions. Members may also be able to take advantage of reciprocal arrangements with other facilities, guided tours, educational programs for both children and adults, film programs, gallery talks, and so on. If you're curious about a particular museum's offerings, all you have to do is call or write. You can also check *The Official Museum Directory* and the *American Art Directory,* both of which list specific museum activities.

Those of you who want to maximize your museum involvement can join museum collectors groups. Not all museums have them, but those who do offer them as an adjunct to membership. Collectors groups go by names like donors forum, president's circle, collecting circle and collectors forum. Their activities include special museum tours, visits to artists' studios and commercial art galleries, and even trips to see private collections.

Those of you who want deeper museum involvement can become docents or volunteers. No matter how large or small museums are, they always need help. They need people to work at art openings and other public functions, sit at reception desks, and help with day-to-day operations. This is a great way to make direct contact with museum personnel, fellow museum members and collectors. It's also a great way to learn. You don't have to know anything about art to volunteer your services. Museum personnel and fellow docents will teach you everything you need to know. In the meantime, you get to talk about the art you love and develop your collecting skills.

The key to all museum-related activities is that they provide opportunities for you to meet people with similar interests who can share their experiences with you. No matter how involved you decide to get, introduce yourself and speak with these people whenever possible. Whether you're just starting out or have been buying art for a while, the single best way to get the best art at the fairest prices is to have access to qualified individuals who can advise you on all aspects of your collecting.

If, at this point, museums still intimidate you, call a local museum or one that specializes in what you want to collect and speak with a curator or someone involved in administration. In the great majority of cases, these people are easily accessible and are happy to answer all of your questions. See for yourself just how easy they are to talk to. Curators and other administrators will tell you that a major emphasis of what they do is to make art and art collecting non-threatening to novices. They'll assess your situation and recommend what's best for you. As the old saying goes: Try it; you'll like it.

Museum Sales and Rental Galleries

Few people are aware that they can even buy art through museums. Many operate sales and rental galleries that are open to the public. The artists whose work is on display are usually local or regional, but they can also be nationally or internationally known. Depending on the location and size of the operation, anywhere from dozens to a thousand or so artists can be represented by a single museum gallery. As with commercial galleries, artists are required to submit slides or examples of their work and must be accepted by these galleries in order to show.

Museum galleries have several advantages over other types of galleries. They tend to be strong on local and regional art. They're great places to see lots of art without feeling pressured to buy, as you might be in for-profit settings. The larger establishments offer huge varieties of art and are able to satisfy just about any collector's requirements.

Because museum galleries are non-profit, their prices tend to be lower than those of their for-profit counterparts. They rarely take standard full retail markups on art and they also pride themselves on catering to all collectors, especially those with modest budgets. This means that in addition to more expensive art, you can almost always find art in the lower price ranges, often for as little as $50 or $75.

The rental option is great for collectors who aren't sure whether or not to buy particular pieces. For modest fees, they can rent the art for several weeks or months. Many galleries offer payment plans and rent or lease-to-own plans in addition to their normal sales and rental arrangements.

On the minus side, the art at these galleries is by no means representative of all available art. As with any other gallery, what they show is a product of the tastes and requirements of the people in charge. At worst, it can be subject to strict, conservative or narrow admissions guidelines. Understand also that the direct affiliation that these galleries have with museums does not automatically insure that their art is great or good or any better or worse than that of any other gallery.

Museum galleries are just one of many art buying options. If you're just starting out, they're great places to look at art because they're so safe. You'll be hard-pressed to find a more comfortable and supportive atmosphere in which to browse and shop. Keep them in their proper perspective, though, and don't use them as an excuse to ignore or avoid what the rest of the art world has to offer.

In spite of their sales and rental galleries, remember that art museums are basically noncommercial islands in a sea of art business. They provide shelter and sustenance for art lovers who want to learn in relaxed, non-conflicted, non-biased environments. Sooner or later, though, art lovers who aspire to become art owners must set sail for those destinations where capitalism reigns, where art is bought and sold for profit. Established art galleries are the logical first stop.

7 Buying from Established Art Galleries

If you're like most people, when you think about places to buy art, you immediately think of established art galleries—those places that you tend to see in malls, city centers, shopping districts and vacation spots. Without question, these are obvious places to buy art. They're comfortable to shop, conveniently located and buyer oriented. Their sole purpose is to sell art and they want your business.

From the standpoint of affordable art, though, the big problem with established galleries, as previously discussed, is the perception that the art they sell is anything but affordable. On the surface, there seems to be no getting around the fact that the overwhelming majority of art that these galleries have to offer is expensive. The result is that most people avoid them because they don't believe they can find anything to buy.

True, the art that established galleries generally show or highlight is of the expensive variety, but this does not necessarily mean that all the art they sell is equally pricey. Galleries prefer to sell expensive art rather than less expensive art, of course, but when faced with the choice of either selling something or selling nothing, most galleries choose to sell something. And if selling something means selling something affordable, that's the choice they make.

The great majority of established galleries do have affordable art for sale. They may not have a lot and it may not be what you want, but then again, you may be surprised. For those of you who either like the idea of buying through these galleries or at least want to give them a try before moving on to less conventional and more affordable sources, here's how to proceed.

Getting Started

The first and most important step in locating affordable art at established galleries is to enter the galleries. This sounds silly, but many people feel so

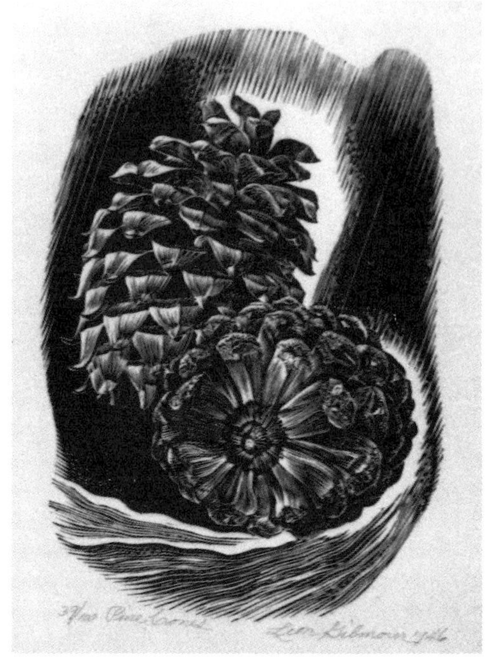

"Pine Cones" by nationally known wood engraver Leon Gilmour. Wood engraving, pencil signed and dated 1946, 9 by 6 inches. Courtesy of The Old Print Barn, Meredith, NH.

uncomfortable or intimidated around art, especially expensive art, that they never get beyond peeking through entrance ways or show windows.

When you pass by a gallery and see anything at all that catches your eye, walk in, look around, look at everything, go into every room in the gallery. Even when nothing excites you that much, checking out the inside is still a good idea—there's always something you can learn. If you don't want to speak with anyone and an owner or employee approaches you, tell them that you're just browsing. Take the time to look around. You will find there are many gallery features that are not always visible from the street:

- They may have several shows running simultaneously.
- They may represent a number of artists, but show only one at a time.
- They may show only one artist or type of art per room and not all rooms are visible from the street.
- They almost always have art that they're not currently showing in back rooms and storage areas.
- They almost always have albums or catalogues of art or artists that they represent or have access to in addition to what's on display.

Fully explore any gallery that you decide to visit. The only time you should leave prematurely is when you feel pressured or uncomfortable in any way. A small minority of dealers may press you about your art interests, insist on showing you everything that they have in stock, or attempt to sell you art that you have little or no interest in. This is never pleasant and if it happens, leave immediately. If, however, you feel at ease and you see art you like, no matter how many thousands or tens of thousands of dollars it costs, you've got to explore further. The affordable art may be only a moment away.

How to Locate the Affordable Art

Affordable art is rarely visible at established galleries. What you see on display is the best and usually the most expensive art that they have to offer. The affordable art is around, though. All you have to do is ask for it.

Begin by introducing yourself to an owner or staff person. Show him the art you like and tell him as much as you can about what you're interested in collecting. State your price range right up front and don't feel embarrassed about it. The sooner you get the dollars and cents specifics out in the open, the better. The person you're speaking with will then know exactly what you want and be able to address your situation without wasting any time, either yours or his.

Talk about how much you like whatever art you're focusing on. The more enthusiastic you are, the better the chances that staff people will spend time with you and the better your chances of coming away with something. Art dealers hate to disappoint people who are genuinely interested in owning art, regardless of how large or small a sale is involved.

No matter how much you're taken with the art that you've pointed out or how accurately you describe what you're looking for, some gallery personnel may have no idea how to respond to your situation. Affordable art encounters do not happen often in established galleries and you could be met with a blank stare. In this case, you may have to help the seller out in order to get what you want or to find out whether it even exists.

For instance, if you're told that the gallery has nothing like the art you want in stock, ask whether the artist creates anything similar in your price range. If the answer is no, ask whether the artist would be willing to create it. If not, find out whether the artist creates anything at all in your price range and, if so, what. If you're met with yet another no, find out whether the artist would be willing to create anything at all in your price range and, if so, what. When a particular artist's art is simply not available in your price range, find out whether any other artists whose work the gallery has access to create similar art that is in your price range.

If you're still coming up empty-handed, don't give up quite yet. As a last resort, ask whether the gallery sells any art at all in your price range. This is a long shot, but the dealer may say yes and the art he shows you may be something you like. If you come up against another brick wall, call it quits. There are many situations where nothing exists in your price range and that's that. At least you tried.

From here on, specific suggestions and ideas for buying affordable art or forming affordable collections will be listed at the close of every chapter and within the contexts of those chapters. These suggestions are exactly that—suggestions. They by no means include all possible types of collections nor do they represent preferred types of collections. They are meant merely to stimulate your thinking. Whatever you like the most is what you should collect.

Artful Collections

Preliminary drawings. Artists make preparatory drawings or sketches for expensive major paintings or sculptures. They normally keep these and hundreds or thousands of other sketches in their studios. Ask dealers whether they are willing to contact artists on your behalf and make this request.

Alternative techniques. Consider buying drawings, sketches, pastels, pen and inks, or watercolors with subject matters similar to those of the expensive paintings that you like the most.

Small format pictures. The same subject matters as in large expensive pieces may be portrayed by smaller pictures. Unless an artist is a miniaturist, the smaller the piece, the lower the price.

Original prints. The type of subject matter you prefer may be available in print form. Only buy these if they are original works of art, not copy prints made by printing companies as discussed in Chapter 5. The artist who paints the pictures you like should be the printmaker.

Close-outs. Just about every gallery has art that did not sell left over from old shows. It's perfectly good art, but the dealers have no further use for it. Always ask about it; you can make some great buys.

▩ The major drawback to shopping established galleries for affordable art is that you always have to settle for minor pieces. You're never going be able to buy anything big, substantial, detailed, significant or important because it will be well beyond your budget. Any selection that you are presented with will consist of the least expensive and, therefore, the least significant works of art that any gallery has to offer.

Because the great majority of affordable art buyers would rather own art that is significant, shopping established galleries is impractical. Shopping for affordably priced significant and substantial works of art at less established galleries or in less conventional gallery type settings makes far more sense. These places may not be high profile, they may not be conveniently located, they may not be heavily staffed, finely furnished or professionally decorated, they may be very casual, they may not even be indoors. But they do exist, they can be found within any art community and, most importantly, they can be great places to buy art. The next chapter talks about the remarkable amount of options available to you.

8

Buying Outside Established Galleries

Art is for sale everywhere, not just at established galleries. Artists show their work at cafes, restaurants, bookstores, open exhibitions, art fairs, street fairs, community galleries, alternative galleries, emerging artist galleries, artist owned galleries, and open-studio events. Not all of this art is affordable, but your chances of being able to buy within your budget are far greater than they are if you confine your searches only to established galleries.

Utilizing these types of resources involves some compromise, but not that much. They're generally less convenient, less conventional and a bit harder to locate than established operations. On the other hand, shopping them is more fun, more adventurous, more exciting and certainly more engaging than shopping their comparatively sterile and insulated counterparts. If getting closer to the inner workings of the art world appeals to you, prepare to have a great time.

A corollary to the fun and adventure associated with locating these places is the art you find once you get there. Established galleries basically represent the tip of the iceberg—they show only a small percentage of all available art and, on top of that, they tend to stay conservative. The range, variety and sheer volume of art that you find elsewhere can be far more fascinating, engaging and entertaining. You still see art that's tasteful, decorative and in the mainstream, but you also see art that's outrageous, cutting edge, thought-provoking and progressive.

Some people hesitate to shop outside of the mainstream because they're worried about the significance or the quality of the art that they might find. These worries are unfounded. The quality of art at established high-profile galleries can be just as uneven as the art on display elsewhere. Look on the plus side—an inconsequential work of art purchased from an established gallery will almost always cost substantially more than an equally inconsequential one acquired from a less-established resource.

Another point to keep in mind is that today's famous artists were not always famous. No artist is born famous. All artists have to start out somewhere and the great majority of them start out at the types of places outlined in this chapter. Artists have always begun and will continue to begin their careers wherever they can talk people into exhibiting their art—a process that will never change.

This doesn't mean that you patronize less-established resources for the sole purpose of discovering the next Picasso or Van Gogh. Experienced artists also exhibit their work at these places because they have little or no interest in the major gallery rat race, prefer to market their own art or have more casual attitudes toward selling. As with any other profession, artists choose to make their livings in all sorts of ways and to sell at all sorts of places.

Cafes, Restaurants and Bookstores

The broader category here might be better described as non-art-related businesses. If a hardware store or laundromat, for example, decides to offer a display space for art, you can bet that artists will line up at their doors for opportunities to show. Cafes, restaurants and, to a lesser extent, bookstores happen to be the places that yield their walls to artists most frequently.

The art on display at these locations is generally affordable and sometimes even inexpensive—under $100 per piece. Many times, businesses put you into direct contact with artists because they show art only as a sidelight and don't care to get bogged down in sales. This gives you opportunities to deal with artists directly, visit them at their studios and see what else they have for sale. As in other viewing situations, when you like what you see, but can't afford it, find out whether the artist has anything available in your price range.

Be advised that buying under these circumstances is not the same as buying at art galleries. These places are not art galleries and they're not owned by art dealers. In other words, staff people on hand are rarely qualified to give accurate overviews as to the quality of the art on display or the reputations of the artists. You have to do that yourself by personally speaking with the artists, obtaining and examining their resumes, checking their credentials with outside experts or experienced collectors, and generally following the guidelines listed in Chapter 3.

Open Exhibitions, Competitions and Art Fairs

These events range anywhere from casual artist gatherings to highly competitive juried exhibitions with strict admission requirements. Hundreds of major shows and thousands of minor ones take place annually at local, regional and national levels. They are held at museums, community galleries, community centers, exhibition halls, public parks, malls, and state and county fairs.

Convenience is a major advantage in these situations. The work of dozens and often hundreds of artists is on display at one location, thereby allowing you to see a huge amount of art with very little effort. You can compare and contrast the specific artworks you like without having to travel from gallery to gallery or place to place. Having it all right there in front of you at the same time is one of the best ways to determine what art or whose style really thrills you the most.

The ability to compare prices is another big advantage. You see what amount of money buys you what amount of art from a variety of different artists. You can ask artists how they set their prices, you can speak with one about another's prices, you can find out whether one artist is willing to give you a little more for your money in light of another artist's prices and so on. Learning about art and money is far easier when you can receive instant feedback from numerous sources than it is when you confine your activities to single gallery settings.

On the whole, selling prices tend to be lower at these events than they are at galleries. This is true not only because so many artists compete for sales at a single location, but also because organizers are usually groups like non-profit or community service organizations. These groups have more interest in showing art than they do in making money and, as a result, they tend to take smaller percentages of final selling prices than galleries do.

Juried shows and other awards competitions have an additional advantage. The best pieces in the show are selected by panels of art experts which makes your job of evaluating easier than it would otherwise be. You can have show organizers and helpers explain how judges select prize-winning pieces and what selection criteria they use.

One final point: When you see art you like, you don't necessarily have to buy immediately. Find out what else the artists have to offer. Ask whether you can visit them at their studios and see the full range of their work. You may find pieces that you like even more and that can be yours at more affordable prices. Studio visits also bring you closer to the artists and give you fuller understandings of their art. You'll learn more about this in Chapter 10.

The best way to find out about these types of events is by reading artist trade publications. Two major resources are *Art Calendar,* an East Coast publication, and *Artweek,* a West Coast publication. When combined, the two list most significant art shows in this country. If your primary interests lie in specialty arts, such as weavings, glass, ceramics, or furniture, consult specific art organizations and trade publications within those fields (see Chapter 9). If your interests are more geographical in nature, arts councils and visitors bureaus cover local and regional art activities (see Chapter 9). Appendix 1 lists artist trade publications that you'll find helpful, like *Art Calendar* and *Artweek,* and Chapter 10 provides additional ideas on how to use them to your collecting advantage.

Another good way to locate art show information, particularly relating to local and regional events, is to check the entertainment sections of your local papers. Most smaller art fairs are publicized in gallery or datebook-type listings.

Alternative and Emerging Artist Galleries

These two types of galleries tend to be newer businesses owned and operated by young, progressive art dealers who are willing to show art that the more established galleries avoid. Many of the exhibiting artists are young or at an early stage in their careers, but all artists with something to say and a competent body of work to back it up are given consideration by gallery owners.

If you like what's trendy, new, fresh, fun and unusual, these are great places to shop. On infrequent occasions, the art on display is so avant-garde that it stresses the limits of tolerance, but this is the rare exception rather than the rule. These galleries have to stay in business and they can't do so by offending the public. Overall, gallery owners are very familiar with the local art scene and are able to provide superior overviews of who's doing what, who the most promising artists are, and what the larger trends are. They educate you not only with the art they choose to show, but also by their abilities to explain what it's all about and to put it in its proper perspective.

As for affordability, prices reflect the fact that much of the art is new or

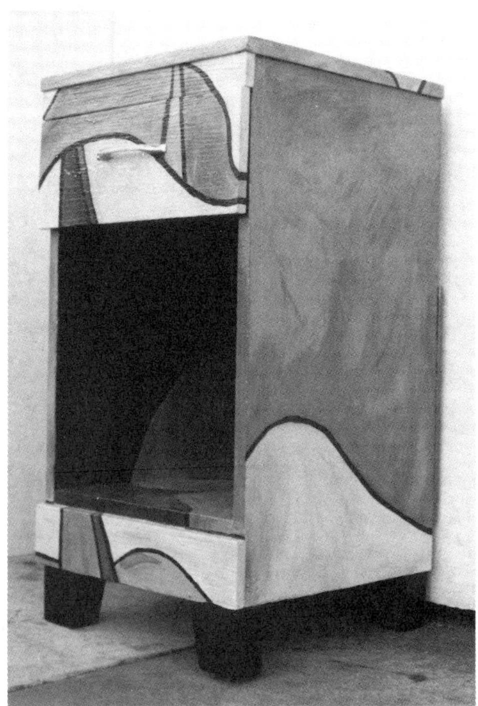

Painted furniture by Vivien Arnold. Height: 30 inches. Courtesy of Art Attack Gallery, San Francisco.

experimental and many of the artists are early in their careers. Finding works of art for well under $100 is by no means an impossible task.

Don't be afraid to visit alternative or emerging artist galleries. If you find yourself surrounded by art that's not right for you, don't automatically assume that everything in that particular gallery or at these galleries in general will impact you in the same way. Wherever you are, ask to see examples of all the art or artists that the galleries represent or have represented but are not currently showing. Get on their mailing lists, keep track of upcoming shows and give them a chance before you give up.

These places are some of the more vibrant and exciting venues in which to see and buy art. The segment of the art community that they represent is never boring. You'll meet people with vision who are willing to take risks. The most talented among them will go on to become tomorrow's established artists and respected art dealers.

You usually have to do a little digging within an art community to find out where these galleries are located. The best people to ask are artists, art students, art school administrators, recent art school graduates and art professors. Also check local newspaper entertainment sections or datebooks. Some of these galleries, but not all, list current and upcoming shows.

Artist-Owned Galleries, Co-ops or Collectives

Artist-owned galleries can be another great source of affordable art, but you've got to be a little more careful here. The best and most respected ones serve their communities, are often non-profit, and have special goals or purposes in addition to selling art. Some offer classes or are dedicated to educating the public about various types of art, such as sculpture or fiber arts. Other focus on under-recognized groups of artists, such as women artists, Hispanic artists, African-American artists, or younger artists who don't have the credentials to show their work elsewhere. For these galleries, getting the word out about their art is paramount and if that means working within a collector's modest budget, that's what they'll do. Prices start as low as $10 to $20 in many instances.

A small percentage of artist galleries are less noble in their missions. They serve primarily as power bases for the artists who control them, and anyone else who is interested in getting involved is pretty much locked out. The galleries have little more reason for existing than to make money for the controlling artists, while ignoring the needs of other segments of their art communities.

Prices can also be too high. The artists attempt to mimic established galleries by selling art at comparable prices while cutting out the middle men—the dealers who perform valuable services as disseminators of education as well as art. These are not the places to shop and you probably won't shop them anyway because little, if any, of their art is affordable.

You can find out about artist galleries in your area or the area of your choice by checking with local artists, art schools, art professors and others active in the art community. Also contact the National Association of Artists' Organizations. They have information on over 300 artist-run organizations in the United States, including galleries. Write them at 918 F Street NW, Washington, DC 20004, or call 202-347-6350.

Open Studios

Certain parts of the country, most notably the major cities, have large artist populations. A number of smaller communities are also known as art centers and have significant artist colonies. Anywhere that you have concentrations of artists, you also have events known as open studios, art walks, or art trails.

Once or twice a year, artists get together and open their studios to the public. These are special opportunities for you to meet dozens and sometimes hundreds of artists in person, speak with them about their art, tour their studios, see how they live, see the best selections of their art available anywhere and, of course, buy at the best possible prices. After all, no less-expensive or easier way exists for artists to sell art than right out of their own studios, so they can afford to be flexible with their prices.

Attending open studios is one of the best ways to find affordable art. In addition to great prices, you also see the work of many artists at once, get as close to artists as you're ever going to get, and, of course, you can enjoy the festive atmosphere of these events. For those of you who want personal involvement with the artists you patronize, nothing's better.

Dealing directly with artists is perhaps the greatest advantage of open studios. If, for example, you really love an artist's work but the prices are a little beyond your budget, you can state your case and see how the artist responds. The artist has a chance to evaluate you as a collector and admirer and, in the great majority of cases, will attempt to accommodate your needs. See Chapter 10 for more complete information about the best ways to buy from artists.

Oddly enough, dealing directly with artists can also be a drawback to buying at open studios, especially when you don't know that much about art. Because you're pretty much on your own, you have no professionals like dealers or other art experts available to provide critical overviews of what you're looking at. If you're not careful, you can end up patronizing artists who know how to sell much better than they know to paint. When you're just starting out, make every effort to attend these events with people who know the territory.

Another occasional problem with open studios is that artists can respond inappropriately to the increased public exposure. For instance, some mark up their prices for these events or put more reasonably priced work out of sight and only display their most expensive pieces. If you find yourself in a situation where you like the art but can't afford it, state your budget and your preferences and see whether the artist is willing to work with you or has something hidden away.

Open studios are always highly publicized within local art communities. Find out about where and when they take place by speaking with artists, art museum staff people, art galleries that show work by local artists, and by reading the art listings in the entertainment or datebook sections of your local papers. The National Association of Artists' Organizations is also a good place to call or write, especially if you are interested in open studios in other parts of the country. They maintain a list of over fifty artist colonies.

Artful Collections

Regional art. Concentrate on art by artists from a particular city, state or region. Most artists show and sell the great bulk of their work close to home. Use the methods discussed in this chapter to locate them.

Works from particular artistic events. Individual events often have reputations for focusing on certain types of art. Find a good-sized show that caters to your tastes and you're all set.

Award-winning art. Confine your purchases to art that wins awards at competitions. If you're on a modest budget, you may have to limit your buying to art from smaller local shows or to pieces that win lesser awards.

Art by artists who share your views. The best way to locate this art is by attending open studios and other events where you can personally speak with many artists at once. Select pieces from the artists who share your goals or artworks that depict a message you agree with.

The art business, unlike most other businesses, is not known for its structure or ability to disseminate comprehensive trade information through easily accessible agencies or organizations. Overall, its pretty fragmented. In order to take advantage of any of this chapter's affordable art options, you might have to investigate for an hour or two before you find a knowledgeable individual who has the answers you're looking for. Art organizations do exist, though, and they can be great resources for affordable art information. The next chapter tells you what these organizations are, how to locate them and how to use them to your advantage.

9 Art Organizations

Local, regional and national art organizations have been established to serve just about every type of art, every type of artist and every art community in existence. These organizations can be divided into two distinct categories—private membership groups and public or governmental agencies.

Private groups are composed primarily of artists and their close supporters. They serve specific segments of art communities, such as sculptors, illustrators, abstract artists, wildlife artists, fabric artists, Colorado artists, Cleveland artists, African-American artists, Southern artists, or ceramic artists. These can almost be called artist trade organizations and they have names like the American Society of Contemporary Artists, Eastern Shore Art Association, National Watercolor Society, Women's Caucus for Art, Boston Art Club, Society of Western Artists, and National Association of Chicano Artists & Entertainers.

Public or governmental art agencies, usually called arts councils or arts commissions, are far broader in scope than private groups. They are involved with all aspects of art and perform services like funding non-profit art centers and art programs, sponsoring shows and competitions, awarding grants to artists and overseeing public arts projects. They are generally dedicated to furthering interest in the arts within every segment of the communities in the geographical areas that they serve.

The one thing that both public and private art organizations have in common is that they are all great repositories and clearinghouses of information. Many have little or nothing to do with selling art, especially government agencies, but each one knows its territory and can tell you where to go or who to contact to get the art you want. Depending on your needs, a few well-placed phone calls can net you names, dates, locations and other specifics about dozens of art-buying opportunities.

For the most part, art organizations operate independently of each other. In other words, one is not necessarily aware of what the next is doing or even

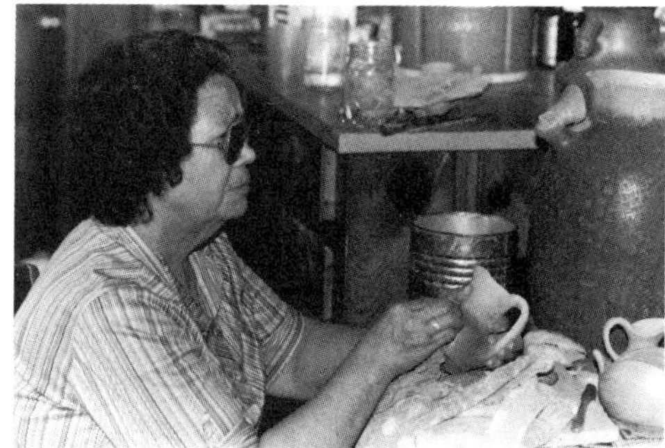

Sara Ayers applying glaze. Courtesy of the South Carolina Arts Commission.

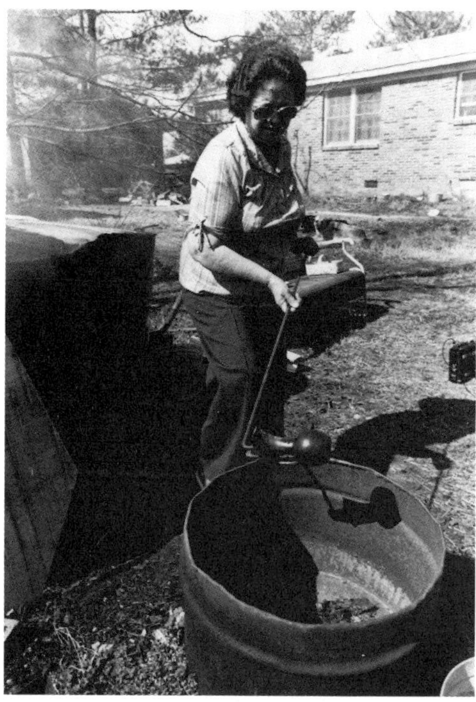

Sara Ayers, South Carolina Catawba Indian potter, firing pots. Courtesy of the South Carolina Arts Commission.

that the next exists. You cannot contact one central agency and expect to get answers to every question you have, whether its about art or about other agencies. A little exploring is necessary in order to locate those groups that will best serve your needs.

Get a feel for the vast amount and variety of organizations you have to choose from by consulting the *American Art Directory* under the headings, "Art Organizations" and "State Arts Councils." You'll find the names of hundreds of national, regional and local groups within the United States and Canada, both public and private. Many listings contain basic information like statements of purpose, publications and activities offered. Also check your local Yellow Pages under the heading "Arts Organizations and Information" to find out what's available in your immediate vicinity. Larger metropolitan areas can have dozes of entries under this heading. And don't forget the chamber of commerce. They often have information about local artist groups, especially those that hold regular public exhibitions.

The best way for you to take advantage of what any organization has to offer is to be precise about your needs, your budget and what types of art you are looking for. The more information you give, the more suggestions or recommendations you'll get. Not all groups will have what you want and when one doesn't or cannot answer your questions, ask whether they are aware of any others that can help you. When you hit a dead end, move on to the next name on your list and repeat the procedure. Once you learn your way around the organizational world, making contacts and acquiring useable information becomes second nature. The following specifics on what organizations are about, how to contact them and what to ask them will help you get started.

Private Membership Organizations

Access a private membership organization and you access dozens, hundreds and sometimes thousands of artists at once—professionals, semi-professionals and amateurs. A simple call on the phone is usually enough to get you started; a few organizations prefer written inquiries. No matter who you contact or how you contact them, the procedure for acquiring information is always basically the same.

First, you've got to determine whether you like their art and the only way to do that is to see it. Find out when and where members exhibit their work, ask whether any publications or catalogues are available that show members' work, find out whether any computer files, registries or slide banks catalogue this art and, if so, whether they're open to the public. When you speak with a national group that's headquartered out of your vicinity, find out whether they have local or regional chapters or representatives in your area and contact them. When no such options exist, ask whether any member artists live in your area. Contact these artists directly to learn about art-related activities or possible artist groups in your locale.

When you see selections of art and decide that you like at least some of it, focus in on those artists whose work you like the most. Rather than buy immediately at shows or other sales events, wait to contact the artists directly. This gives you the widest range of art from which to choose in terms of size, subject matter, medium and price. Organizations almost always refer you to artists at no charge; some do not give out member addresses or phone numbers, but all will contact them on your behalf. The artists then decide when, where or how they want to meet with you.

As far as staying within your budget, major exhibitions sponsored by national or regional organizations are not generally the best places to see affordable art. What you see are the most important, most expensive pieces submitted by the most prominent artists. Not to worry, though. When art is out of your price range, contact the artists anyway and see whether they have anything less substantial at their studios that you can afford—some will. When you come up empty-handed, find out whether they know other artists with similar styles whose work is less pricey—many do.

If you're really on a budget, focus more on local shows, local chapters, smaller-scale events, less-established organizations, younger artists, and local artists in general. That's where you'll find the least expensive art. The Yellow Pages or local chambers of commerce are especially good resources for locating these types of groups.

When you like what a particular organization has to offer but can't afford much of it, try contacting members who don't exhibit at shows or only keep examples of their work in artist registries or files that are difficult to access. These artists may be amateurs or part-timers, less motivated to compete with other artists, more private, or not concerned about showing. Their art tends to be less expensive, and, regardless of their reasons for not showing, virtually all of them are interested in selling and will do so given the opportunity. By the way, never automatically assume that art by artists who don't show is not worth your while. You can make some great discoveries by seeking out low-profile members.

Not knowing who these artists are or what their art looks like may seem like an insurmountable hurdle in terms of ever being able to see or buy anything, but it's not. All you have to do is advertise your wants in organizational newsletters or other membership publications. Most have classified sections or will print your copy in small display ads for only a few dollars per issue. Be as specific or as general as you want. A sample ad might read:

If you have coastal scene watercolors for sale for under $150, please write to John Doe, 123 Main St., Townville, NY 22222 or call (444) 111-2222.

Advertising to buy art directly from artists is one of the most effective ways to get what you want, no matter what publications you advertise in. Always consider it as an option. In addition to ferreting out at least some low-profile members, more-active artists will contact you too. You'll be surprised at how many responses you get. An added benefit is that by stating your preferences and your budget up front, you hear only from those artists who have what you want.

When an organization turns out to be particularly helpful, consider joining it. Non-artists are always welcome and annual membership dues are usually nominal. In return, you receive newsletters, regular updates on activities, and the latest information about upcoming shows and competitions. Many organizations also offer opportunities for you to meet other members, hear lectures or attend special artist functions. As for affordability, artist members are almost always favorably predisposed to selling their art to fellow members at special prices.

Public and Governmental Organizations

Local, regional and state arts councils and arts commissions are some of the best all-around places to learn about and locate affordable art. No matter where in the United States you live, you are served by at least one such organization. Appendix 2 lists the fifty state arts councils. A phone call is all that's necessary to find out what's happening in your state or in any geographical area that interests you. If, for example, you want information exclusively about art in your city or county, your state council will refer you to the local council or agency that best serves your needs.

As always, be specific about what you're looking for. Staff people are happy to help you and spend time with you, but you have to direct them. They are aware of so many programs and other options that they can't be expected to list them all. When they mention specific programs, events or places, get the addresses and phone numbers, the names of contact people, and ask whether any further information can be sent to you in the mail (most arts councils have regular newsletters that detail their activities).

Arts council employees are not in the art business but rather in the business of advancing and encouraging interest the arts and, in that capacity, tell you what you need to know and gladly make referrals. They are educated about art and intensely involved. Because their organizations often control arts funding and provide other forms of public assistance, they are in continual contact with numerous artists and, more importantly, virtually all arts programs as either grant applicants or recipients.

These programs range from the established to the progressive, the fascinating to the original. They include art centers, artist colonies, art museums, cultural centers, alternative exhibition spaces, community galleries, art exhibitions, art competitions, art fairs, and non-profit organizations. Groups served focus on traditional arts, folk arts, immigrant arts, ethnic arts, rural arts, art by children, art by the elderly, and just about any other noteworthy activity taking place within the arts community. See Part IV for detailed descriptions and information about these and other specific types of art.

Some programs are so new that hardly anyone outside of arts councils and the inner cores of arts communities is even aware of them. If you like to explore, don't forget to ask about programs or groups that have recently formed or been funded for the first time. Another good way to get this information is to ask arts council employees which art programs or groups they personally find the most interesting and why. You'll always get great answers and sometimes the responses will introduce you to whole new realms of art.

Those of you who don't quite know what to ask for, or who are given so many options that you can't digest them all, should find out what sorts of printed information arts councils make available to the public. Most publish newsletters, updates, events calendars, lists and descriptions of arts organizations, names of grant and fund recipients and lists of opportunities for artists (which translate into opportunities for you to see and buy art). Request specific items or ask that your name be placed on their mailing lists. You might have to pay for certain publications, but costs are always nominal and well worth the amount of information you get in return. Having everything in front of you in writing can be far more enlightening than trying to understand details over the phone.

In addition to their own publications, many arts councils maintain small libraries or files of publications from other arts councils. These are great places to do research if, for example, you're going on vacation and you want

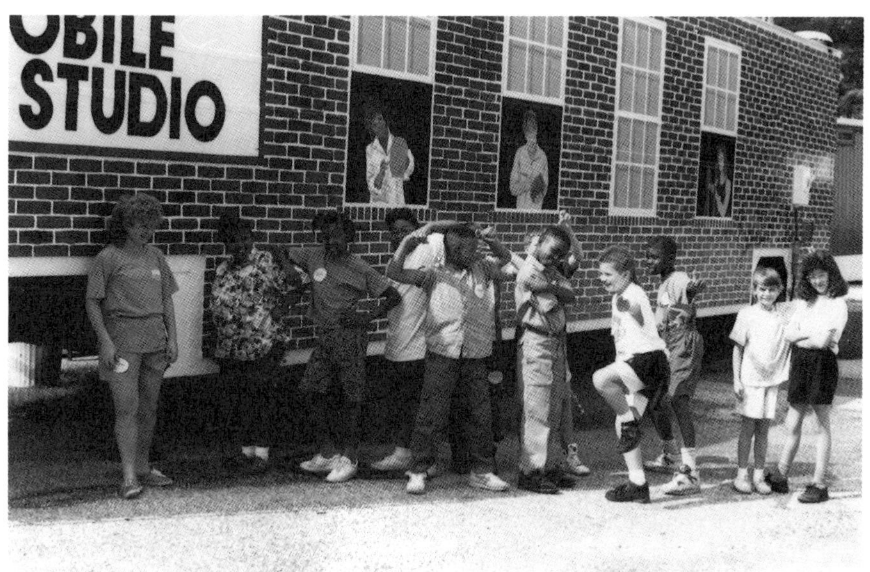

One of South Carolina's mobile art studios with a mural by Ralph Waldrop. These mobile studios, operated by the Arts Commission, serve even the remotest areas of the state and conduct programs for artists of all ages. Courtesy of the South Carolina Arts Commission.

to see art while you're there, or you're looking for special types of programs that you are pretty sure exist but are not in your area. Taken in their entirety, arts council publications cover thousands of art-buying opportunities.

Some agency libraries also keep artist registries and slide files. All you have to do is make an appointment to come in and take a look. Instead of visiting artist after artist, or program after program, you can one-stop-shop, see hundreds of pieces of art at once, decide what artists or art groups you find the most appealing, get their names and personally contact them. Agencies that don't maintain files can often refer you to groups within your fields of interest that do.

Affordability is one of the central features of the great majority of art that you learn about through arts councils and arts commissions. Much of this art emanates from sources well outside of the established art business. It is often sold in casual, comfortable surroundings and with little in the way of hype or high prices. Because the goals of the sellers are rarely to get famous or make lots of money, but rather to encourage and support art, you can discover some of the most reasonably priced art that you'll find anywhere.

Artful Collections

By organization. Confine your purchases to pieces done by artists who belong to a particular organization or club. Becoming involved with the same group of artists over a significant period of time can be a highly rewarding experience. You are able to see careers evolve, styles change and skills develop.

By funding source. Collect art by artists from art programs that receive funding from a particular state or regional arts council. You can assume that any such artists or art programs have at least some merit based on the fact that they have been chosen from among many competing applicants to receive government funding.

Many art-buying options that you have read about so far involve meeting artists and, assuming you that like their art, visiting them at their studios. Personal visits with artists are great ways to see the full scope of their work, speak with them, view their work environments, see how they live, exchange ideas and, if everything works out, buy art. This type of contact always results in a deeper understanding and appreciation of what you end up owning. Buying directly from artists is an art in itself, though, and the next chapter will help you make the best of all such opportunities.

10 Buying Directly from Artists

Buying directly from artists is a great way to save money on art. When no dealers operate as middlemen, you are often able to save one-third to one-half and sometimes even more over what the art would cost at galleries. Dealer commissions account for substantial percentages of retail art prices.

Dealers deserve those commissions, though. Without them, being able to see and buy art on a regular basis would be a lot more difficult. They bring artists to the public's attention by professionally presenting the art in their galleries and marketing it in ways that few artists are capable of doing or interested in getting involved with. Dealers educate, inform and provide valuable overviews of art, artists and the art market. When they are successful, they build solid collections for their clients, help establish reputations for artists, and create appreciation and demand for art.

Don't simply remove dealers from art business transactions in order to save money. You have to respect what they do and not attempt to go around them. Seeing an artist's work on display at a gallery, for example, and deliberately trying to exclude the dealer by contacting the artist on your own is totally inappropriate. You end up alienating not only the dealer but, most likely, the artist too.

The right way to eliminate dealers from the commission picture is either to cut back on or give up the gallery habit. Instead of waiting for dealers to bring art to their galleries so that you can go see it, bring yourself to the art. By going directly to the artists, you eliminate the dealers and save yourself the money that dealers charge to bring the art to you.

"But," you say, "The only good art is art you see at galleries."

Not true. Galleries by no means have a corner on good art. They show only a minute percentage of all existing art and cannot even come close to showing all the good art. The great majority of artists—many of whom are good—never exhibit at galleries.

You have already been introduced to a variety of situations in which you can come into contact with artists. Most of these are organized or formal events, though, and many artists never participate in these sorts of activities. You have to find out where they live and work so that you can attempt to make contact with them.

Ways to Meet Artists

As mentioned in the previous chapter, a fantastic way to meet artists is by taking out simple classified ads in artist trade papers and magazines. State your preferences. State your budget. State your name, address and phone number so that artists can contact you without too much difficulty. You may wish to mention that you are a private collector, although that's not really necessary. Depending on your requirements, advertise in those publications that are either general interest or specific to the types of art that you want to collect (see Appendix 1).

Advertising your wants on community bulletin boards is another good way to meet artists, especially when you're interested in buying locally or within particular geographic regions. Contact area arts councils, art schools, art galleries, art supply stores, museums and museum sales and rental galleries to find out where artist studios are concentrated. Most of these resources freely give this information and when they do, get specific names, addresses and neighborhoods whenever possible. For example, many major metropolitan areas have converted warehouses or warehouse districts where hundreds of artists live and work. Get these names as well as those of nearby businesses where artists congregate socially or do their shopping. Most of these locations will have community bulletin boards where you can post your art-collecting requirements.

And don't forget artist files and registries. Local and regional arts councils and non-profit arts organizations are particularly good resources, but no matter who you speak with, always ask whether they know of or can direct you to additional files. The more you have access to, the more art you can see at single locations and the less running around you have to do.

However you proceed, you eventually assemble a list of artists who may possibly have art for you. At that point, begin making more in-depth contact. Speak with these artists about their art and, whenever appropriate, make appointments to see their work.

Your goal is not only to locate art that you like at prices you can afford to pay, but also to recognize those artists who respect your financial situation. In order to establish mutually satisfying relationships, you need a basic understanding of the types of artists you will meet and the circumstances under which your art transactions will take place.

Profile of an "Affordable Artist"

In any artist encounter, decide as soon as possible whether you're speaking with *an affordable artist* or *an artist who has art that you can afford.*

Just about all artists on your list will have art that you can afford. Not that many of them are affordable artists, however. Understanding this difference is crucial to your art buying effectiveness.

Every artist you meet has their own ideas about what you deserve and how much they are prepared to give in terms of art, time, attention and respect when they learn how much money you have to spend. At one end of the continuum is the artist who sits down with you, answers all of your questions, wants you to have a good piece of art, stays in touch with you after your purchase, and keeps you updated on career developments. At the other end is the artist who offers you only inferior and insignificant pieces of art and can only be bothered with you for as long as it takes to sell you art and collect your money. The former is an affordable artist; the latter is an artist who has art that you can afford.

If you're like most people, you want to do business with affordable artists. These artists value you as an art lover, as a person who appreciates their art and as someone whose art interests deserve to be encouraged. When your budget is modest, you'll rarely get the biggest, most important piece of art no matter who you buy from, but if you stick with affordable artists, you'll at least be able to get something nice in terms of quality, care, detail and concern.

Not only do you end up with better pieces of art when you buy this way, but the affordable artist philosophy also happens to be the philosophy of success. These artists tend to be positive, selfless, generous, flexible, interested in enriching people's lives with their art and not obsessed with money or fame. As a result, they generally progress smoothly in their careers and their work is more likely to be sought after by collectors. On the other hand, artists who are difficult to deal with and are primarily interested in money, fame and ego impede their own success.

Some ways to identify affordable artists:

- They believe that their art is for all people, not only those who can afford to pay high prices.
- If you really want their art, they'll bend over backwards to make sure that you get it.
- They want as many people as possible to have and enjoy their art.
- Creating art and expressing themselves is more important than getting ahead in their careers.

Some representative quotes that you are likely to hear from affordable artists:

- "The most important thing is for people to see what I do."
- "I don't want to be my only collector."
- "Sharing my art is what's important."
- "I love meeting people who really appreciate my work."
- "I want my art to go to good homes."

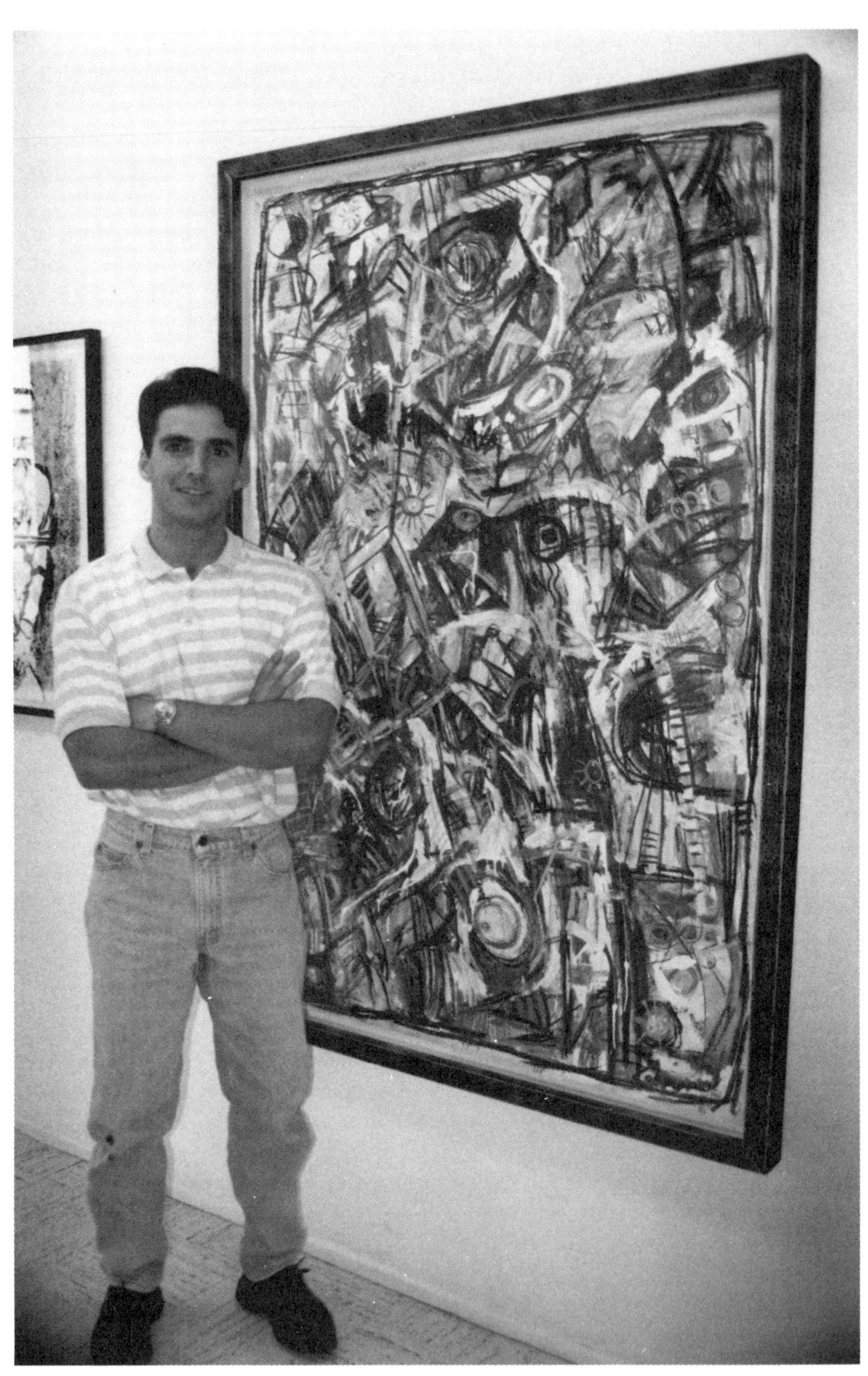

Los Angeles area artist Zohar Wertheim believes that everyone who wants to own original art should be able to and will work with all collectors, no matter how small their budgets.

Even if you have to go through ten or twenty encounters before you find one artist who satisfies the affordable artist criteria, you'll be glad you waited. Affordable artists are wonderful people to meet and do business with—when you find one, you'll know it.

ARTISTS TO AVOID

Some mention has already been made of qualities in artists that make neither for good relationships nor good buys. Most are centered around money, fame and ego issues, but to be more specific, these additional pointers will help you recognize when the time has come to end one encounter and move on to the next:

- The artist refuses to be flexible in selling prices.
- The artist makes you feel inferior.
- The artist is only willing to meet with you if he's relatively certain that you are going to buy art.
- Money is a central aspect of everything the artist says and does.
- The artist wants to charge you the same amount of money that galleries charge for his art, even though no dealer participates in your transaction.
- The artist thinks he should be better known than he is.
- The artist compares his work to that of expensive artists, says it's just as good, and bases his asking prices on what those artists charge.
- The artist has bitter or hostile feelings about the art world or the way his career has progressed.
- The artist has nothing good to say about fellow artists.
- The artist flat-out refuses to consider making a smaller, less detailed or cheaper version of a piece that you really like but can't afford.
- The artist has a "take it or leave it" attitude about your interest in buying his art.
- The artist is willing to sell you something for what you want to pay, but complains or is unhappy about it.
- The artist only offers you the most insignificant pieces in his studio and stresses how little he has to give for what you want to pay.

NEGOTIATING WITH AN ARTIST

Whenever you find an artist whose work you like and who you get along well with, follow a fairly simple routine. See all his art before making any decisions. Allow the artist to show you around his studio and pay special attention when he explains his work. Never be too quick to dismiss art without hearing the story behind it because a piece that you don't find attractive at first may take on new meaning, beauty or significance once you understand the artist's intentions. Find out selling prices along the way and

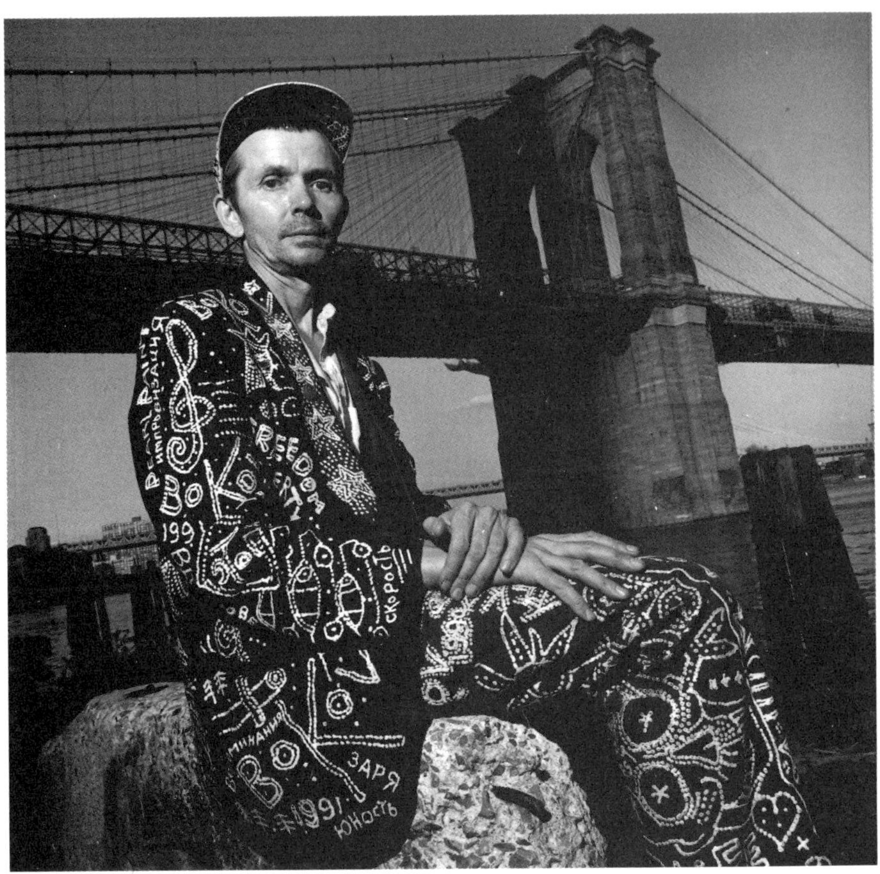

New York artist Konstantin Bokov by the Brooklyn Bridge, 1992, Copyrighted by Juliana Thomas. Bokov, whose art has sold into the thousands of dollars, believes that anyone who wants to should be able to own his art and that his mission is to serve society as an artist.

set aside those pieces that you like the most, even when they might be a little beyond your price limit.

Keep in mind that when you buy directly from an artist, with no dealer involvement, you should pay wholesale, not retail, prices. Don't pay an artist a dealer's commission. The only exception to this rule is when an artist is under exclusive contract to a dealer and is prohibited from selling any art for less than the dealer sells it for. Any time that you're unclear on this issue, have the artist explain his pricing policy or price structure.

When the time comes to buy, sit down with the artist, review your selections and ask whatever remaining questions you have. If what you've chosen comes close to what you want, but doesn't quite satisfy you and you'd really love a particular type of piece that you believe the artist is capable of making for you, describe it and find out whether that can be done.

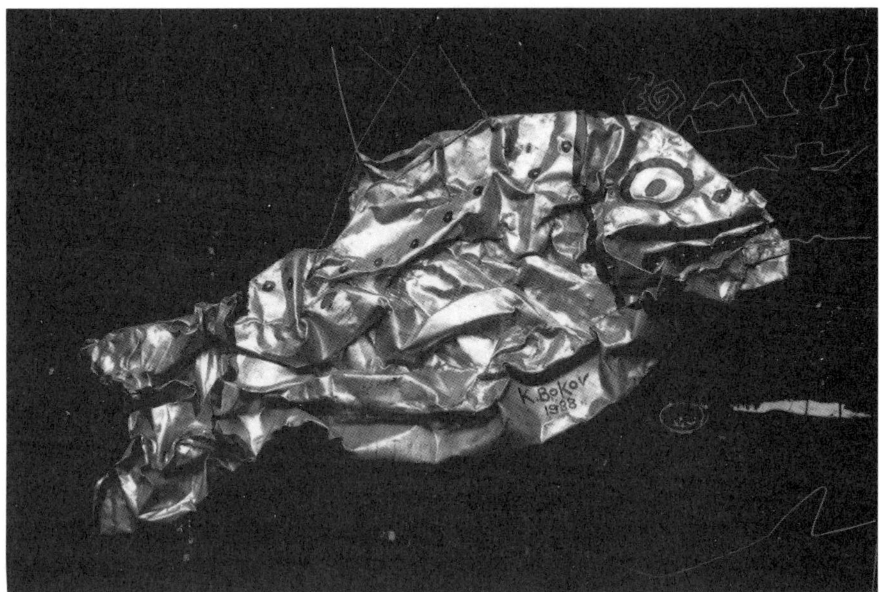

"Fish," by Konstantin Bokov (1988).

You never know unless you ask. For those of you who are ready to buy except for the fact that you would like to pay a little less than the artist wants, here are some negotiating do's and don'ts:

- When you like the art, say so. Artists enjoy hearing compliments. You may think that artists will hold firm in their prices if you show your enthusiasm, but the opposite is much more often the case. They'll be more flexible.
- If you can't afford something but really like it, be truthful about your feelings as well as your financial situation. Most artists will work with you. There is nothing they want more than to sell their art to people who love it. The extent of your admiration may be almost more important than the money involved.
- If you can't afford to pay for it all at once, ask whether you can pay over time. Most artists are amenable to these sorts of arrangements.
- If you want to pay a lower price, make a reasonable offer and support it with constructive reasons.
- Never disparage a work of art to get the price down.
- Never criticize an artist's pricing policy or compare it in negative terms to how other artists price their art.
- Don't insult with lowball offers.
- Don't play games to get a better price. Artists can tell when this is what you're up to and it's the quickest and easiest way to alienate them.

BARTER

Barter is one of the better kept secrets of the art business. Art insiders know about it, but relatively few retail buyers are aware that it's a very viable option. That's because most people are used to shopping at galleries and galleries rarely barter.

Artists love to barter, however. They barter art among themselves and with their friends all the time. Virtually all artists will accept goods or services from anyone in exchange for their art. Barter is a great way to obtain art that costs more than you can ever afford to pay and it's also a great way to acquire art while conserving your cash.

In your meetings with artists, always bring up the subject of barter. Find out what sorts of things they need and tell them what you have to offer or have special access to. The more ideas that you exchange with each other, the greater the chances that barter will play a part in your transactions.

When barter does appear to be a possibility, don't insist on all-barter, no-cash arrangements unless the artist is really enthusiastic about what you have to offer. You'll find that barter will go further towards a purchase price when you pay a portion of that price in cash. This way, the artist gets the best of both worlds.

Artful Collections

By subject matter. Commission artists to do small paintings, drawings or watercolors that all have similar subject matters. This type of collection shows how different artists handle the same situation. Possible subject matters might include members of your family, your house or property, abstract designs in reds and blues, farm scenes, animal scenes, the inside of a room, or a particular point of interest in your city or town.

Self-portraits. Try to obtain a self-portrait by every artist whose work you like.

Studios. Collect pictures showing the studio or workplace of artists whose work you like.

By price. Give each artist the same amount of money—$100, for example—and let them make whatever they want to for you.

Older pieces. Many artists price these to sell because they move on to other things. Paradoxically, early works frequently become the most collectible in the long run.

By now, you have all the basic tools necessary to navigate the art world and locate those individuals or groups that have art for you. You've been given hints about the vast variety of art that's available out there, but not much in the way of particulars. Part IV, the final part of this book, talks about specific types of affordable art, describes what they are and tells you how to go about finding them. This is the fun part—discovering exactly what and how much you can get for just a little bit of money.

Part IV

Specific Types of Affordable Art

11 How You Can Afford the Work of Famous Artists

Those of you who have always wanted to own originals by Picasso, Chagall, Miro or other world-class artists but believed that the only way to accomplish that would be to mortgage your house, need not despair. Believe it or not, you can purchase works by these and many other big-name artists for as little as $50 each. Imagine showing your friends your collection of modern masters and having them wonder what your source of hidden wealth could possibly be!

Few people are aware of the famous artist affordable art option for two main reasons. First of all, the art is not ordinarily found in the form of individual framed pieces and secondly, it is not often found at art galleries. It comes in the form of original prints that are found almost exclusively in books, portfolios, periodicals, magazines and exhibition catalogues. What makes them so inexpensive is that they're almost always unsigned and were published in large edition sizes. They are originals, however, and that's what counts.

Original prints have been included in books, portfolios and other publications for centuries. Not until the latter part of the nineteenth century, though, did these items really begin to proliferate in the marketplace. This was due in large part to the evolution of public education and the expansion of public museums. At the same time, advances in the publishing industry allowed for quality publications to be printed at very reasonable costs. The stage was set for the dissemination of fine art to the masses.

Deluxe art publications were initiated and marketed to satisfy the increased demand for information about art and artists as well as for the art itself. Original prints were included alongside the texts to increase these publications' salability, desirability and prestige. In many instances, the prints also helped to publicize major art exhibitions and, in general, aided in broadening the collector-base for their artists and the dealers who represented them. Artists were always eager to contribute their prints because they

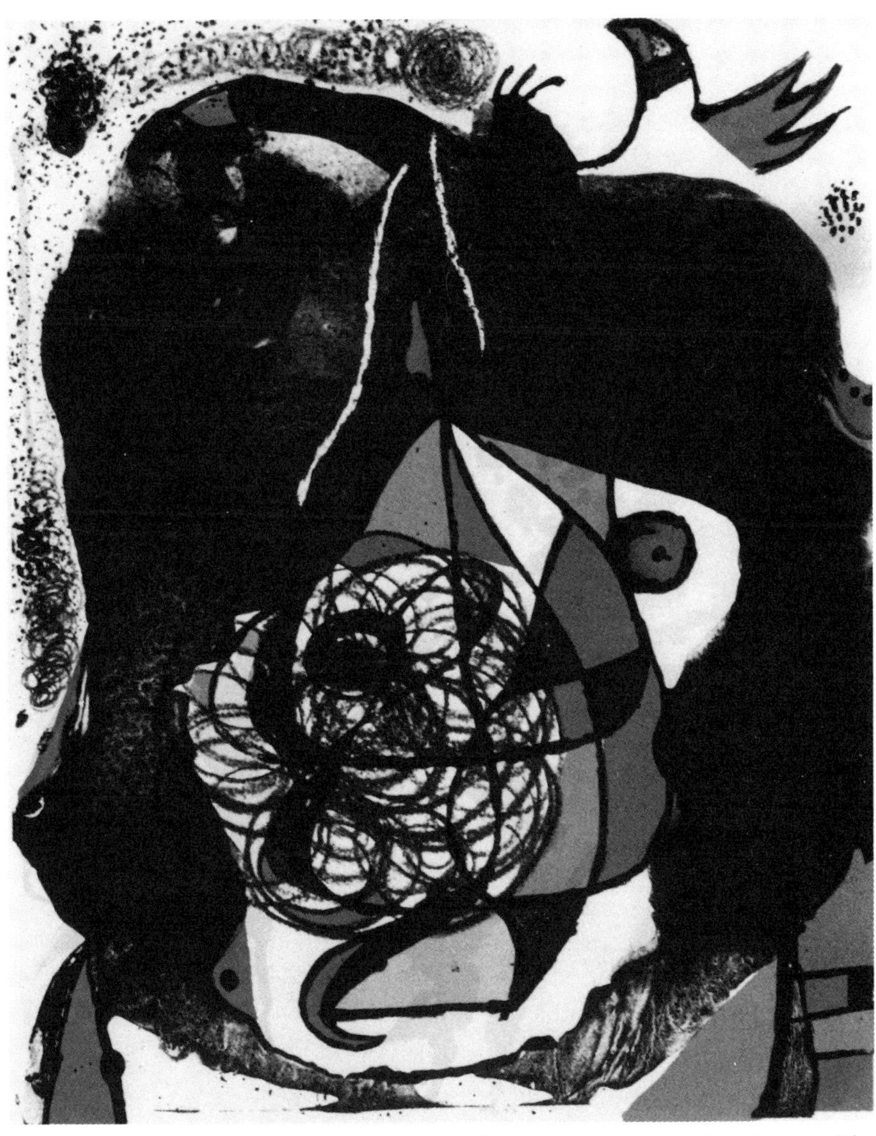

One of two original Miro lithographs contained in the book Revolutions in Stage Design of the XXth Century *by Denis Bablet (Paris, Leon Amiel, 1977). Dimensions: 13½ by 10 inches.*

made such great advertisements and were seen by so many more people than the usual gallery goers and art insiders.

In spite of the fact that these publications contained original art, they were not initially marketed as collectibles. They were priced significantly higher than average books, periodicals or catalogues, but were very affordable and far cheaper than what original art pieces cost at the galleries. Edition sizes were large and often ranged well up into the thousands—well beyond the limits of what any serious dealer or collector would have considered to be representative of "real art" during those time periods. Those who wanted the genuine signed, limited and original pieces still had to shop the galleries.

As time passed, though, and gallery prices rose higher and higher, publications with original prints took on new significance as collectibles in and of themselves. For art lovers with little to spend, they became the only way to afford originals by famous artists. Since the 1970s, their popularity has continued to grow, until today the most collectible of these publications have become rather expensive and difficult to find. However, there's still plenty of quality material available to collectors of modest means.

What You Get for Your Money

Understand at the outset that for the amount of money you spend on these prints, you buy at the low end of artists' outputs in terms of collectibility and significance. Don't confuse this art with multimillion dollar masterpieces that you read and hear about. Regardless of their limitations, though, these prints are still by well-known or world-famous artists and you're still talking about some pretty good-looking art. The overwhelming majority are beautifully composed, were produced by some of the world's great fine art printers and, when properly framed and displayed, they can look every bit as imposing as signed limited editions or even one-of-a-kind originals.

You also get names. To some collectors, name is everything, nothing else matters and nothing else satisfies. To others, the look is more important, but the name is still what makes the art work. Whether you love Picasso or you want to impress your friends or you feel that a big name automatically legitimizes a work of art, these prints accomplish such objectives.

Lastly and most importantly, you get original art and not reproductions of original art. These prints were conceived by artists as prints alone and not created first in other mediums and then reproduced as prints of those originals by third parties (review Chapter 5 for a full explanation of this statement). The artists themselves produced the surfaces from which these prints were printed and then worked with fine art printers to insure that the finished products were accurate and acceptable.

How Much to Spend

Even within this realm of collecting, the amount of money that you can spend from one print or publication to the next varies substantially. Expect to pay at least $50 apiece for prints by the more famous artists, but be careful when per-piece costs begin to exceed several hundred dollars—some sellers occasionally overestimate values because they believe that anything by famous artists must automatically be expensive. Remember that you're buying at the bottom of the output continuum, so shop around, familiarize yourself with the market and pay accordingly.

Quite often, individual publications have more than one print in them. Depending on how famous the artists are and the total number of prints, you can pay anywhere from $50 to several thousand dollars per item. The advantage to buying a single publication with multiple prints is that per-print costs tend to be lower than if you purchase the prints separately. You're buying in bulk, so to speak, which gives you a better overall price.

If you take the time to look and learn who the likely suppliers are, you can find books or periodicals that contain multiple prints, frame them all, acquire your entire art collection in one or two or three separate purchases,

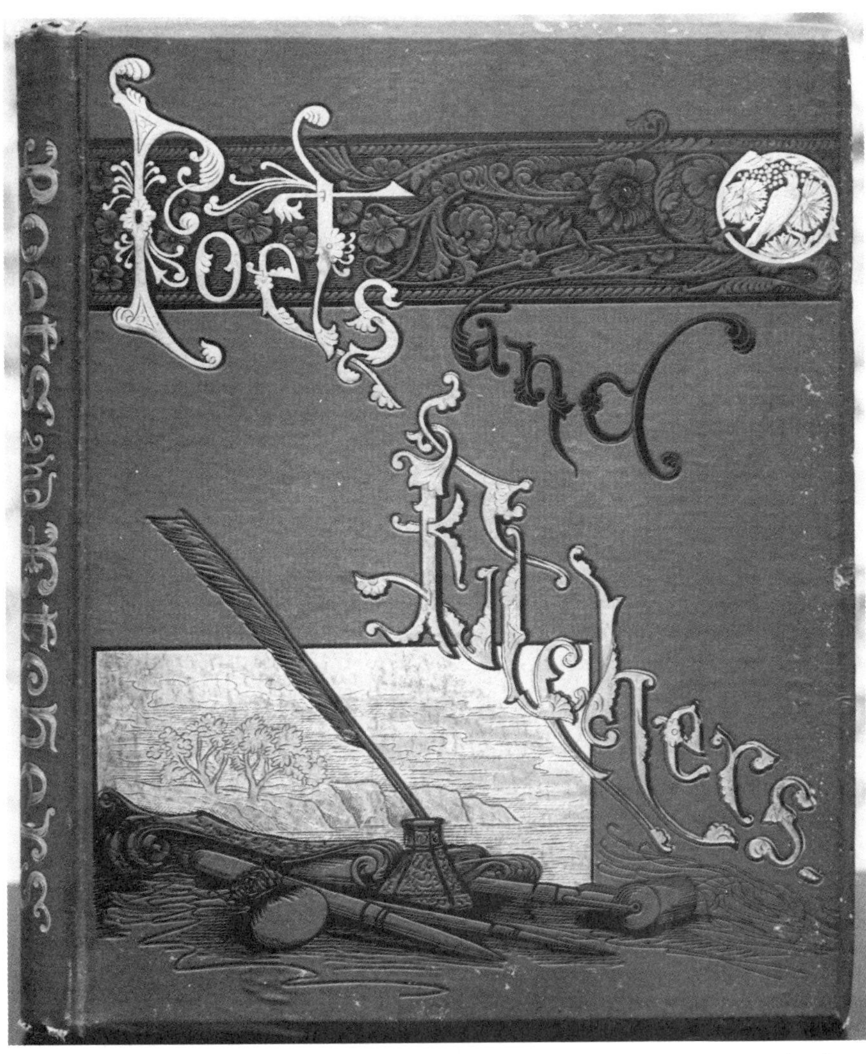

The book, Poets and Etchers *(Boston, James R. Osgood, 1882), contains twenty original etchings by five important 19th-century American artists.*

and never have to buy again. The other option with bulk buying is to keep only the prints you want, take those you don't want and either sell, trade or give them as gifts. The more contacts and resources that you develop in this area, on the buying as well as the selling or trading end, the easier a time you'll have putting together a quality collection.

Those of you who prefer to pay less than $50 per print won't be able to buy the biggest names, but lesser-known artists with decent reputations have also produced original prints for various publications. Depending on the artist, these prints can sometimes be had for as little as $5 or $10 each. In particular, works by lesser-knowns can often be found in art-related books, periodicals, catalogues and portfolios that have been published in France and Germany since the early part of this century. When you see publications with prints you like, but don't recognize the names of the artists, don't automatically assume that they're worthless. Use techniques outlined in Chapter 3 to locate and evaluate biographical information. Depending on the quality of the prints and the amount of information you find, pay accordingly.

You can also save money by meeting dealers and collectors of more expensive prints and offering to buy the ones that they don't want or that don't fit into their collections. Sometimes these people have to buy prints in bulk just to get one or two that they want, and they're always happy to sell the rest off at very good prices. Finally, keep an eye out for publications that contain original prints as well as prints that reproduce pre-existing works of art in other mediums. Sometimes, both are printed by the same fine art printer using the identical techniques, and even though the reproductions are equally as beautiful and dramatic as the originals, they're far cheaper simply because they're not original compositions. Ways to distinguish between the two are discussed in this chapter under the heading, "How to Identify Original Prints."

How to Find Prints

A few mainstream art dealers and galleries sell single prints that have been removed from their publications and framed or matted, but this is not a recommended way to buy because, you're paying full retail for the prints plus additional dealer markups on framing costs. Another problem with buying like this is that these dealers tend to overprice and overhype these pieces by placing too much emphasis on the reputations of the artists and too little on the insignificance of the art. They won't necessarily tell you that the prints have been taken from publications and issued in large-edition sizes.

Find prints at better prices by checking used and rare bookstores, specialist art bookstores and booksellers, used and rare book fairs, book auctions and antiques or collectibles shows where booksellers participate. These are all places where you can find complete publications with their prints intact. Also look through boxes or file drawers of miscellaneous prints whenever you see them at shops or shows because many dealers keep all of their odd prints together and you never know what you might find. As always, be specific about what you're looking for and never come and go without asking for it.

Find bookstores by checking your local Yellow Pages or those of nearby major cities under the heading "Book Dealers–Used and Rare." Find out about book auctions and book fairs from book dealers. Find out about antiques and collectibles shows from antiques dealers or check schedules in local or regional antiques trade papers (often distributed free at antiques shops) and in local newspaper classifieds under art, antiques, collectibles or general merchandise headings.

Booksellers are your single best resource for finding prints. Call or visit all used and rare bookstores in your area and see what they have. When you come up empty-handed at specific stores, speak with the owners and ask who might have what you're looking for. Booksellers are a close-knit group and can usually direct you to the right dealers or specialists.

Also contact *AB Bookman's Weekly* (PO Box AB, Clifton, NJ 07015; 201-772-0020), the largest used and rare bookseller trade publication in the country, and ask for a copy of their *AB Bookman's Yearbook*. This annual directory lists thousands of dealers by city and state as well as by specialty and costs only $25. It also lists regional bookselling associations, some of which have hundreds of members, and book auction houses from around the country. Through it, you can place your name on dozens of mailing lists and receive regular sales catalogues as well as personal quotes from dealers who think they've found what you're looking for. If you really want to get serious, subscribe to *AB Bookman's Weekly* and keep current with who's selling or auctioning what. If you really, really want to get serious, advertise your wants there—you will get responses.

How to Identify Original Prints

It is important to be able to separate out the originals from the reproductions of pre-existing works of art in other mediums. The techniques used to produce both the originals and reproductions are sometimes identical, even within the same publication. Fortunately, there are two basic ways of figuring out what's what.

The simplest way is to check inside the publications themselves. At the beginnings or ends of many of them, you will find either lists of illustrations, publisher statements or limitation statements telling how many copies have been printed and what types of art they contain. Prints are often listed as being original or the publication will include a sentence such as "The original lithograph opposite page 33 was created specially for this issue by the artist." These statements are not always in English, especially in foreign publications, so you may have to have them translated.

When you are unable to determine from a publication whether or not a

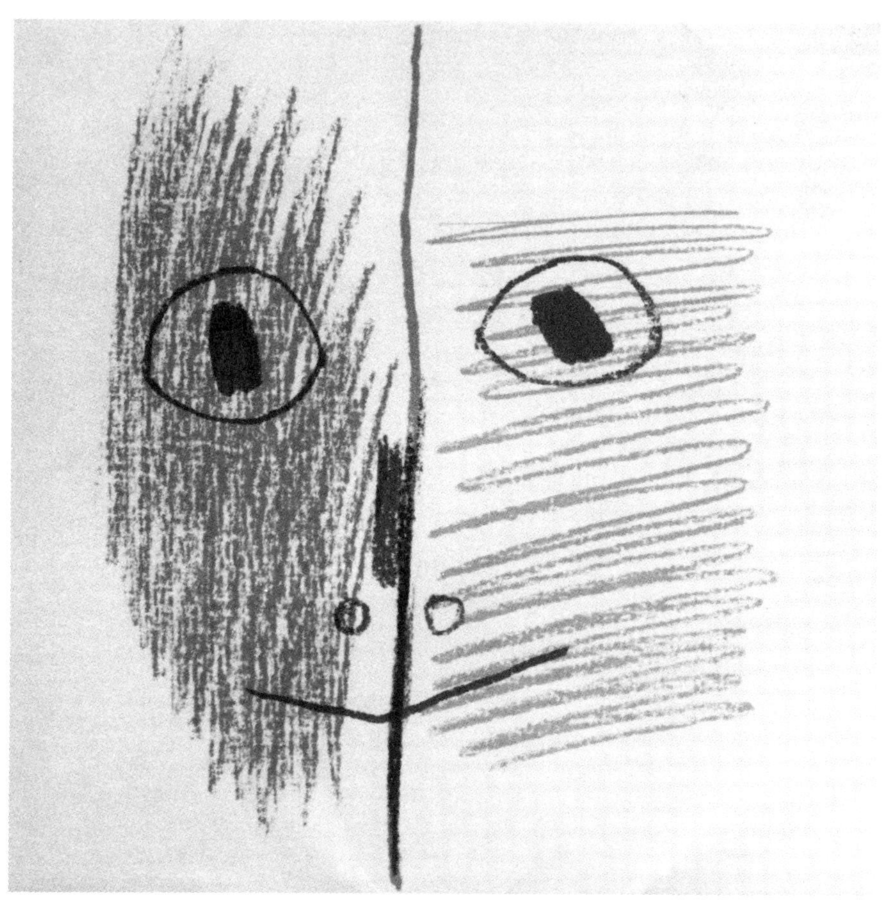

Original cover lithograph by Picasso from a Picasso exhibition catalogue and show at Galerie Louise Leiris, Paris, 1957. Dimensions: 6½ by 6⅝ inches.

print is original or you are considering buying a single print, you can check art reference books called *catalogues raisonné*. This type of book has been written about most famous and near-famous artists. A *catalogue raisonné* lists all the prints, paintings or other works of art produced by a particular artist during his career.

Museums and other institutions with significant print collections usually have all major print *catalogues raisonné* in their libraries. Check *The Official Museum Directory* or museums in your area for names of libraries or research facilities that would best be able to help you. Once you locate a good resource, give the librarian all essential information about the print—what publication it was in, its date, subject matter, size and so on. If the print is listed in the *catalogue raisonné,* it's original and you can proceed with your purchase.

When a print is not listed, you can either forget about buying it or pay substantially less for it than you would for an original. As mentioned above, some of the reproductions of original works of art printed by fine art printers are identical in quality and beauty to the original prints. You would not be collecting originals by buying this way, but you would be collecting the arts of the printer. You can read more about this type of affordable art in Chapter 15.

Specific Sources of Prints

Although thousands of publications include original prints, some are more well-known and popular among collectors than others because they contain prints by relatively important artists. There are a few that you should keep an eye out for.

In the category of periodicals and magazines, the three most popular ones are all French—*XXe Siecle* (published from the 1930s through the 1980s), *Verve* (published from the 1930s through the 1950s) and *Derriere Le Miroir* (published from the 1940s through the 1980s). All contain prints by near-famous artists and famous ones like Miro (1893–1983), Chagall (1887–1985), Picasso (1881–1973), Kandinsky (1866–1944), and Matisse (1869–1954). *XXe Siecle* and *Verve* were bound with prints bound in; *Derriere Le Miroir* was published in a portfolio format with loose prints laid in and easily removable. Another advantage to *Derriere Le Miroir* is its large format. Single-page prints measure approximately 15 by 11 inches, double-page prints about 15 by 22 inches.

Exhibition and show catalogues with original prints have been and continue to be published by museums, art dealers and fine art printing companies. Many times, the covers of these catalogues are original prints which can be removed and framed. Those published by art dealers are usually more affordable than museum catalogues and would be what you'd look for if you were really on a budget. For example, Paris art dealers, Berggruen & Cie, has published numerous show catalogues with cover lithographs by Miro, Chagall, Matta (1911–?) and other world-renowned artists. Among museum show catalogues, "Prints from the Mourlot Press" is one of the most collectible. Published in 1964, it honors the accomplishments of this great French fine art printing company, contains nearly twenty original lithographs by artists like Picasso, Chagall, Miro, Matisse and Calder (1898–1976) and can be usually be purchased for several hundred dollars.

Books and portfolios with original prints are generally deluxe publications published in smaller or limited editions. Many of them are about the artists themselves and contain anywhere from one print to as many as ten or twenty in exceptional cases. For example, *catalogues raisonné* of the prints of some of the major artists like Chagall, Miro and Picasso, contain original prints. If you're on a budget, American and European painter-etcher publica-

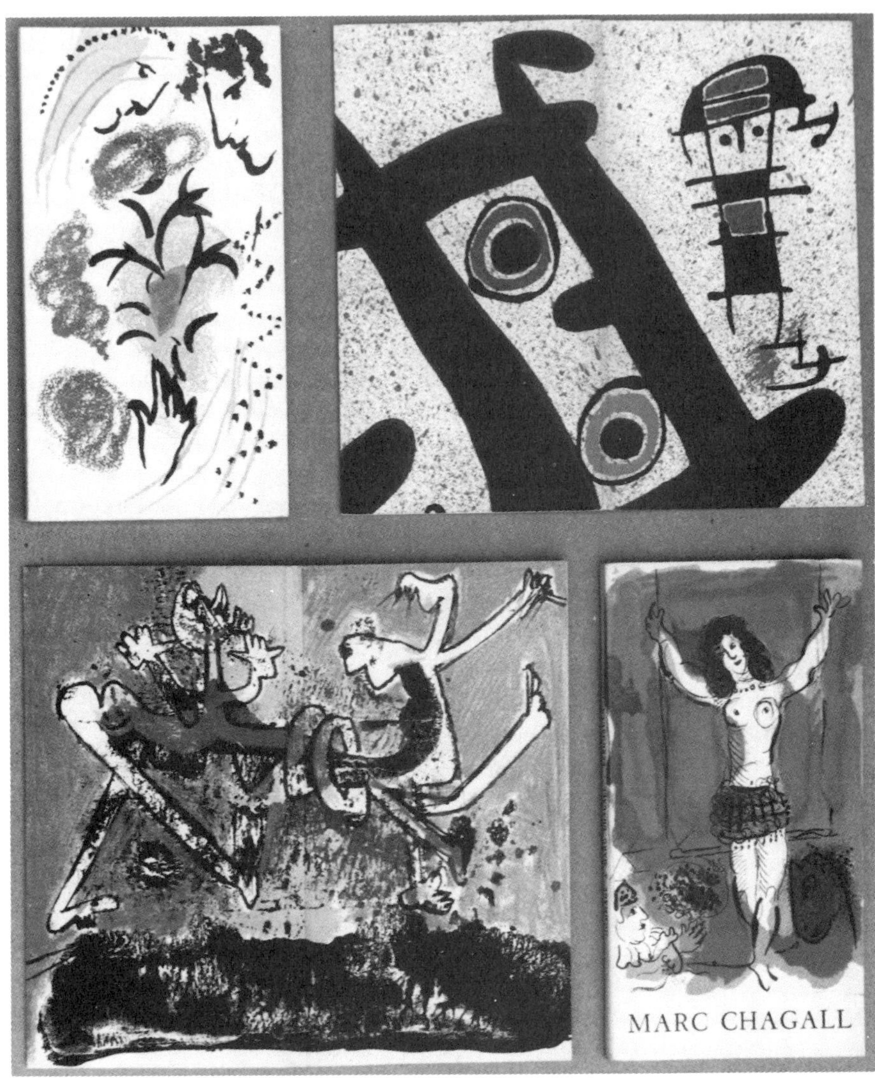

Four exhibition catalogues with original lithographic covers from Berggruen & Cie, Paris, circa 1965–1973. Top: Chagall, 8¾ by 4½ inches; Miro, 9⅜ by 8½ inches. Bottom: Matta, 9⅜ by 8½ inches; Chagall, 8¾ by 4½ inches.

tions produced in the latter part of the nineteenth century such as *Poets and Etchers* are good sources of etchings—complete books or portfolios of etchings often cost out to as little as $10 or $20 per print.

How to Handle Your Prints

When you buy a publication that contains original prints, the first thing you want to consider is whether or not to keep it intact. Removing the prints can sometimes diminish the value of the piece as a whole, especially when the text is integral to the appreciation and understanding of the prints. In these cases, you may wish to leave it as is. You can appreciate the art just as easily by looking at it in its original settings as you can by removing and framing it.

Other times, the prints are meant to be removed. This is especially true of portfolios or publications that are not bound together but contain loose prints. If you have any questions in this area, consult an expert before separating out any prints.

When you decide to remove prints that are bound in, always have them removed by a professional who is experienced in taking books, magazines or catalogues apart without losing any surface area of the prints. Don't do this yourself. Even though these prints have only modest value, that value is still heavily dependent upon condition, intactness and absence of damage.

As for framing, have this professionally done too. Use acid-free mats and backing and observe standard rules for display such as avoiding direct sunlight, temperature extremes and excessive humidity or dryness. Proper framing and hanging assures that your prints will remain in excellent condition and hold their value over time.

Artful Collections

Prints by one artist. Select an artist whose work you love and is not too expensive and concentrate on collecting his prints. If you don't have much money to spend, pick one who didn't do very many prints for publications.

Exhibition catalogues. Base your collection on original prints from dealer or gallery exhibition catalogues. You could even center your collection on the cover art from this type of catalogue.

Prints from a single publication. Collect all the prints from one book, catalogue, portfolio or other publication. Buy a large enough piece and you can have your entire art collection at once.

By publication date. Collect all of the prints published by a particular gallery or publication during a given time period. For example, you might collect those prints issued during the year of your birth.

■ Fine art photography is another field of collecting where the work of relatively famous artists can be had at reasonable and even bargain prices. After decades of being overlooked and ignored, photographs are becoming increasingly popular with collectors. Even so, the photographic world is still underexplored, and dealers as well as collectors are continually discovering and rediscovering substantial amounts of worthwhile material. As you're about to see, this means that lower-priced items are relatively more common than they are in more established fields of collecting.

12 Collecting Original Photographs

Of all the affordable art options that were researched for this book, the most astonishing findings center around opportunities for collecting photographs. In no other area can so much quality work be purchased so inexpensively. The amount of available material is huge, bargains abound and if photography as fine art appeals to you, you'll love what you're about to read.

You only have to look at newspapers, magazines and browse through photographically illustrated books at your local newsstand, bookstore or library to realize how many tens of thousands of beautiful, professional-quality photographs have been taken. For every one of those published photos, thousands more unpublished ones fill the files of photographers' studios around the world. To get an idea of how many photographers make their livings by taking pictures, open up any good-sized city's Yellow Pages and take a look under the headings "Photographers–Commercial" and "Photographers–Portrait." Add to this the amount of competent amateurs, hobbyists, part-timers and lower-profile professionals who don't list their names. Then consider the amount of vintage photographs that have been taken by competent or professional photographers since the invention of the camera. You are talking about millions upon millions of original works of art.

Photography dealers only scratch the surface with what they offer at their galleries. If they made the most modest attempts to represent everything of merit, they'd be overwhelmed in an instant. The amount of serious collectors is far too small to even begin to absorb all the quality material that's available. At this point in time, dealers sell the best of the best, stick with what has proven track records and pretty much ignore the rest. "The rest" is what you're about to be introduced to.

General Guidelines for Collecting

Because photograph collecting is so new and because so much material is available, dealers and collectors sometimes have the attitude that the only photographs worth collecting are those by the world's great photographers. That leaves a surplus of undiscovered and unexplored territory from which newcomers can put together groupings or collections that no one else has thought of yet. As with other areas of collecting, look at a variety of photographic images, decide what you like and how much you like it, research and act according to guidelines listed in Chapter 3, avoid the hype or lack thereof and buy what you feel comfortable buying. Here are some additional guidelines for evaluating photographs:

Evaluate the content of the image. The more unusual, historical, detailed, thought-provoking, or engaging it is, the more collectible it will be. See whether you can read any writing on the image itself (you may need a magnifying glass for this). Also attempt to identify fashions, styles, dates, individuals, events, or locations. Always ask yourself what places a particular image apart from the great majority of ordinary photographs.

Document the photograph with related information. When you're buying a vintage print, find out whatever you can from the seller. This includes names of previous owners or relevant family histories, background data that helps to explain the image, and any additional details, like those suggested in the previous paragraph, that are not evident from the image itself. When you're buying a contemporary image, get this information from either the photographer or the dealer. The photographer's statement is particularly important and always adds value to the photograph. Whenever possible, have anyone who tells you anything interesting put it in writing or do so yourself.

Inspect the condition of any photograph before you buy. Damage seriously reduces the value of all but the rarest, most important images. First, check the overall physical condition of the photograph and the mount (when there is one). Remove a mat or frame so that you can see everything. Notice any rips, tears, scratches, rubbing, soiling, or other defects. Next, inspect the condition of the image itself. Watch out for fading, problems with color reproduction, tarnishing, darkening and unevenness. Under ordinary circumstances, confine your buying to images that are fresh, clear, in focus, have good contrast, are well-defined and show little or no signs of damage, mishandling or wear.

Identify the photographer. With contemporary photographers, simply get biographical information or resumes whenever you buy. For collectors of vintage photography, this procedure is not so easy. While much has been written about the most famous photographers, little information is available about the legions of lesser-knowns. Nevertheless, piece together as many clues as possible pertaining to any photographers you identify because, once again, the more you know, the more you enhance the values of the photographs.

Often, you can get photographers' names and addresses from the photographs themselves—either off of the fronts or backs of the mounts or stamped or signed on the images themselves. More recent photographs may have local or regional exhibit stickers on the backs of the mounts in addition to signatures. Look up these names in dictionaries, bibliographies or indexes of photographers (art departments at major public and institutional libraries usually have these). If you come up empty-handed, check *The Official Museum Directory* for museums that have photography departments or for specialized photography museums that might be able to help you. Local historical societies, geneologists and old city directories might also have the information you're looking for.

For example, the George Eastman House Library (900 East Avenue, Rochester, NY 14607, 716-271-3361) is a major research facility that is equipped to handle all photographically related questions. They maintain a data base with over 14,000 names of individual photographers from all time periods and all nationalities, as well as numerous other references that you might find helpful. Call or write them and they'll be happy to research any name for you. All inquiries are answered.

If you'd rather learn how to do the research yourself, get a hold of the book *Photographers: A Sourcebook for Historical Research* edited by Peter Palmquist (Carl Mautz Publishing, P.O. Box 9, Brownsville, CA 95919). It contains essays on the hows, whys and wheres of photographic research as well as worldwide bibliography of directories of photographers by Richard Rudisill. Use this book as a springboard to accessing information on tens of thousands of photographers of all time periods and all nationalities.

When a photograph is unsigned or the photographer is unknown, don't automatically assume that it's worthless. If the image is good, the condition is good and the background information is interesting, you can still have a winner.

Successful research and evaluation means that you learn the who, what, when, where and why behind every photo you own. You know their stories, you can caption them, you understand what makes them special. This not only increases their value, but it also increases their meaning, significance and the pleasure they provide to you and anyone who sees or owns them in the future.

Opportunities in Vintage Photography

Vintage photographs are everywhere. Antiques shops, secondhand stores, flea markets, antiques malls, rummage sales, collector fairs, auctions, used and rare bookstores, estate sales—just about any place where secondhand goods are sold is a great place to look. Photos can be found in boxes, drawers, folders, file cabinets, albums, hanging framed on walls, lying on tables, or propped up on chairs.

Certain types of vintage photographs are already heavily collected, very

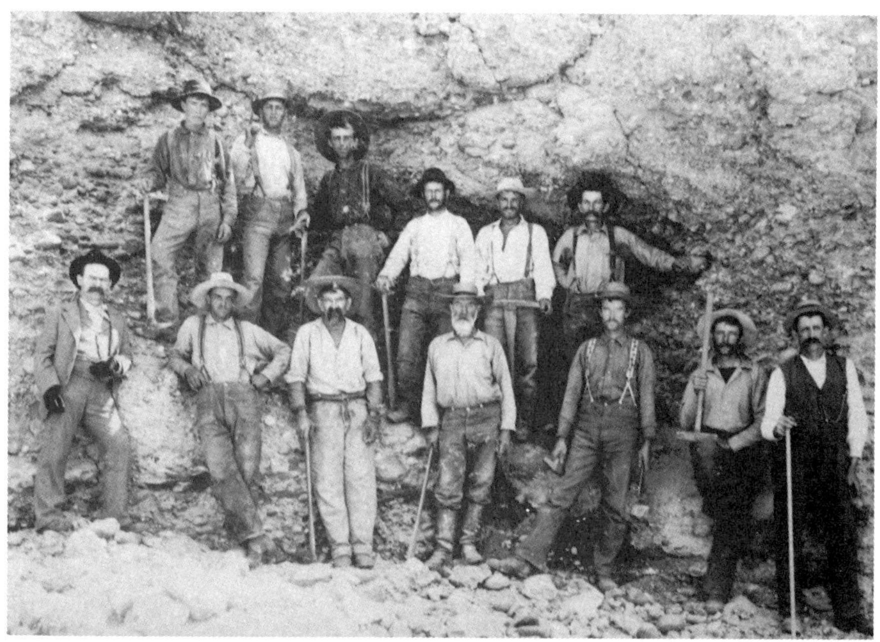

Northern California miners. Albumen print, circa 1895, $5^{1}/_{2}$ by $7^{3}/_{4}$ inches. Courtesy of Argonaut Book Shop, San Francisco.

expensive and difficult to find. Numerous others are not, however, and can be had for prices starting as low as fifty cents or a dollar each. Here are some frequently ignored categories where collectors still have a large choice:

Old family portraits. You'll find a huge amount of material available in this area, which translates into a huge amount of collecting opportunities. Few people have ever thought seriously about collecting them because they are so common and, besides that, many people never considered putting other people's relatives on their walls.

If you view them as original works of art, though, and not as people you never knew, the situation dramatically changes. For example, you can collect the works of one or two or several photographers. Or how about collecting only photographs that were taken in a particular city or state? Or perhaps you'd rather collect by date, fashion style, age or sex of the sitters, the number of sitters per photograph, whether anyone is wearing uniforms, types of backgrounds used, whether animals are present, whether people are seated, standing, leaning against things, or have mustaches or beards. You name it—create your own collection and do it on a shoestring budget.

Nineteenth- and early twentieth-century views of famous buildings, landmarks, interiors and works of art. Collectors have traditionally paid little or no attention to photographs whose subject matters look exactly the same today as they did at the time they were taken. This tends to be true even when they're in perfect condition, beautifully done or have been taken by

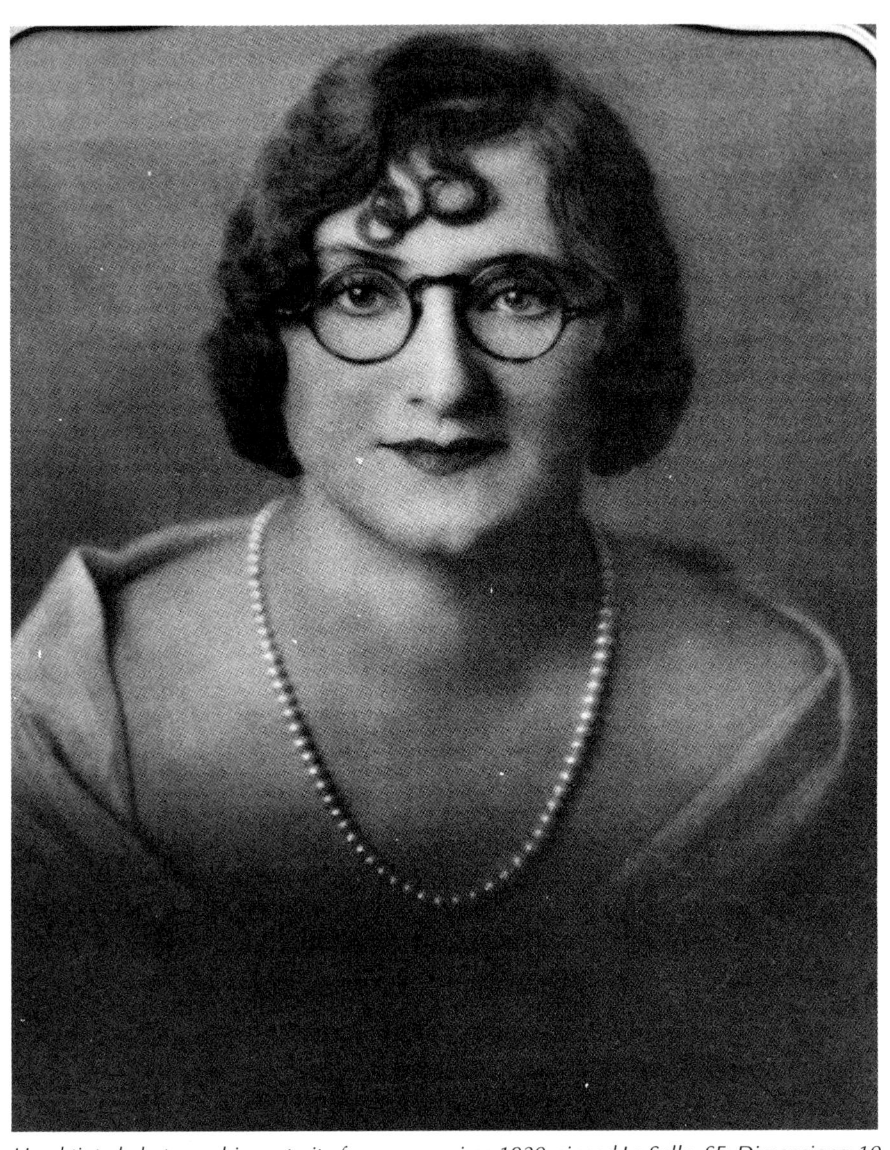

Hand-tinted photographic portrait of a woman, circa 1920, signed La Salle, SF. Dimensions: 10 by 8 inches.

well-known photographers. Possible collections you could form are images of statuary, paintings, hallways, churches, altars, particular types of rooms, or interiors and exteriors of famous museums or public buildings. You might also think about collecting by country, photographer, city, date, physical size of the image, whether mountains are visible, fountains are present, doors are open or modes of transportation are visible.

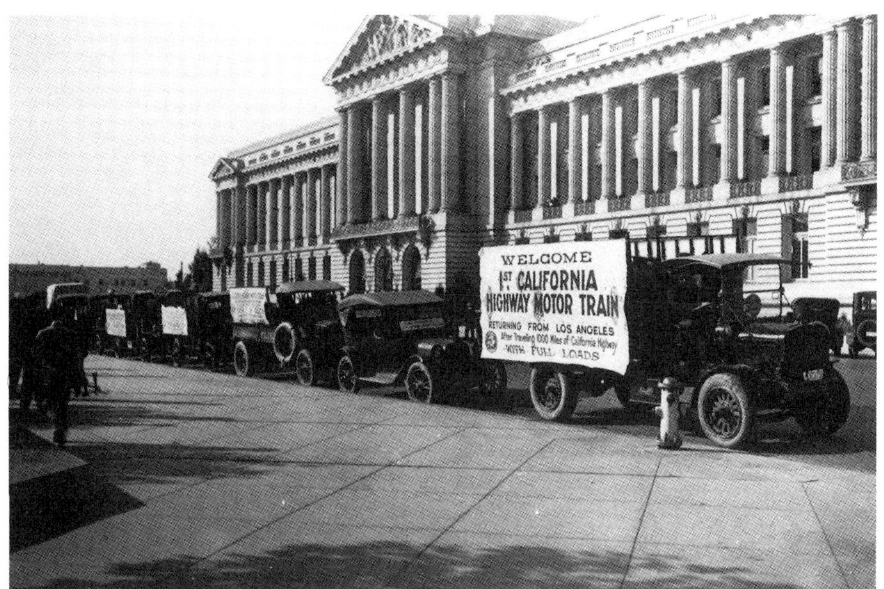

First California Motor Train returning to San Francisco after traveling 1,000 miles to Los Angeles and back. Vintage photograph by Charles H. Hiller, San Francisco, 1919, 7½ by 11 inches.

Photographs taken by unknown or amateur photographers. You can keep costs down by collecting the types of images that serious collectors collect, but without being as particular about the identities of the photographers. Collecting suggestions include images of places that no longer look the same as they did when the photographs were taken, city scenes showing lots of activity, or pictures of remote and faraway places that few people travel to. Page through any book of famous old photographs for many, many more ideas about what to look for.

Panoramas. These photographs are much longer than they are tall and commonly depict subjects like city views, ceremonies or events, military units, graduating classes, conventions or conferences, and other large groups or gatherings of people. Prime panoramic views, like all highly collectible photographs, are scarce and expensive, but once again, if you go after what's left, there's still plenty to choose from. Consider panoramas as collectibles in and of themselves without overemphasizing subject matter, and form collections based on variables like who the photographers are, when the photographs were taken, whether the sitters are all male or female, whether buildings are visible or what types of ceremonies or events are involved.

Early photographic processes. Focus on particular types of photographs rather than what they show or who took them. For example, two of the more unusual types that are still readily available are tintypes and cyanotypes. Tintypes are photographs on thin sheets of iron that were most popular from the 1860s through the 1890s and were produced well into the

1900s. Cyanotypes, popular from the 1880s through about 1920, are always recognizable by their matte finish and bright blue image color. If this field of collecting interests you, the Eastman Kodak Company publishes a wonderful identification guide to all major nineteenth- and early twentieth-century photographic processes. To order yours, send $5 to the Image Permanence Institute, Rochester Institute of Technology, Frank E. Gannett Memorial Building, P.O. Box 9887, Rochester, NY 14623-0887; or call 716-475-5199.

Negatives. The great majority of photograph collectors are only interested in positive images and, as a result, negatives are almost totally ignored and very affordable. Occasionally you can find boxes of old glass negatives or envelopes of old plastic negatives at antiques shops, secondhand stores or flea markets, but more often you find these items at estate sales or general auctions where complete contents of single or multiple estates are being dispersed. One great thing about negatives is that you can have them printed to your specifications. Most businesses that do photo-finishing will work from old negatives, but prices vary so call around or check your local Yellow Pages under the heading "Photo Finishing–Retail."

Albums of Photographs. Photograph albums that contain significant images or pieces by known photographers are expensive, but once again, plenty of less sought after and very reasonably priced albums are available, particularly those put together by amateurs. Old family photo albums, for example, can be found at used and rare bookstores, antiques shops, flea markets, and estate sales. Good albums either contain at least a few better-quality or unusual photographs, or they tell stories, and the more fascinating or engaging those stories are, the better. For example, keep an eye out for albums that show trips to remote places, document local visits by important people, show out-of-the-ordinary events or activities that were once common but no longer take place.

Other less avidly collected vintage photographs that you might also look into are old news photographs, photographic post cards and publicity stills relating to movies, plays, musicians and other preforming arts and artists. Use your imagination. If a type of photograph that hasn't been mentioned appeals to you, go ahead and collect it.

Contemporary Printings of Significant Vintage Images

This grossly underexplored area of collecting is a way to obtain rare and historic images, prints by the world's great photographers and pictures from your favorite eras or of your favorite subject matters, whatever those may be, for tiny fractions of what vintage originals would cost. The best part is that these prints are made directly from the photographers' original negatives—almost like owning the real thing!

Museums, historical societies and other educational institutions have used this method for years and you can also take advantage of photoduplication services that are available at many major museums, historical societies, libraries and other public and governmental facilities with substantial photographic holdings. The primary objective of any institution's photoduplication service is to provide quality photographic reproductions of material in their collections for clients who are interested in exhibiting or publishing the material. Anyone can acquire and use these photographs for

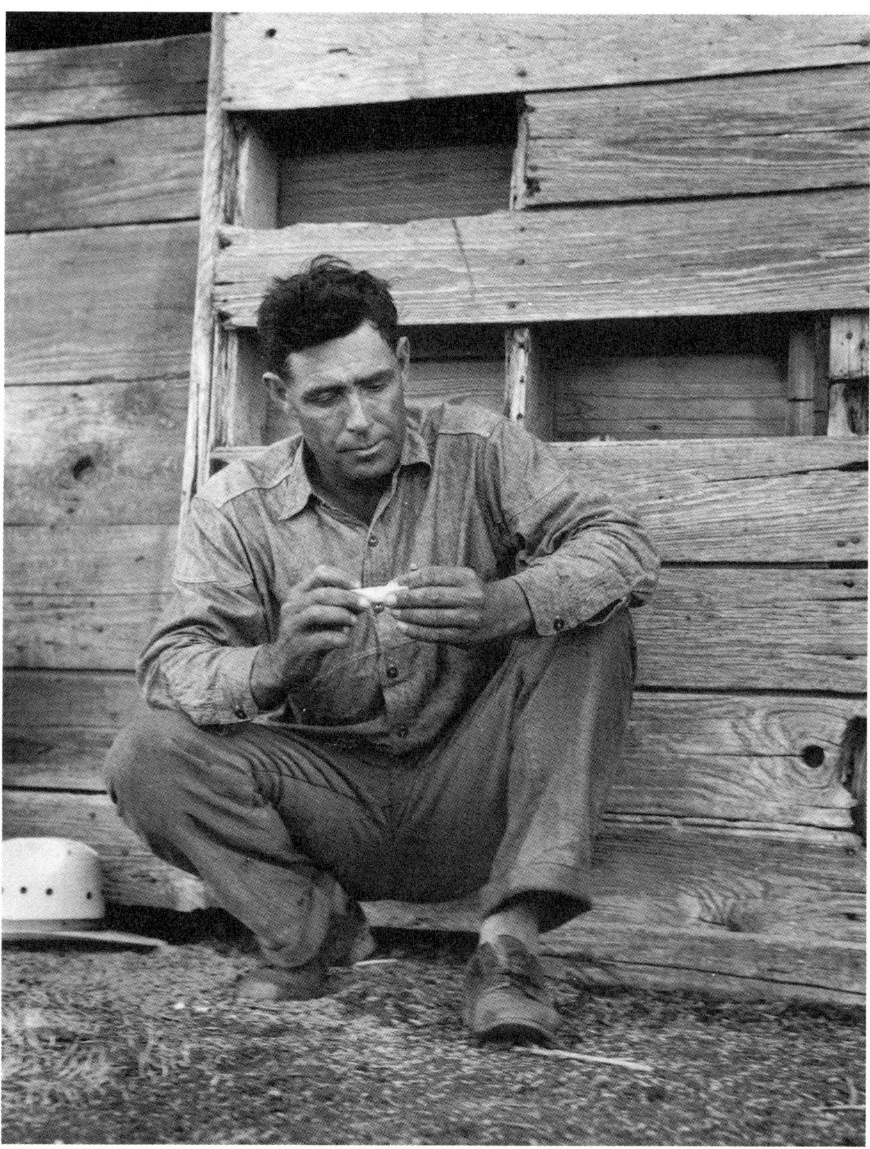

Goodliet, Hardman County, Texas, by Dorothea Lange, Farm Security Administration, June 1938. Available through the Library of Congress photoduplication service. Photograph number USF 34-18277.

whatever purposes they wish (assuming basic regulations are adhered to and proper credit is given in certain situations).

The Library of Congress, for example, offers one of the major photoduplication services in the country. Their collection consists of some 10,000,000 images—the largest in the world—any of which you can own as long as they've been catalogued and are accessible by file number (quite a few have yet to be). These images include important events in American history; pictures taken by major photographers like Ansel Adams (1902–1984) or Matthew Brady (1823–1896); photographs of famous people like presidents, supreme court justices, scientists, sports figures and military heroes; photographs taken by Farm Security Administration photographers during the Great Depression; city views; land surveys; and just about anything else you can think of. The library also regularly assembles special groupings of photographs for exhibition and display, like views of the Statue of Liberty, Capitol views, images relating to women acquiring the right to vote, Ellis Island related imagery and photographs from the Prohibition era.

The best way to select your photographs is to visit the library in person, view a range of images in the appropriate collections and decide which ones you like the most. Every photograph you wish to have duplicated has a corresponding number. The Photoduplication Services Counter across the street will process and mail your order.

When you can't appear in person, contact Prints and Photographs Division, Library of Congress, Washington, DC 20540; or call 202-707-6394. Staffers on duty can perform a limited amount of research. Simplify their job by supplying as much information as possible about what you're looking for, such as names of photographers, subject matters, dates, and locations. Whenever possible, send photocopies of either the exact images or images that are similar to those you're looking for. If you're not quite sure about what you want or what the library has to offer, be as specific as possible and the researchers will tell you how to proceed. Those of you who require lots of research or want a significant number of photographs will either have to appear in person and do your own legwork or hire outside researchers recommended by the librarians. Once you have your image numbers, write Photoduplication Services, The Library of Congress, Washington, DC 20540; or FAX your order to 202-707-1771 (all orders must be in writing). Checks, Mastercard and Visa are accepted.

Many institutions offer photoduplication services, but procedures vary from institution to institution, so always call ahead and find out the ground rules. Some photoduplication collecting tips:

Always specify that you do not want copy negatives. When negatives are fragile or damaged or have had many copies made from them, institutions retire them and replace them with copy negatives made by photographing the original photographs. You don't want these because even with today's sophisticated equipment, subtleties can still be lost in the translation. The central feature of photoduplication collecting is that you are getting prints made from the original negatives and aside from their superior quality, you will, in a sense, own limited editions once those negatives are retired. By the way, people who work at photoduplication services will tell you that, as a result of technological advances, the images they produce are often better than the original images ever were—another reason why this is such a great collecting area.

Always request exhibition-quality photographs. You pay more for these than you do for basic photoduplications, but their quality is far superior, the materials used hold up far better over time, and they're still incredibly inexpensive compared to what the originals would cost. For example, the Library of Congress only charges $45 for an 8-by-10-inch exhibition-quality black-and-white print made from a film negative, or $55 for one made from a glass negative. If you would rather the print measure 20 by 24 inches, costs are only $90 and $100, respectively.

One caution: Private galleries are beginning to produce special limited editions of famous vintage prints and are marketing them at high prices. Always avoid them no matter how they are packaged—signed and numbered, with certificates of authenticity, etc. You now know how to get your own directly from the source at small fractions of gallery selling prices. If you see an image you like at a gallery, you'll surely be able to locate something similar or maybe even identical from among the millions of images housed in public archives and repositories around the country.

Buying from Contemporary Photographers

Fine artist photographers create the photographs that you normally see for sale at galleries, open studios, and art fairs. As with other fine artists, their work can get pretty expensive, but if you look around, you'll be able to find prints in all price ranges—some starting at low as $10 to $20 each. Buying directly from fine artist photographers is very similar to buying from any other fine artists, so review Chapter 10 if this affordable option appeals to you. Here are several additional tips on how to proceed when meeting with photographers or their representatives:

Ask about the availability of work prints. Work prints are interim prints that are made in the process of reaching final images and are similar to first, second or third states of etchings, for example. They may not quite possess all of the qualities that artists are attempting to capture, but are often good solid images regardless. Artists who sell them usually sell them for substantially less than they do their final-state images. Bear in mind that not all photographers are interested in selling these, however, and some won't even show them.

Look at smaller-sized images when you can't afford the larger ones. These are usually more reasonably priced than major works.

Focus on earlier work. Photographers, as do most other artists, often have earlier work that is not particularly representative of what they are

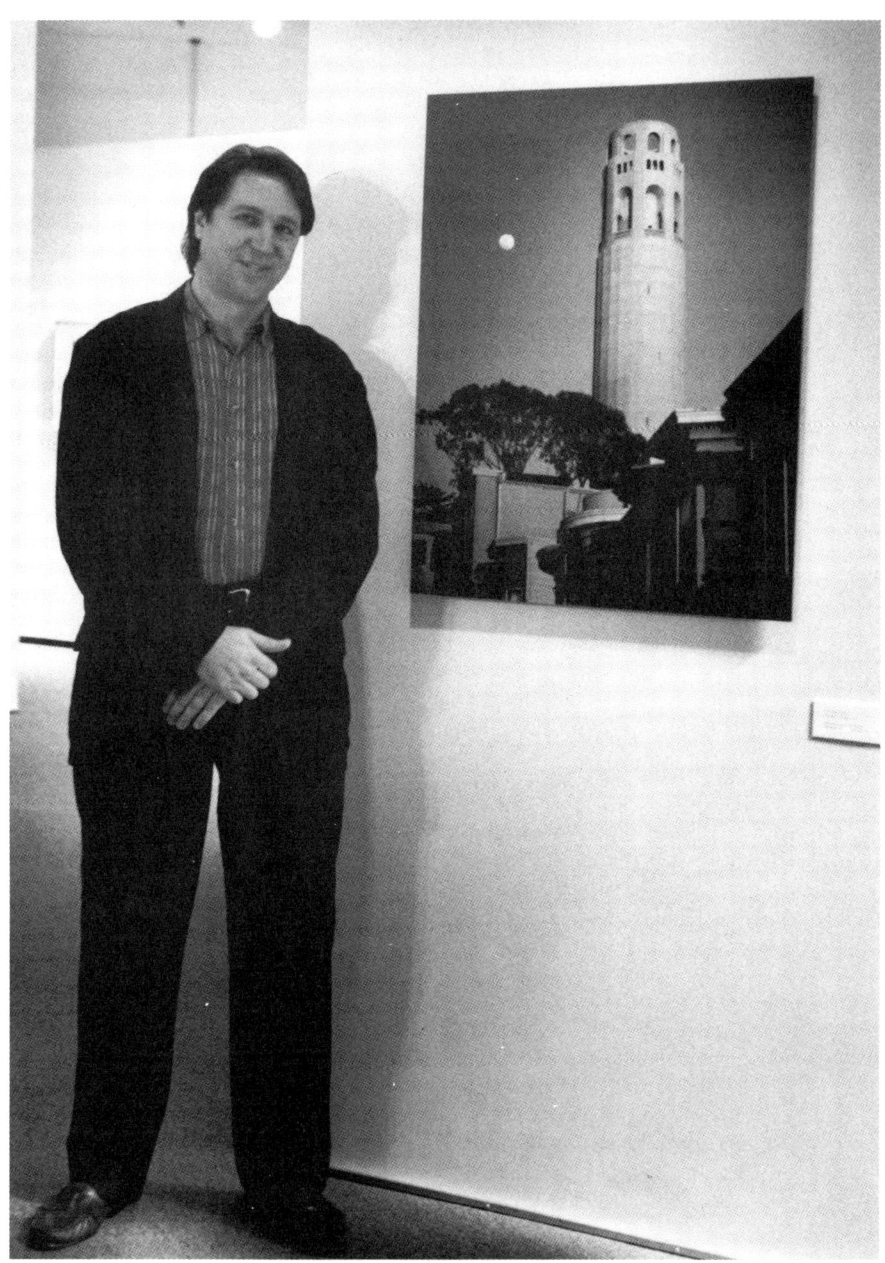

Professional photographer Bennett Hall whose clients include Huey Lewis and the News, TriStar Pictures, Charles Schwab, Inc. and the Sheraton Palace Hotel sells his fine art photographs for as little as $35 at his San Francisco gallery.

doing now. As a result, they tend to be more flexible about selling it for less than their current work. Earlier work is not necessarily inferior in quality; it's just that the artists have personally progressed beyond it.

Look for odd items that are not parts of particular series or projects. These, in a sense, are working prints too. They are taken in between projects, as research or as explorations of ideas. Once again, they are not necessarily inferior in quality to the works in projects or series. Whatever their reasons, the photographers have decided not to fully explore what these represent and have moved on to other pursuits.

Larger-edition sizes are usually less expensive. Unique prints are always the most difficult and time-consuming to produce and are, therefore, the most expensive. Some photographers sell images rather than individual prints, though, and print their best-selling images either in limited or open editions. Production costs are kept to a minimum and prices can be extremely reasonable when compared with one-of-a-kind images.

Gather documentation. Get written or printed explanations, and have prints that you buy signed, dated and titled whenever possible. Also request any other documentation that the photographer has available such as gallery invitations, exhibit catalogues, and news articles.

Additional Opportunities in Contemporary Photography

Fine artist photographers are only one source for collecting photographs—contemporary collecting opportunities are everywhere. You can collect images from specialists such as those who do work for newspapers,

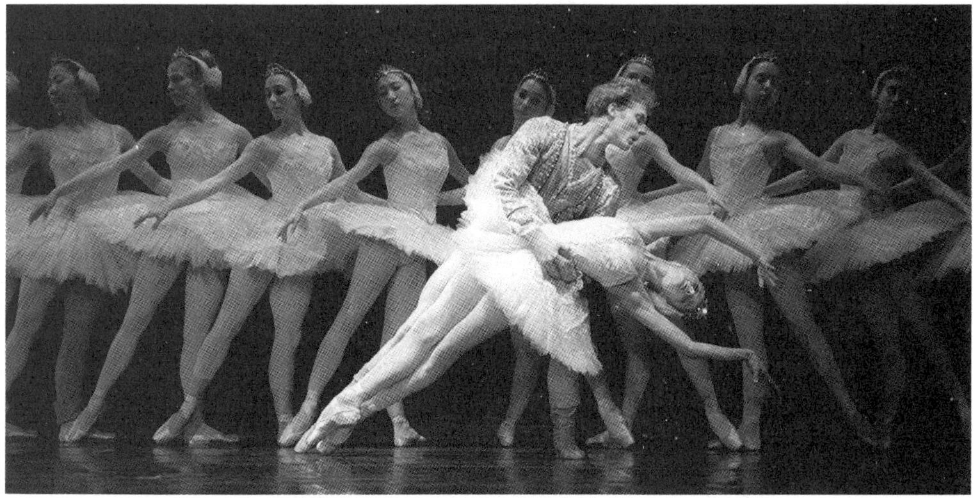

"Swan Lake" by Chris Hardy. Contemporary photograph, 8½ by 11 inches. Courtesy of the San Francisco Examiner *photoduplication service.*

magazines, the fashion industry, or the government. There are also photographers who do coffee table books, portraits, underwater or scientific images, and wedding or advertising pictures. These photographers are all good, the great majority of them are always happy to sell their work and, once again, you can make some terrific buys.

Photographers such as those just mentioned all have one thing in common—they are professionals who make their livings in fields other than that of fine art photography. This means that acquiring their work is not quite the same as buying fine art photographs at galleries or from photographers at their studios. Professional commercial photographers tend not to show their work and they tend not to be all that accessible, but once you learn how to reach them, you should have no trouble locating the images you want.

Whenever you see a photograph that interests you, whether it's in a book, newspaper, magazine, advertising brochure, government publication, mail order catalogue, on a poster or anywhere else, go after it. Call or write the publisher, printer or organization involved, identify yourself and speak briefly about your collecting interests. Find out whether you can get a copy of the photograph in question and ask how much it will cost.

Many times, prints are available through photoduplication-type services at the organizations themselves. This is the most affordable way to go. Newspapers, for example, can send you prints of any photographs they publish that are credited to them. Costs usually range from around $10 to $20 per print, even if you're getting the work of a Pulitzer Prize winning photographer.

Suppose, for instance, that you're fascinated by the freeway and bridge collapses that took place in the San Francisco Bay area during the 1989 earthquake. You can order some incredibly dramatic views taken at the scenes almost immediately after the quake by California Department of Transportation photographer Bob Colin. Full-color images developed directly from the negatives are available from the California Department of Transportation and priced at less than $10 per print for the 8-by-10-inch size and about $20 for a 16-by-20-inch size.

Sometimes in your searches, you'll be referred directly to the photographers. Although this is often a more expensive route, prices vary dramatically from photographer to photographer, so shop around before you buy. When photographs you're interested in are beyond your budget, speak frankly about how much you can afford to spend and find out whether you can get anything similar in that price range. Never be embarrassed to contact photographers, no matter how well-known they are—they love hearing from people who appreciate their work.

In any of these situations, photoduplication or otherwise, always ask whether the photographers will sign, date and title the photographs. These touches enhance value above and beyond that of comparable but unsigned prints and also lend an air of exclusivity to the images. Photographers may

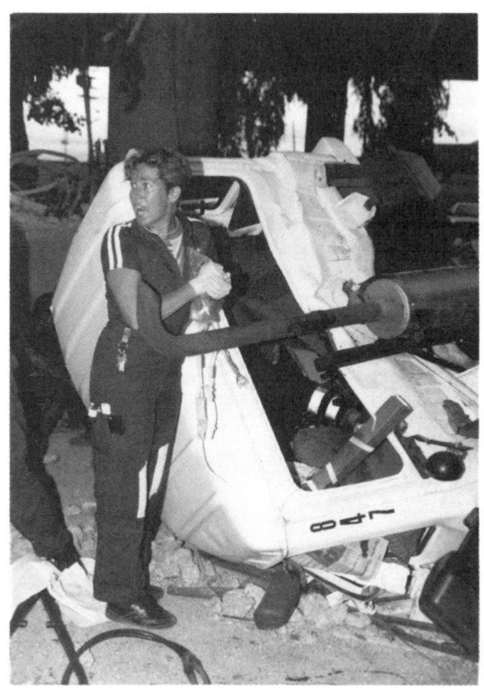

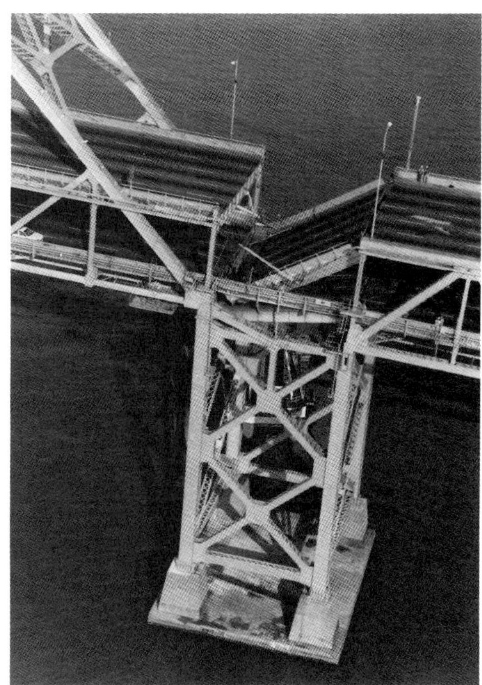

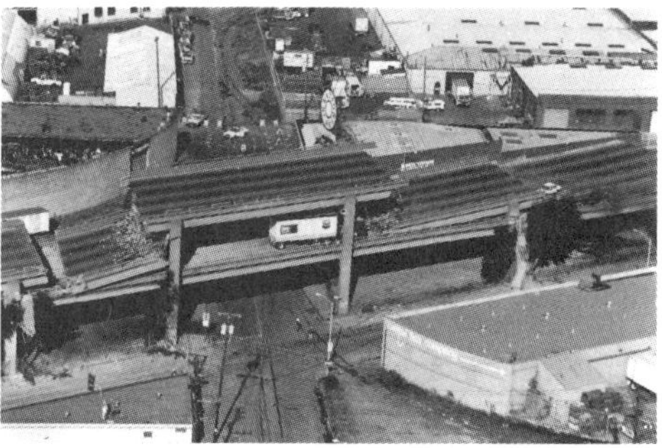

Photographs taken immediately after the San Francisco earthquake of 1989 by California Department of Transportation photographer, Bob Colin. Available in color or black and white through the Caltrans photoduplication service.

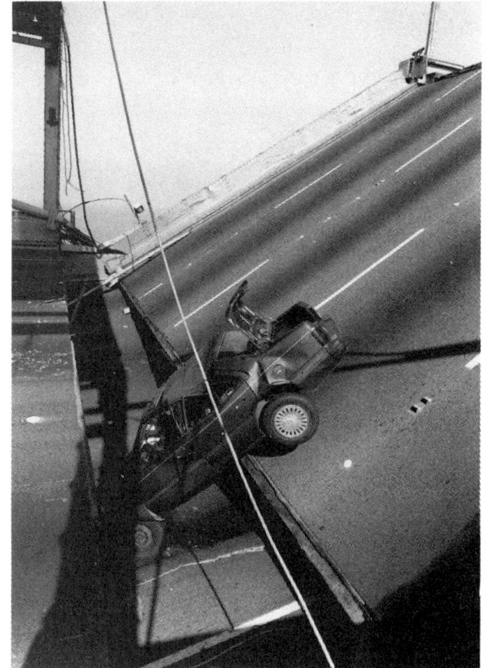

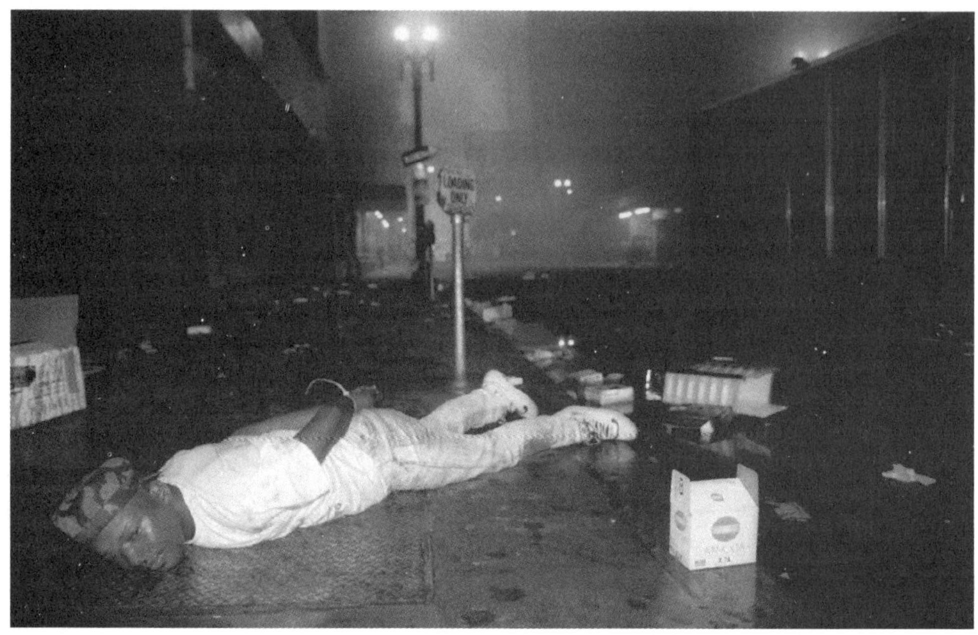

Riot scene by John Storey. Contemporary photograph, 8½ by 11 inches. Courtesy of the San Francisco Examiner *photoduplication service.*

refuse to sign their work for a variety of reasons and may charge a fee if they consent to sign.

Artful Collections

Particular subjects. If you like vintage cars, for example, collect old photographs with cars in them.

Miniature photographs. They cost substantially less than larger ones and some may be no bigger than a quarter.

Unusual shapes. Find photographs that are circular, long and thin, tall and thin, etc.

Identical scenes or subject matter. Choose photos taken by a variety of contemporary photographers whose work you like or those taken by different photographers over a significant period of time.

By price. Give photographers $50 each, for example, and let them photograph the picture of their choice for you.

Additional handwork. Select photographs that have been hand colored or retouched in some way.

Collecting opportunities in the field of photography are limited only by the scope of your imagination and the amount of effort you're willing to put into tracking down whatever you decide to collect. From these last several pages, for instance, you see how many possibilities exist for building collections consisting of the work of professional commercial photographers. The realm of commercial art in general is an area that is almost totally overlooked by collectors and, as a result, plenty of art is available at affordable prices. Opportunities in commercial art collecting will now be addressed.

13

Collecting Art by Commercial Artists

Commercial art is all around us. Every time you see a billboard, a drawing in a newspaper advertisement, an illustration in a book or magazine, pictures on food packages or shopping bags, a scale-model of a new mall, a travel poster or a prototype for a product of the future, you are looking at the work of commercial artists. The idea of collecting shopping bag or newspaper advertisement art or a prototype of a doorknob design is not as strange as you might think.

The appreciation of the functional or useful arts as fine art is nothing new. In 1923, for example, the Spring Salon in New York City, conducted by the Salons of America, Inc., exhibited an original design for a Crane Patent Valve alongside the hundreds of other pieces of fine art in the show. Commercial art is created by professional artists who are just as talented and are just as deserving of collectors' accolades as are the artists who create the paintings and sculptures you see on display at museums and for sale at art galleries.

Art by the most famous commercial artists has been collected for decades. For example, Maxfield Parrish (1870–1966), Norman Rockwell (1894–1978), Dean Cornwell (1892–1960) and J.C. Leyendecker (1874–1951) are household names in this field of collecting. For every well-known and collectible commercial artist, however, there are thousands of less well-known, but entirely competent, practitioners who create or have created commercial art for clients. This means that countless millions of pieces of original commercial art are languishing in drawers, closets, file cabinets and storage areas just waiting to be collected.

As with other areas of undercollected art, when you have a mammoth supply and virtually no demand, prices are right for budget-minded collectors. The problem, however, is that this art is rarely for sale at galleries, stores or other traditional outlets. Your mission, should you choose to collect it, is to coax it out of its hibernation and onto your walls or pedestals.

LOCATING AND PURCHASING COMMERCIAL ART

Your first task, assuming you've decided what to collect, is to get names of the commercial artists who produce it. The best way to do this is to either see or hear about specific professionals whose work you think you might like. When this is not possible, use the Yellow Pages, trade journals or annuals and trade organizations to assemble a list of names. If, for example, you like architectural drawings, you can find names and addresses of architects under the headings "Architects" or "Architectural Illustrators" in the Yellow Pages, in magazines such as *Architectural Digest* or *Unique Homes,* or through trade organizations such as the American Institute of Architects in Washington, DC. Appendix 3 contains the addresses and phone numbers of these and other useful publications and organizations that will be mentioned throughout this chapter.

Once you have names, call, write or visit these professionals and give as much information as possible about why you've contacted them and what you're looking for. Be specific and make your requests simple and direct. Commercial artists tend to be busy and involved with their jobs and will not necessarily be interested in hearing you out if you're too vague. It is a good idea to mention your budget fairly early in your conversations in order to avoid wasting time chasing after work that's too expensive.

Be aware at the outset that few people collect art in this manner and, as a result, commercial artists are not particularly prepared to deal with these types of situations. Many throw their work out as soon as it's served its practical purposes and have never once considered it to be in the realm of fine art, let alone worthwhile saving and eventually selling. Some commercial artists may express concern about your motives in acquiring their art, so be clear that you intend to frame or display it for enjoyment purposes only and nothing else.

Focus on working drawings, models, "rough art," or interim drafts that are produced on the way to developing finished presentation pieces. Not only can final products be expensive, but they often become the property of the clients for whom they are produced. Acquiring them can be difficult because this usually involves getting permission from the artist or commercial firm as well as from the client. Interim pieces, on the other hand, are not that time-consuming to produce or as desirable to either the artists or the clients and are, therefore, more easily accessible and less expensive. Here are some additional types of work to look out for or ask about.

Pieces that have been presented to clients, but have been rejected. The great majority of rejects are perfectly acceptable in terms of quality, but were simply not quite what the clients had in mind.

Pieces that don't relate to specific clients. These are more the result of spare-time activities or ideas that never got off the ground.

Art from old jobs that clients never picked up or expressed any interest in owning. These pieces are either saved in files indefinitely or thrown out if clients fail to request them after set periods of time.

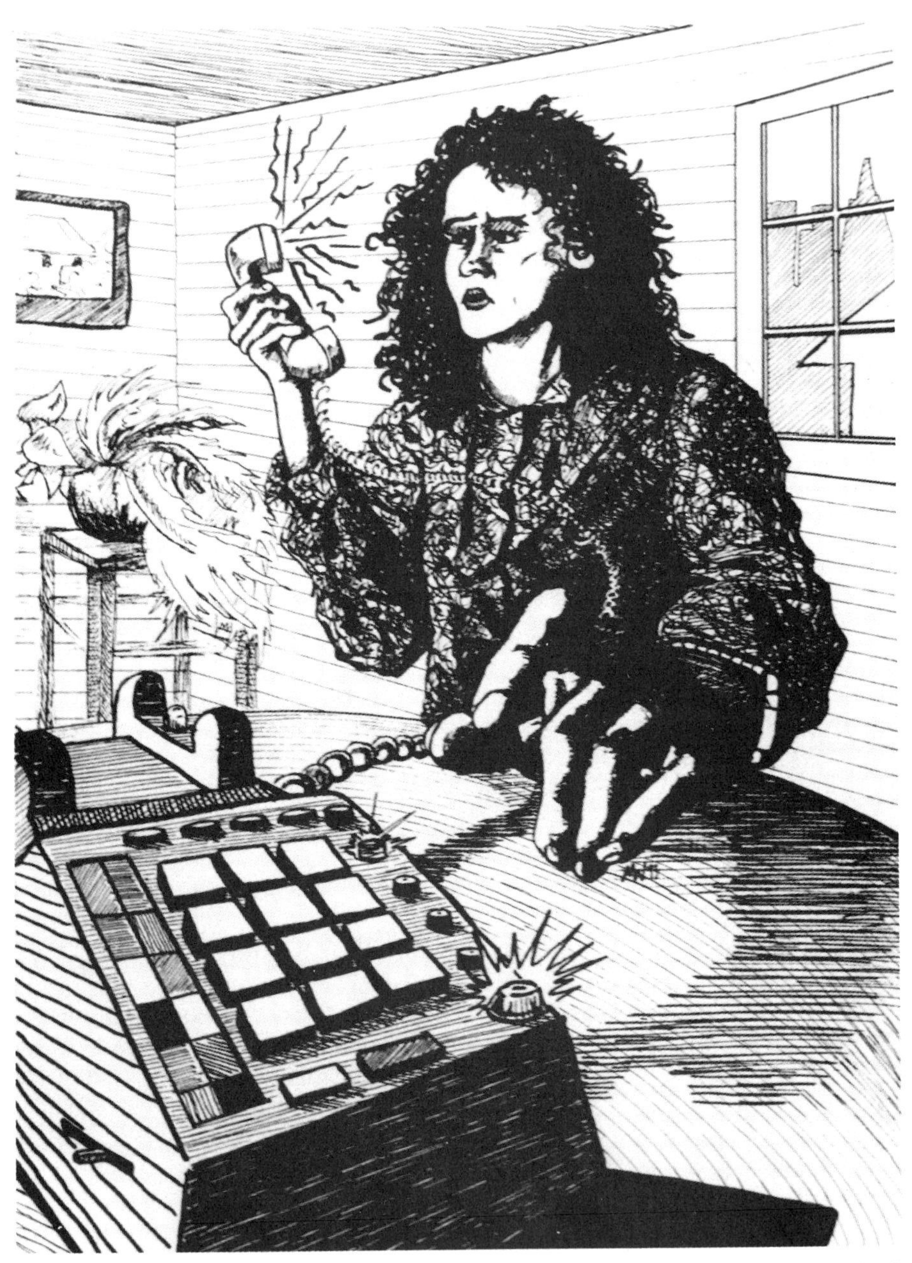

Pen and ink illustration for a consumer advocate newsletter by San Francisco illustrator Michael Waddell. Dimensions: 7 by 10 inches.

Work that you hire the artists to create just for you. Rates can start out as low as $20 to $30 per hour for younger but entirely competent artists, and two to three hours is usually all that's necessary to produce a good-looking piece of work. For those of you on modest budgets, simple sketches may only take a few minutes and be quite reasonable. Commissioning your own art is an especially viable option when you really like a particular artist's work but the artist is unwilling to sell the pieces you want, getting a client's permission is too complicated, or what you like the most is too expensive.

Commercial art from particular sources such as businesses, companies, organizations or publications. When you see art you like in newspapers, magazines, advertisements, retail stores, on billboards or anywhere else, contact the companies or organizations directly rather than the commercial artists who produced it. They may be willing to part with original art in their files or out-of-date pieces. For example, a local clothing store may save all of their old sale signs and allow you to purchase or even have one or two for your collection.

No matter what you're looking to buy, be persistent and don't expect that every encounter will be simple or that you'll get something from everyone you contact. Commercial artists may have trouble deciding what to sell, whether to sell, or what prices to set on what they do decide to sell. You'll also hear a variety of reasons why artists either don't sell or don't wish to part with any of their work. In these cases, ask whether they know of any other artists who might have something for you, thank them for their time and continue with your calls, letters and visits. Sooner or later, you'll get what you want.

Specific Types of Commercial Art

Commercial art originates from a variety of sources. Here are some of the more common types that you might consider collecting along with helpful tips on how to locate and buy:

Commercial illustration. This is the type of illustration that comes the closest to fine art in the look of the finished products. It's the art that you see in books, newspapers, magazines, brochures, leaflets, posters, billboards, and packaging. Illustrators can be found in the Yellow Pages under the heading "Artists–Commercial," in annuals of advertising and illustrator art, or through organizations like the Society of Illustrators in New York City. Most major cities have illustrator organizations, many of which hold periodic shows of members' work. By the way, illustrator art is among the most expensive of all forms of commercial art.

Graphic design. Graphic designers are related to commercial illustrators and produce just about anything visual that clients request. Examples of graphic art are logos, brochures, package designs, advertising art, page layouts, T-shirt designs, catalogues, magazines, exhibits for court cases, posters, record or CD covers, and photo montages. Whatever you see in

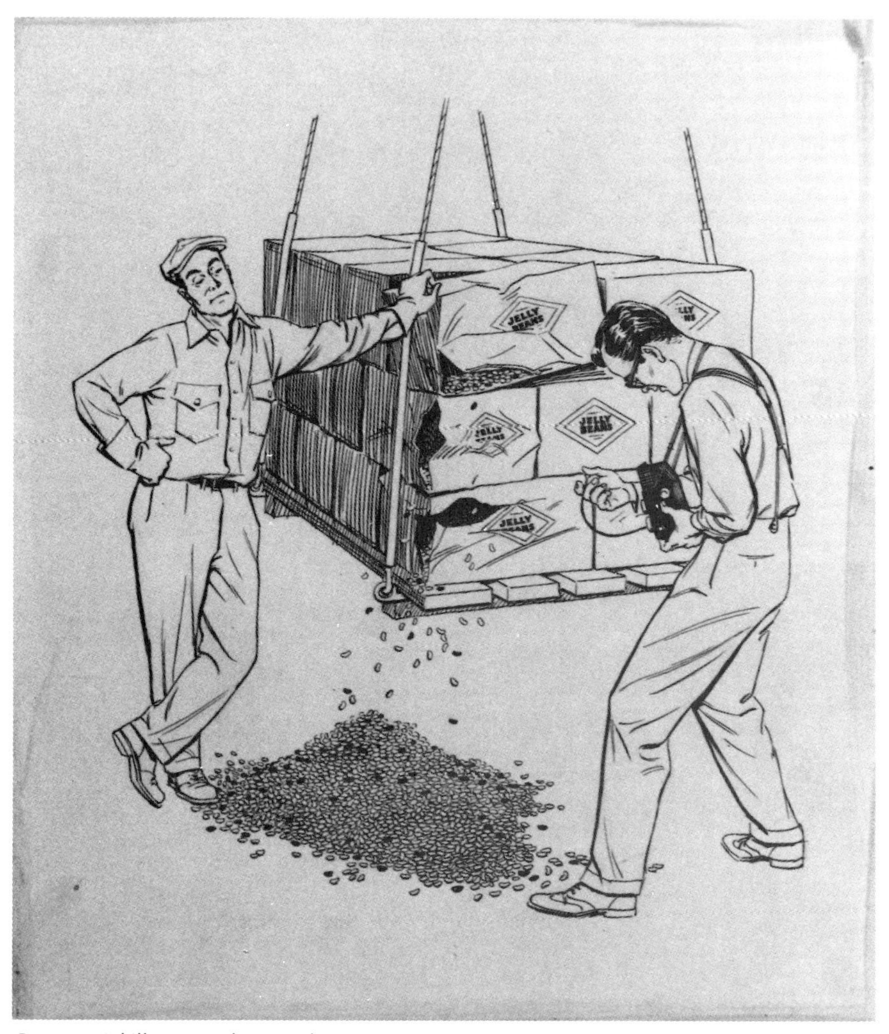

Commercial illustration by an unknown artist, circa 1950. Pen and ink on artists board, 17 by 15 inches.

print, chances are excellent that a graphic designer has had something to do with it.

When contacting these professionals, always find out what their specialties are so that you can really zero in on the best artists for your collecting needs. Find graphic designers listed in the Yellow Pages under the heading "Graphic Designers," in annuals of advertising art or graphic design, through trade publications like *Graphic Design* or *Communication Arts* or through the American Institute of Graphic Arts in New York City.

Architectural drawings, illustrations or scale models. Contact architects if you're looking for drawings; contact architectural illustrators if you're

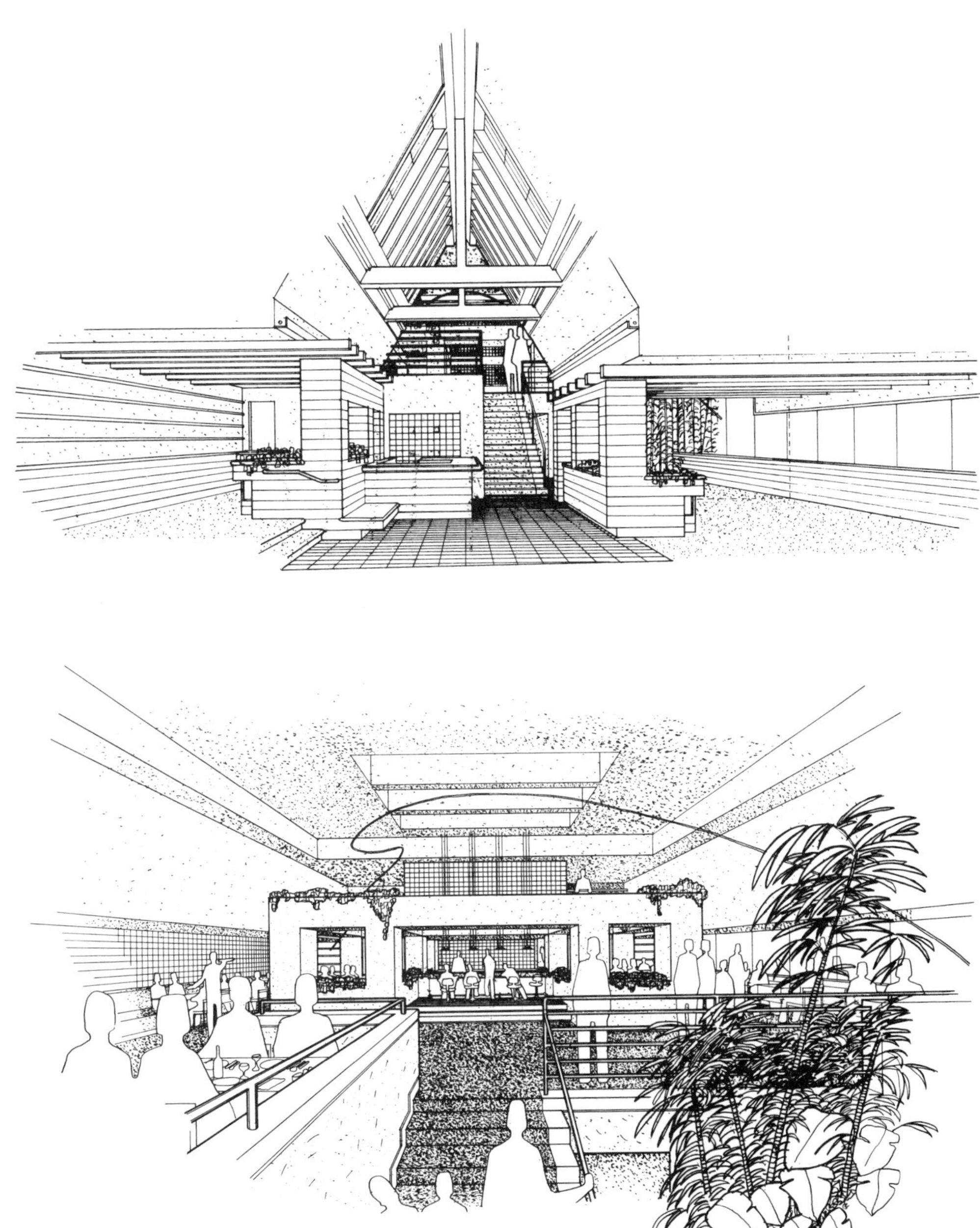

Restaurant interior design by San Francisco architect, Phil Mathews. Each is pencil-on-vellum measuring 24 by 36 inches.

more interested in finished color pictures or scale models. Collecting options include building elevations, examples of interior or exterior detailing, and landscape or interior views.

Practicing architects and architectural illustrators have hundreds and often thousands of drawings that they've produced over the years. Whether or not these professionals will want to sell their originals or how much they'll consider selling them for varies widely from architect to architect, so don't get frustrated if one or two refuse to sell or quote prices that are beyond your budget. One option for obtaining the work of architects who are not interested in selling originals is to ask for professionally reproduced copies of their work. If you go this route, make sure your copies are top quality and permanent, that you do not pay more than $30 or so per copy, and that the artist signs, titles, dates or inscribes them for you.

Fashion illustration. All ideas for clothing and fabric patterns begin as works on paper. Collecting options include black-and-white sketches, sketches with color highlighting and finished drawings. As with other areas of commercial art, a signed illustration by a world famous designer is expensive, but there are thousands of talented local and regional designers and clothingmakers who market their work through small-scale operations, such as single stores, studios or street and craft fairs. These are the artists to contact. Ask to see their drawings and find out how much they would charge to produce originals for you—some designers might be willing to work by the hour or do quick sketches for modest fees.

In terms of locating these artists, the fashion industry is not as well organized as other areas of commercial art. No national organization serves as an informational clearinghouse, but for a start, you can look in the Yellow Pages under "Fashion Designers" and "Designers–Apparel" or check the trade publication, *Women's Wear Daily*. Also keep an eye out in your travels for small shops or co-ops that specialize in selling clothing by area designers.

Cartoon Art. This is a great area to collect in and one where you can own work by reasonably big-name cartoonists for no more than $100 to $300 each. Work by lesser-knowns can be had for as little as $25 to $50. Cartoon art includes editorial cartoons, cartoon strips, single cartoons as well as cartoon-style illustrations.

Few people are aware that the great majority of cartoonists own all of their published work and are almost always happy to sell it. Successful cartoonists have hundreds of cartoons from which to choose and, assuming they're agreeable, you may wish to browse before purchasing specific pieces that you have seen in print. Some are also amenable to checking their files if you request specific content or subject matters.

The best way to acquire cartoon art is look for cartoons you like in newspapers, magazines or other publications, contact those publications and ask to speak with their cartoonists. The cartoonists will either be on staff or you will be referred to the syndicates or publications that handle their work. Other ways to locate cartoonists are to check the Yellow Pages under "Artists–Commercial" or contact the Association of American Editorial Cartoonists in Raleigh, North Carolina, and the National Cartoonists Society in New York City.

Industrial Design. Industrial designers are the people who design the products that we use in our everyday lives. Everything from coffee cups to alarm clocks to doorknobs to telephones begins as a concept in the mind of an industrial designer. Their ideas take the form of drawings, scale models, working models, watercolors, paintings, transparencies or whatever else is necessary to convey appropriate information to clients.

As usual, this can be an expensive area to buy in if you want art from major design firms. Smaller independent firms can consist of as few as one or two people, however, and they're frequently amenable to selling non-current, preliminary or rejected work for affordable sums of money. Locate industrial designers by checking the Yellow Pages under "Designers–Industrial," looking through the magazine *ID,* or contacting the Industrial Designers Society of America in Great Falls, Virginia.

Many companies, rather than hire outside designers, do their designing in-house, so if you like a particular product line, contact the companies directly and speak with individuals in research and development departments. You probably won't be able to purchase original product designs or prototypes—companies usually keep those—but you may be able to buy nonproduct-related sketches, promotional pieces or other artworks from in-house designers. Smaller local and regional firms are your best bet.

Vintage Commercial Art

Vintage commercial art of all varieties can appear on the market just about anywhere, anyplace and at any time. You can find it at antiques and collectibles shops or co-ops, flea markets, antiques shows, secondhand stores, house sales and so on. Visiting dealer after dealer is not an easy task, though, and finding anything significant is pretty much a function of being in the right place at the right time. You have to be persistent, constantly remind dealers of what you're looking for and ask them to contact you whenever they see something they think you might like. If you work at it, your efforts eventually pay off.

You're a little more likely to get what you want by keeping an eye out for sales or auctions of the estates of commercial artists. Going-out-of-business sales or liquidations and auctions of businesses that have operated for decades are also good sources. This way, you have a chance to buy before the material is dispersed into the marketplace. In the great majority of cases and unless an artist or business was well-known, the art is often sold in bulk lots at reasonable prices and is rarely marketed with any fanfare.

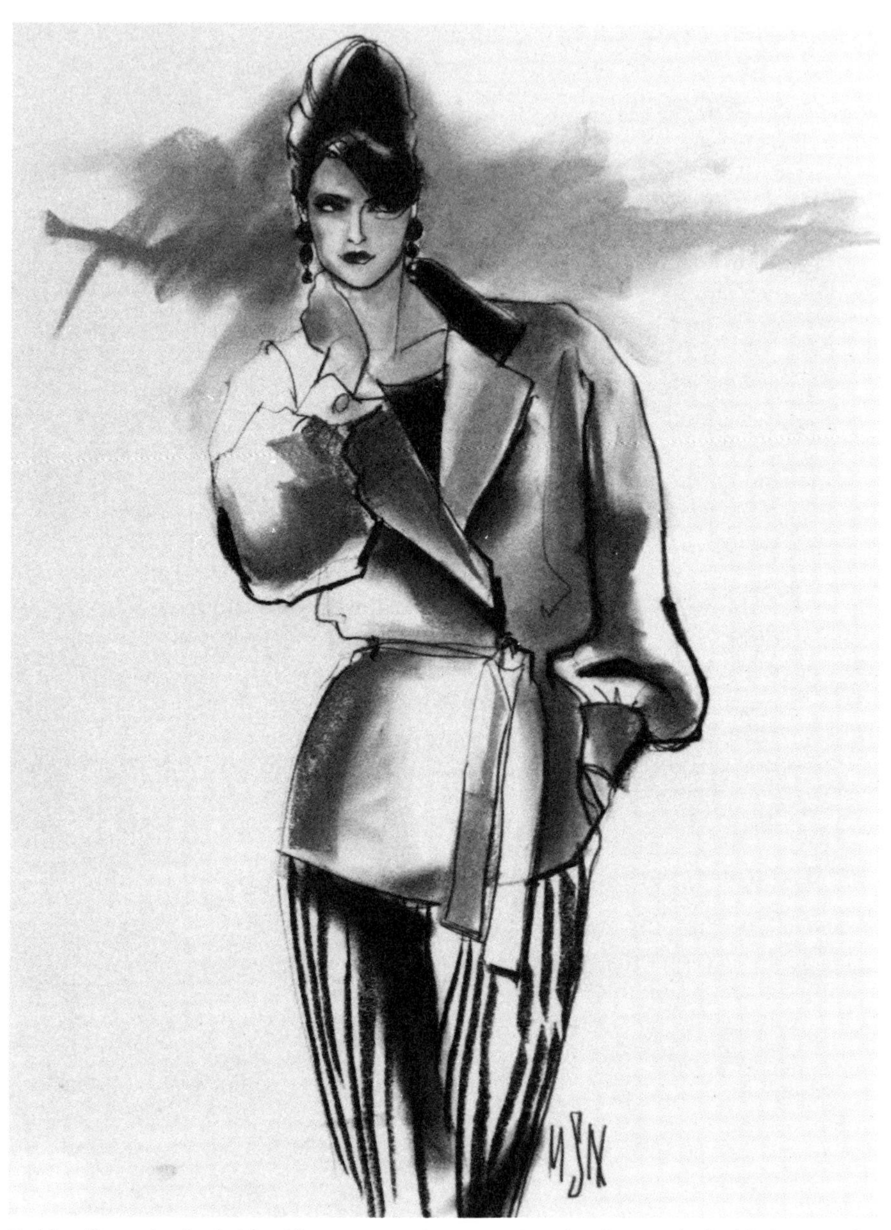

Fashion illustration by fashion illustrator Martin Nunez. Pastel with gouache highlights, $21\frac{3}{4}$ *by* $16\frac{3}{4}$ *inches.*

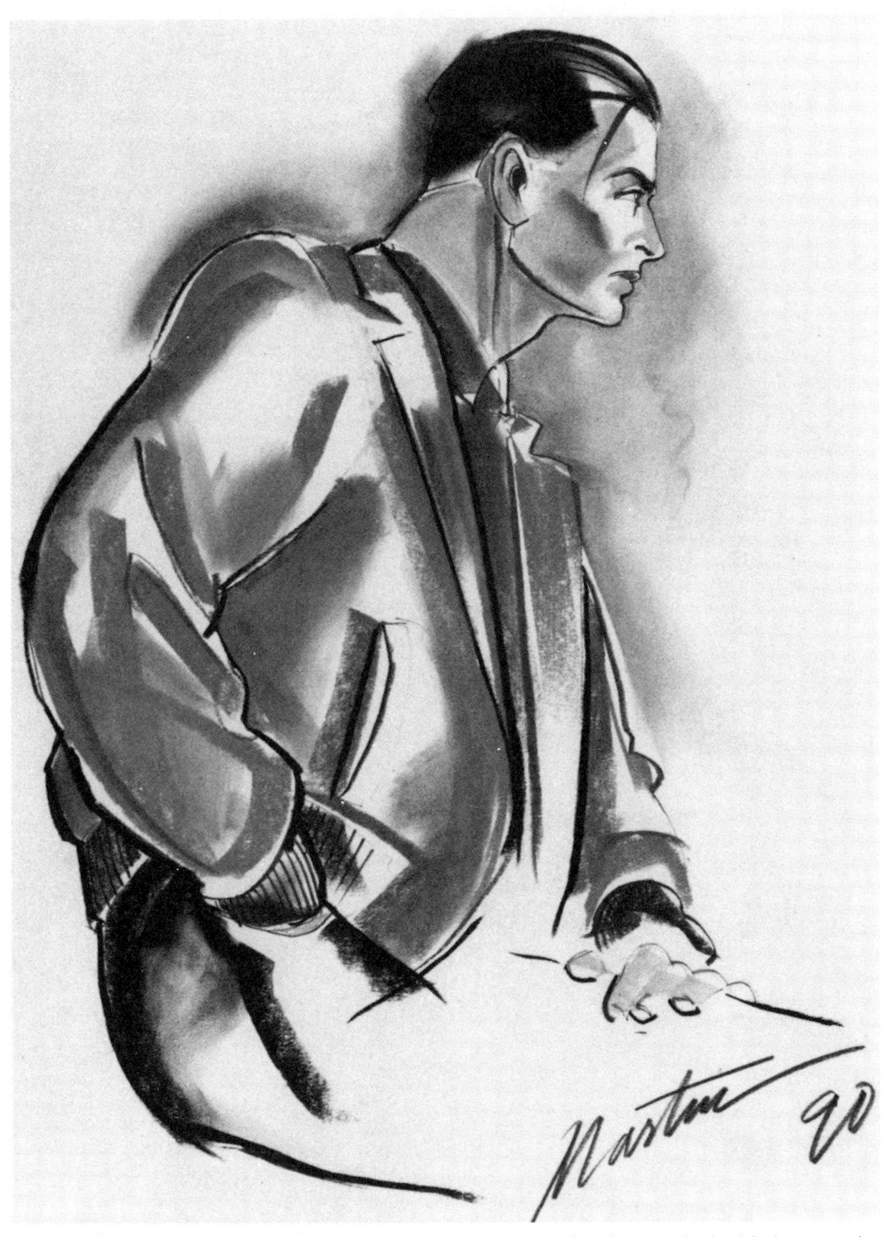

Fashion illustration by fashion illustrator Martin Nunez. Pastel with gouache highlights, 21¾ by 16¾ inches.

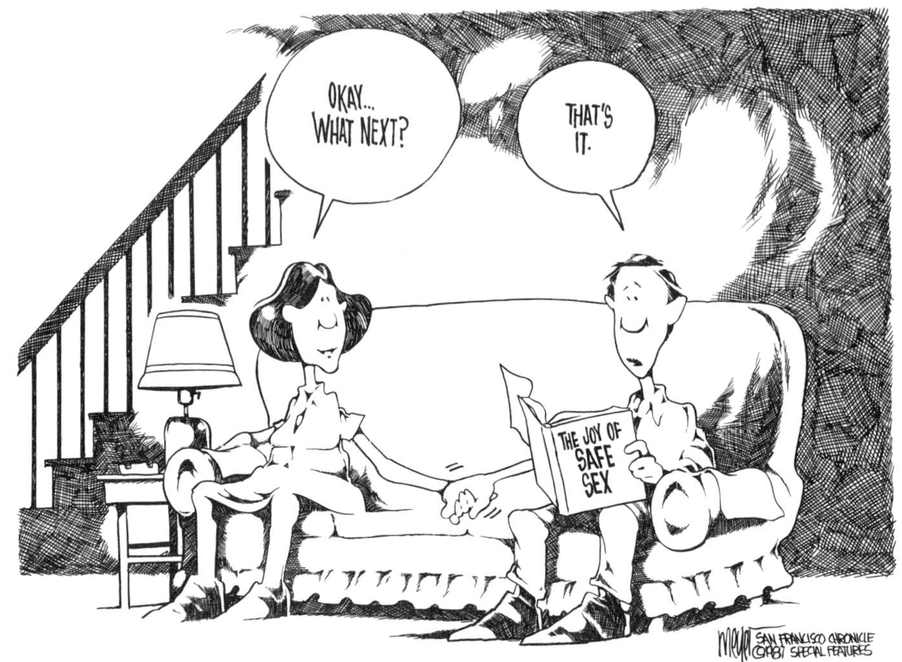

Editorial cartoons by Tom Meyer of the San Francisco Chronicle. *Collectors can "purchase" Meyer original pen and ink drawings by making donations, in amounts determined by Meyer, to a local food bank. Dimensions: 7 by 9 inches.*

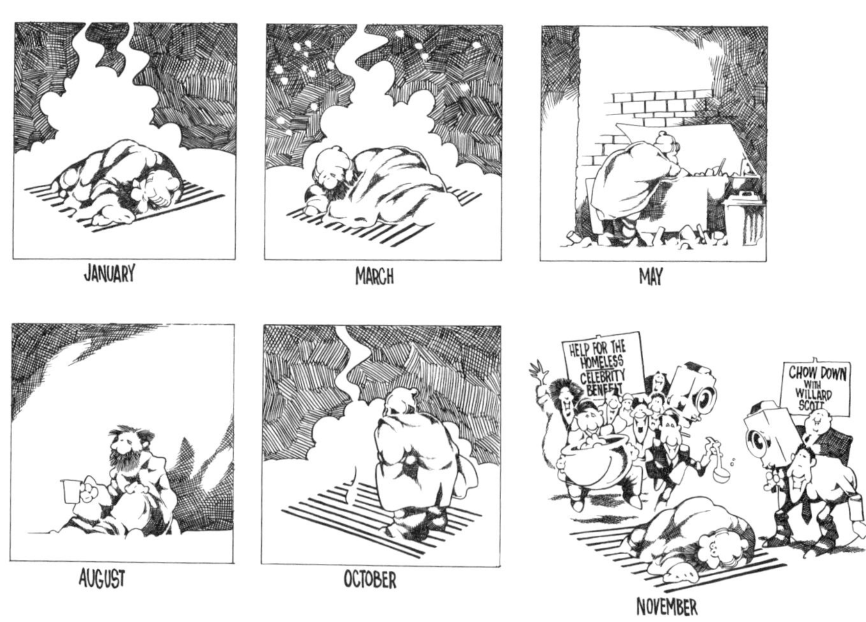

Dimensions: 7½ by 11 inches.

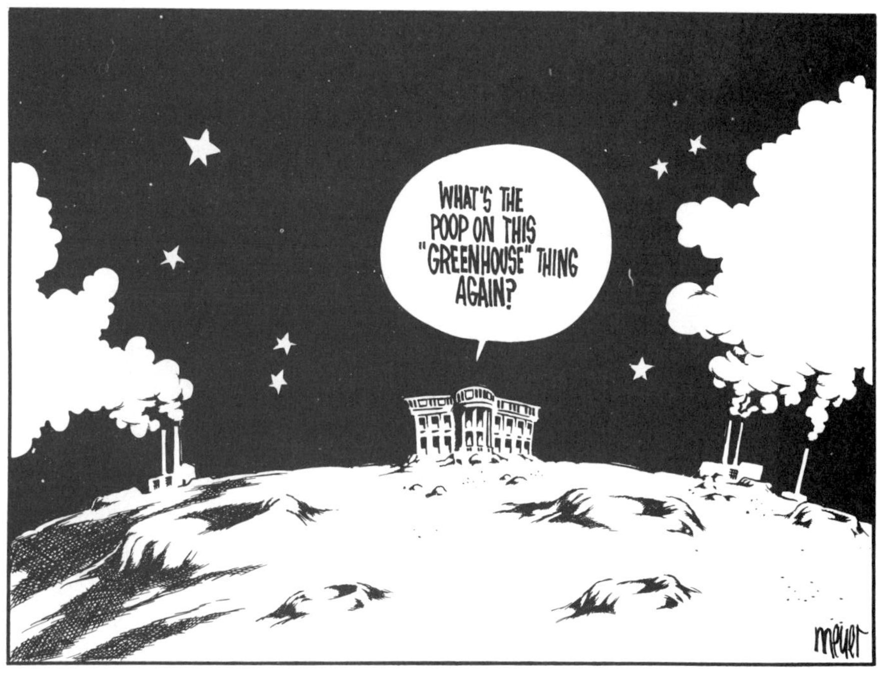

Dimensions: 7 by 9 inches.

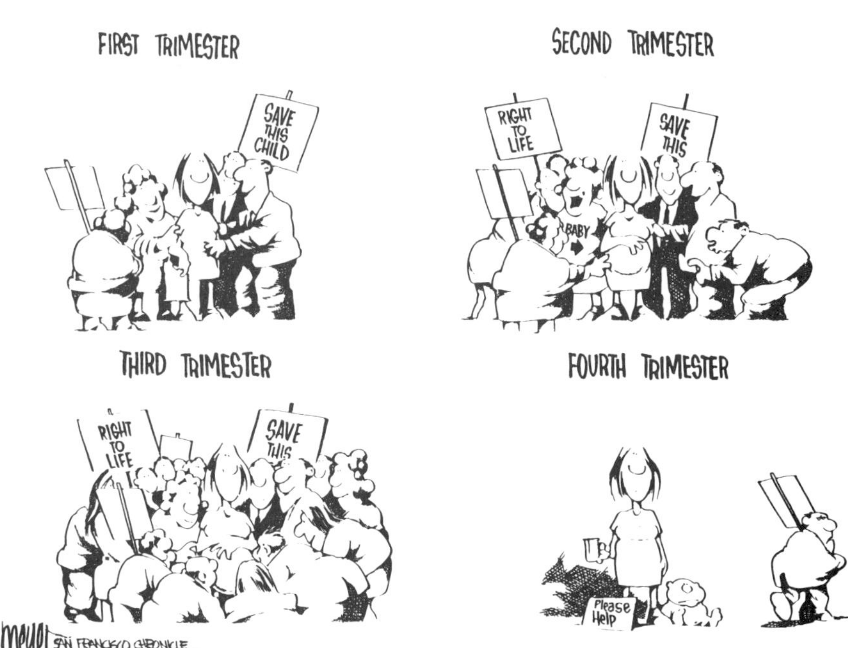

Dimensions: 7 by 9 inches.

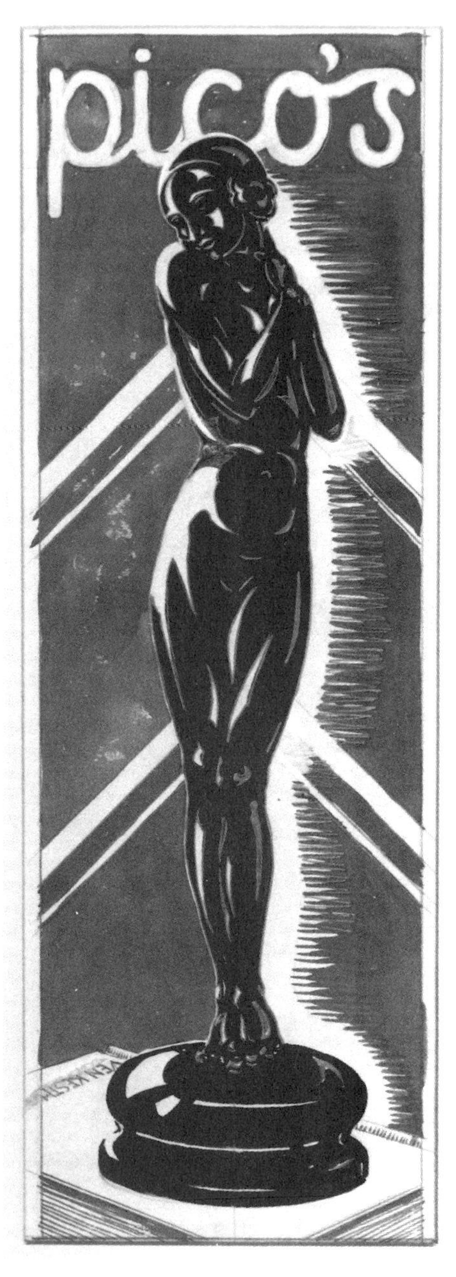

Commercial illustration in ink and watercolor, circa 1930s, by Kenneth S. MacIntyre. Dimensions: 19 by 7 inches.

The best option is to go directly to the source. Contact currently practicing professionals, tell them what you're looking for and find out whether they know of any retired commercial artists in your area. Inquire as to the whereabouts of family members or descendents if the artists are deceased. Old city directories or Yellow Pages are also good resources for locating names (many phone companies and some public libraries maintain stocks of old phone books).

When you make contact with an artist or family member, explain your purpose and ask about the availability of the art. When it's been saved, and many times it has, ask whether you can look through it. If you like what you see and the owners are willing to sell, talk price.

Oddly enough, vintage commercial art can often cost less than contemporary material. Artists or family members may be less attached to it than they were at the times that it was produced, or they may no longer equate its importance or dollar value with how long it took to produce or how much clients originally paid for it. They also tend not to view or value it as fine art, but rather as the products of ordinary everyday careers in the business world.

Outside of work by the major artists, vintage commercial art has only recently been shown some of the respect that it deserves and been considered more in the realm of fine art. The effects of this trend have not yet been felt at all levels of collecting, though. This means that vintage commercial works by lesser-known artists and even some unsigned pieces remain part of a relatively wide-open area in which many great buys can be made.

Tips on Selecting Commercial Art

As with collecting art by any other artists, get an idea of who the better-known and most widely respected commercial artists are in your fields of interest. Depending on your budget, focus on professionals with good local, regional or national reputations. Since you won't have art reference books to rely on (except for the most famous artists, no in-depth ones have been written yet), you pretty much have to go by the opinions of colleagues and contemporaries, so address this issue whenever you speak with knowledgeable and experienced professionals. Consider variables like how long individuals or firms have been in business and how broad or impressive their client bases are.

Also find out whether they've received any awards or commendations from trade organizations, chambers of commerce, or community groups. In some fields of commercial art and in some parts of the country, most notably the major metropolitan areas, annual exhibits or awards events take place. Find out where and when they are held and whether any book or catalogue shows the art or lists the names of the participants. Trade events are great for locating top-quality artists and, whether or not you can afford their art, viewing it allows you to compare quality and originality with what you've been seeing or buying.

As for the art itself, focus on what the artists are particularly proud of and whether or not their clients found it acceptable. Consider the significance of the clients that the art was produced for, too. The more famous or important the clients, the more collectible the art tends to be over the long term. Original Coca-Cola advertising art, for instance, is highly collectible and sells for quite a bit of money.

If you're a less conventional collector, keep an eye out for younger artists and firms who are becoming known for trendy or progressive work. These could well become the most highly regarded professionals of the future and examples of their work would be an asset in any collection. No matter what the future holds, however, collecting in this manner is always an adventure.

Regarding prices, look around and get a feel for who's charging how much for what kind of art before you start buying. Because no formal or structured market exists for most commercial art, asking-prices have a wide range. You pretty much have to create your own structure especially when you find yourself meeting with artists who have never considered selling any of their work in this manner before.

One final tip—always ask commercial artists you meet whether they produce any fine art in their spare time or as a hobby. A fair amount do it for fun or relaxation and when they do, the best of their commercial talents can be appreciated within the context of works of fine art. In addition, a number of commercial artists initially intended to become fine artists, worked at it for a while, built up bodies of work and then changed careers. You also may be able to see and buy these sorts of pieces.

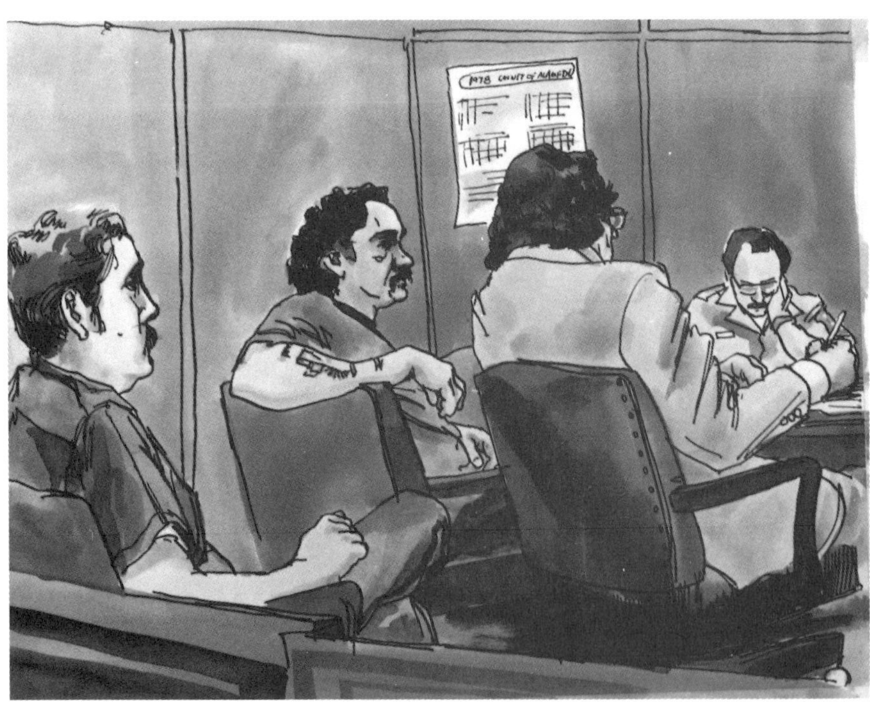

Scene from a Hell''s Angels trial, 1978, showing defendant Sonny Barger (second from left), by courtroom artist Jim Schwering. Watercolor and ink, 13⅝ by 17 inches.

By artist. If you meet a commercial artist whose work you really like and who you get along well with, become a major collector of his work.

By project. Concentrate on commercial art associated with a particular product, era or nation. Perhaps you like advertisements for soft drinks, restaurants, festivals or events, vacation spots or auto races. The field is wide open.

Buildings. Collect drawings of storefronts, single-level homes, multiunit buildings or other specific types of buildings. If you like your local contemporary architecture, for example, meet the architects who are responsible for it and collect samples of their work.

Everyday items. Select art that's on the things you use every day, like T-shirts, coffee cups, letterheads or business cards.

Court art. This is the type of art that you see accompanying television news stories about court cases where no cameras are allowed in the courtrooms. You can find out the names of courtroom artists by contacting local television stations or national networks. Successful courtroom artists often have hundreds of sketches and drawings in their files.

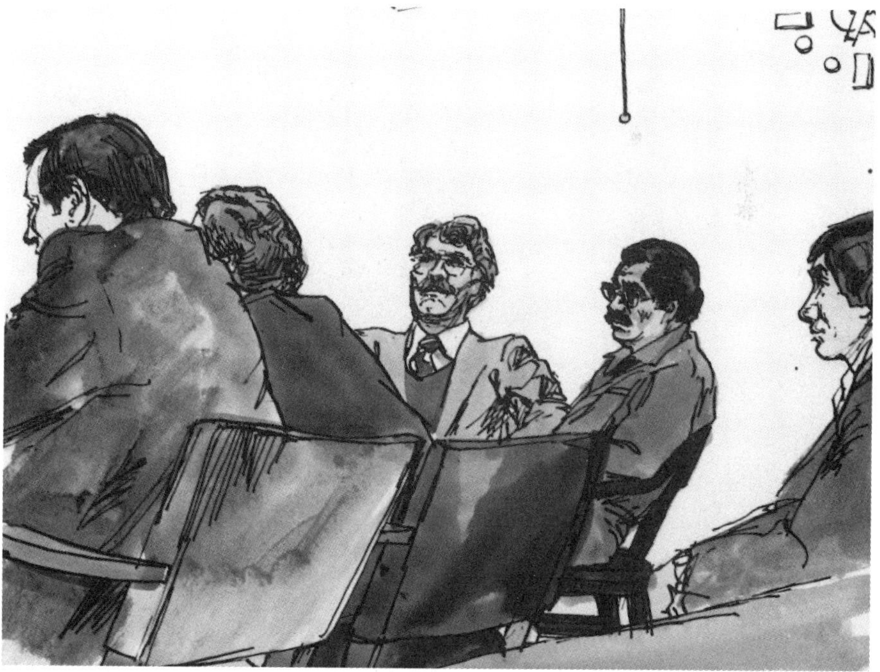

Scene from Juan Corona trial, 1979, showing defendant Juan Corona (second from right), by courtroom artist Jim Schwering. Watercolor and ink, 13⅝ by 17 inches.

Set and costume designs. This is a wonderful collecting area if you enjoy plays, musicals, live theatre, or dance. You can often meet the designers without much effort, especially with smaller local and regional production companies.

Trademarks or logos. These can be appealing for their simplicity and uniqueness.

Portraits by quick-sketch portrait artists. You can find these artists at carnivals, street fairs, tourist areas, parties, conventions, sporting events and other public gatherings. The portrait can either be your own, someone you know, or that of someone famous like a sports figure, actor or politician.

■ As you have seen with commercial art and many areas of photography, one of the keys to buying affordably and effectively is to focus on types of art and artists that are not widely collected. The art is plentiful, competition is light and buying is fun. Another of the more underexplored areas of collecting is that of art created by people who are not normally thought of as artists. They are out of the mainstream, which means that you won't get too soaked when you buy their art, so to speak. Prepare for a flood of fantastic art buying opportunities.

14 Finding Art by Non-Traditional Artists

The great majority of art that you see in average, everyday situations is produced by formally trained and educated artists. The great majority of art in existence is not produced by formally trained and educated artists. Virtually no one goes through life without creating something, at one time or another, that can be classified as art. For convenience sake, the types of art that are produced outside of conventional settings by people other than formally trained artists will subsequently be referred to as non-traditional.

In spite of the sheer quantity of non-traditional art, hardly any one has any idea what its scope and variety really is. For the most part, art galleries don't show it, art dealers don't sell it, museums rarely exhibit it, art collectors don't own it. Perhaps the major reason why this is so is that few of us—dealers, scholars and collectors included—were ever taught to appreciate or take it seriously.

A small percentage of non-traditional art does receive attention and acclaim, for instance early American portrait paintings done by itinerant artists who lacked formal schooling and landscapes such as those done by Grandma Moses (1860–1961). The total amount of art encompassed by the non-traditional realm, however, is far greater than this.

A number of terms such as folk, naive, primitive, visionary, outsider, self-taught and intuitive have been coined to represent specific types of non-traditional art. A certain amount of scholarly activity and research has been dedicated to these topics, especially in recent years, but what you need to know is what this art looks like, who creates it, where to see it and how to buy it, should you decide that you like it.

How to Recognize Non-Traditional Art

The most compelling aspect of non-traditional art is that it can be anything. Freedom to create it is total, no formal training or education is

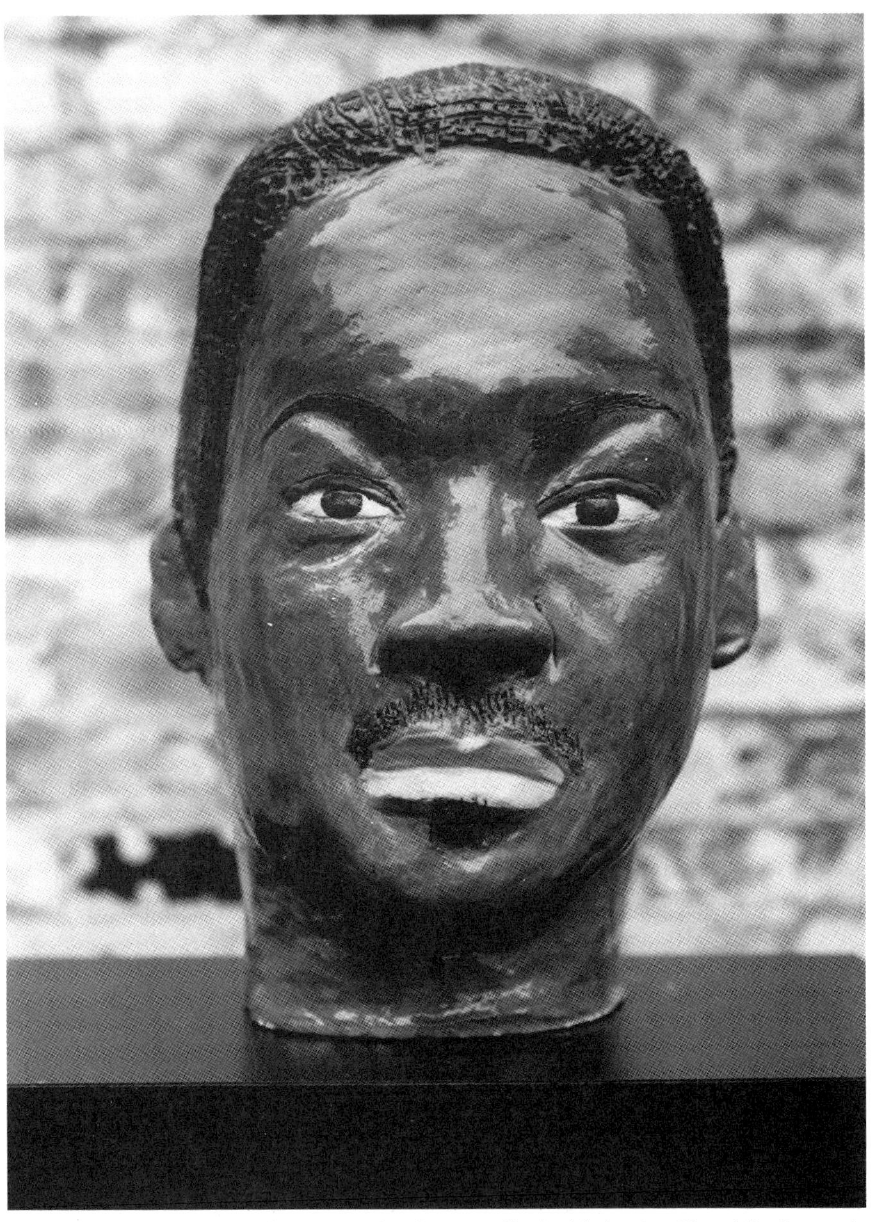

Bust of Eddie Murphy by William Scott, developmentally disabled artist. Glazed fired ceramic. Height: 15 inches.

necessary, there are no rules or guidelines for producing it, anyone can make whatever they wish. And a non-traditional artist can be anyone—the person next door, someone with a physical or mental disability, someone who lives in isolation and is totally cut off from the rest of the world, someone who believes that he is on a mission from God, someone who thinks that making art is the true path to happiness, someone who has nothing but time on his hands—anyone.

This sounds like a pretty confusing situation for art buyers, but in fact, the opposite is the case. Since anything is OK to create, anything is also OK to own or enjoy. The tricky part is that most people don't take this art seriously, let alone understand what it's all about.

The one aspect of non-traditional art that people have the most difficulty with is that much of it has a childlike look because the great majority of the artists are untrained. Viewers not used to seeing this art often make comments like "any eight-year-old can do this" or "the person who did this can't possibly be an artist." On the surface, these statements may be accurate, but on more significant levels, they aren't. Looking beyond the technical abilities of the artists is the key.

Non-traditional art has depth, complexity, maturity and wisdom about it that art created by children cannot possibly have. Subject matters, compositions, themes, ideas expressed, issues conveyed, all emanate from adult perspectives and are confronted in adult fashion. When you allow yourself to appreciate what this art is saying and how it is being said, you can become just as entranced by it as you can by any other kind of art.

But don't ignore the technique (or lack thereof) simply because of its childlike aspects—it is an essential part of the art and can be just as complex,

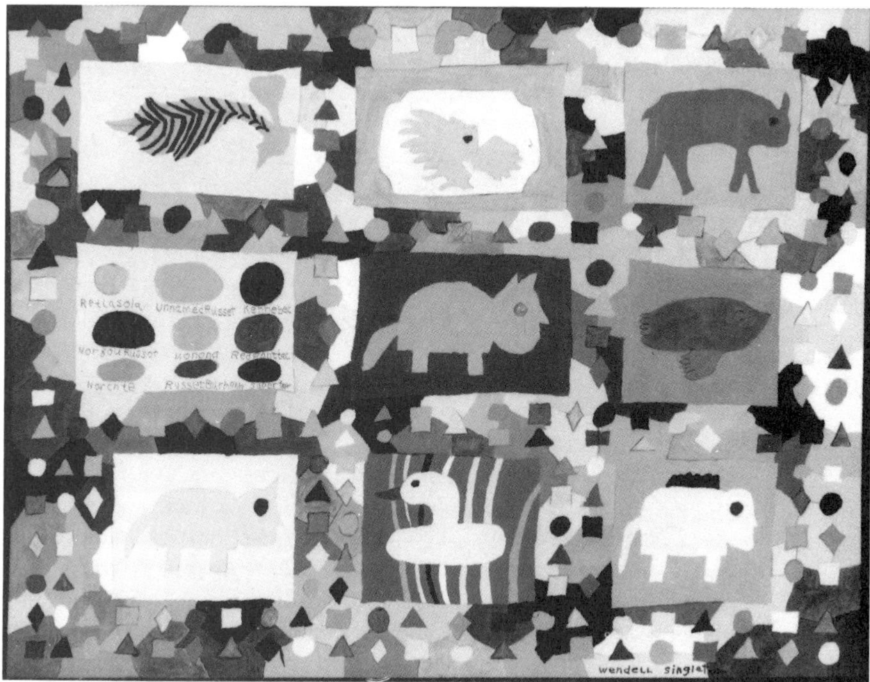

Animal mosaic by Wendell Singleton, an autistic artist in his early thirties. Acrylic on paper, 24 by 30 inches. Courtesy of The National Institute of Art & Disabilities, Richmond, California.

in its own way, as that of any other art. In spite of incredible obstacles that many of these artists face, they produce complete pieces of art that work. They are not simply lucky—they have missions to accomplish and they manage to accomplish them as well as any other artists do. The most talented among them have innate abilities that are rarely seen anywhere in the art world.

Locating Non-Traditional Art

This art has only recently begun to emerge as acceptable to own and even though people continue to relax their stereotypes and educate themselves, non-traditional art collecting is still in its infancy. A few galleries formally show and sell this art, but for the most part, it is shown and sold outside of conventional settings and the market for it is relatively unstructured.

As a result, the non-traditional art world is fragmented, artists are scattered everywhere and attempting to know everything that goes on is incredibly labor-intensive. A number of the artists live and create on their own and since they are not in the art mainstream, very few people know that they exist and their art is not readily available. Many others, however, are affiliated with or take part in organized arts programs that are based in places like correctional institutions, mental health facilities, homeless centers, convalescent facilities and out-patient centers.

For beginning collectors, patronizing non-traditional artists through organized arts programs is the ideal way to start. These places are particularly good resources because they're relatively easy to find and they usually have plenty of art for sale by a variety of artists at very reasonable prices.

Before getting into specifics, a little background information is necessary to help you understand non-traditional arts programs. They did not originally come into being for the purpose of producing art for the marketplace and, even today, few are operated for that reason. Most were born out of the recognition of the therapeutic values of creating art. Participants were often needy in one way or another and completing works of art gave them direction and purpose, provided them with feelings of accomplishment and also boosted their self-esteem. The art was seen almost as a by-product—a means to an end—rather than as something to be treasured for its own merits.

What happened, though, during the course of evolution of these programs is that many genuine talents began to emerge and their art could no longer be ignored. At first, it was appreciated and collected only by those closely affiliated with the participants, but word spread and more and more people became interested. Today, therapeutic benefits continue to be the main reason why most of these programs exist, but in addition, much of the art is now saved, displayed and sold. It is made available to the public either through periodic or ongoing sales or through informal on-site galleries.

Depending on the type of art you are interested in or what artists you

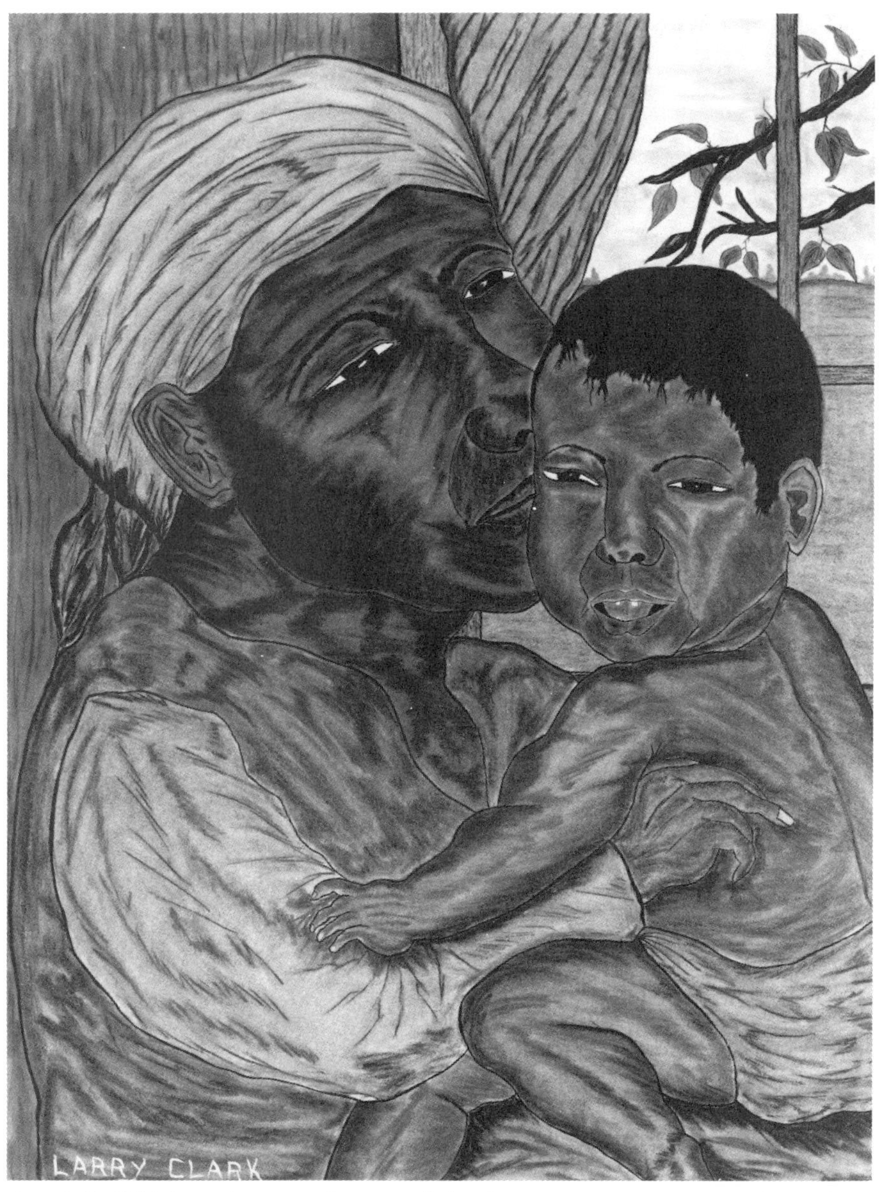

"My Only Child," pastel on paper by Larry Clark, a low-income artist. Courtesy of Central City Hospitality House, San Francisco.

would like to patronize, you can either call organizations or institutions directly and ask about their art programs or contact your local, regional or state arts councils (see Appendix 2) for names of specific programs in your area. Once you make contact with program personnel, ask what arrangements must be made in order to see and buy the art.

TYPES OF NON-TRADITIONAL ART PROGRAMS

You can approach this area of non-traditional art collecting in a variety of ways. You may wish to patronize a particular organization or program, a certain type of artist, or a specific form of art. The following suggestions by no means represent a comprehensive overview of collecting opportunities, but they're definitely enough to get you started.

Art by the physically or developmentally disabled. A substantial number of programs exist to serve these individuals. They are almost entirely non-profit and most receive government funding. This means that they can usually be located through arts councils or state departments of mental health. A good national resource is Very Special Arts (1331 F Street, NW, Suite 800, Washington, DC 20004; 1-800-933-8721), loosely knit umbrella organization with branch offices in all fifty states and a main gallery in the District of Columbia. Branch offices are capable of supplying local and regional program information as well as specifics about where the art is sold. Depending on what part of the country you live in or are curious about, have

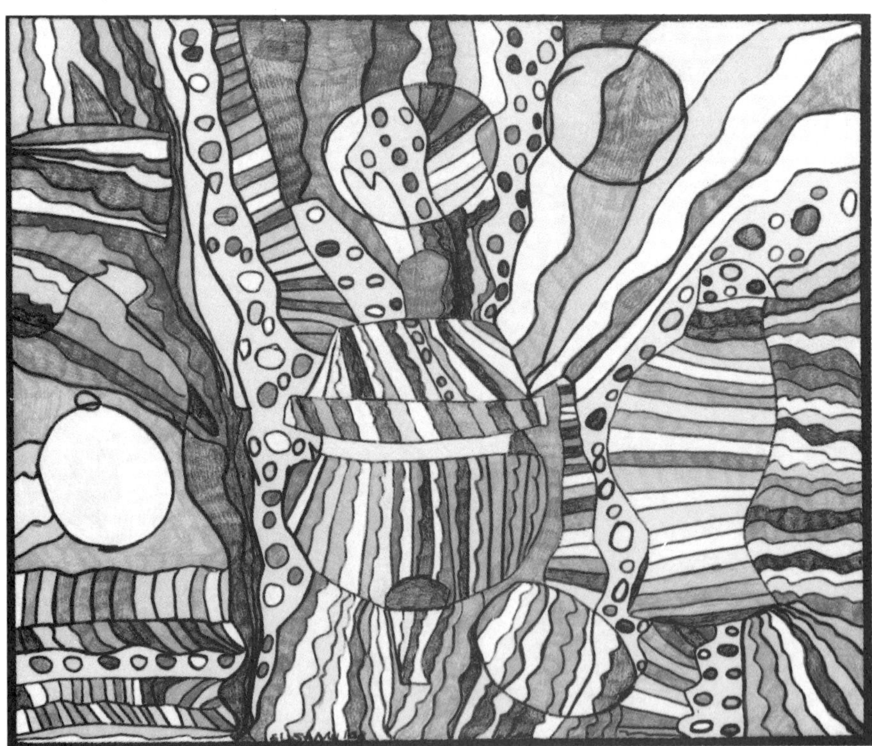

"Vase of Flowers," by Susan Wise, developmentally disabled artist in her mid-forties. Pen and pencil on paper, 26 by 30 inches. Courtesy of the National Institute of Art & Disabilities, Richmond, California.

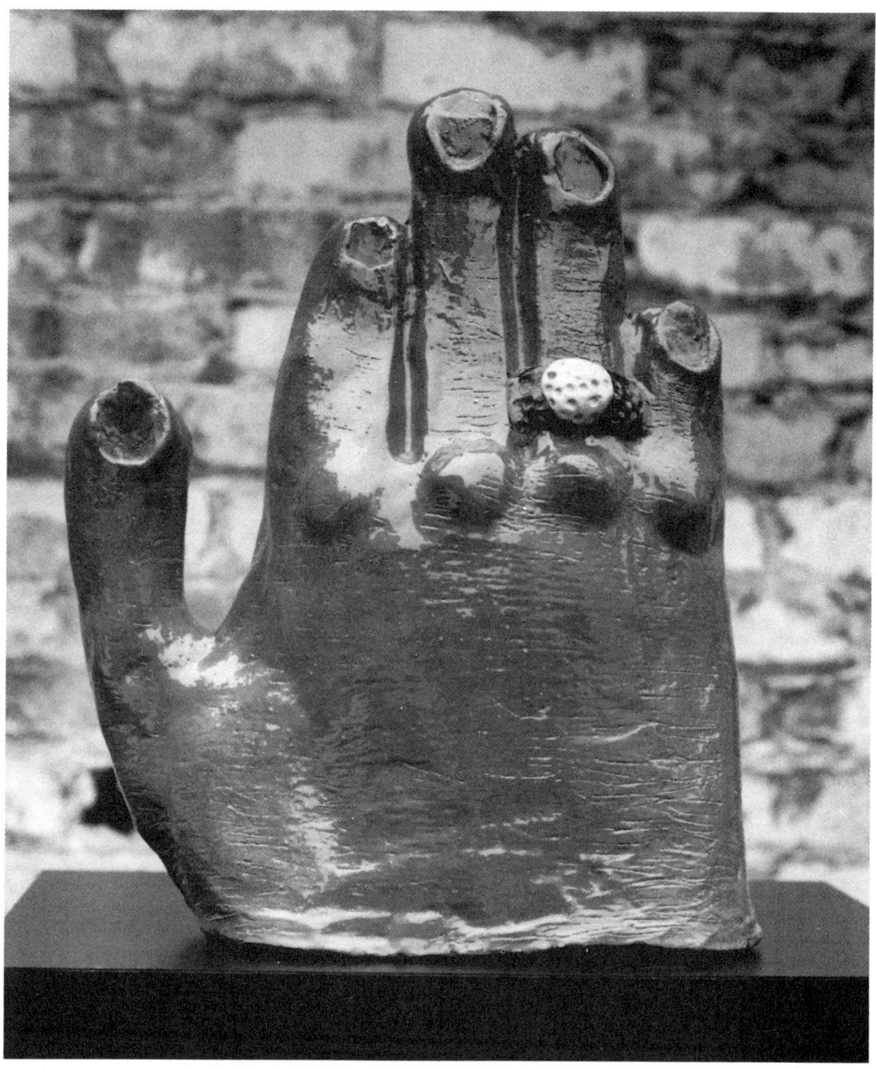

Hand with ring, by Calmer Clark, developmentally disabled artist. Glazed fired ceramic. Height: 15 inches.

the main office provide you with the appropriate names, addresses and phone numbers.

For the most part, programs for the physically or developmentally disabled are located in major metropolitan areas, but some operate in smaller communities. The participants normally spend a certain amount of hours per day or per week together in classlike settings and produce art under the supervision of trained artists and art instructors. These programs are among the more sophisticated in the marketing of their art and often have on-site galleries, sales areas or cooperating outside galleries or retail stores that show the work. The more established programs publish catalogues of artists' work and have hundreds of works on hand from which you can choose.

Art by convalescents. To locate this art, call institutions and ask to speak with recreational or occupational therapists, the individuals who generally supervise art-related activities. You'll have to determine on a case-by-case basis whether participants are interested in selling their art or institutions are amenable to showing it. The better you are at conveying your collecting interests, the better your chances of seeing and buying the art. Art by convalescents is, for the most part, an almost totally unexplored area of collecting.

Art by psychiatric patients. Most mental health facilities have organized art programs. Participants are frequently supervised by professional artists who come in on grants and teach for set periods of time. Some systems, such as California's, have sophisticated statewide programs that involve all state-run institutions. The better programs cultivate highly talented artists of all ages and produce beautiful art. Some can even send you catalogues or publications describing what they do and showcasing their artists' work. To locate programs in your area or the area of your choice, call state or regional arts councils, state departments of mental health and individual public or private institutions for specific program information.

Some mental health facilities have organized arrangements for selling

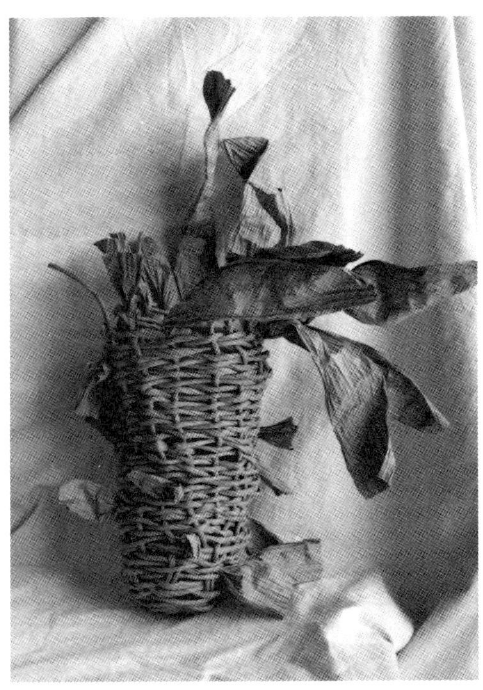

Hanging basket by Jose, a patient at Napa State Hospital, Napa, California. Woven paper twine unraveled at the ends, height 18 inches. Courtesy of the Napa State Hospital Arts in Mental Health Program.

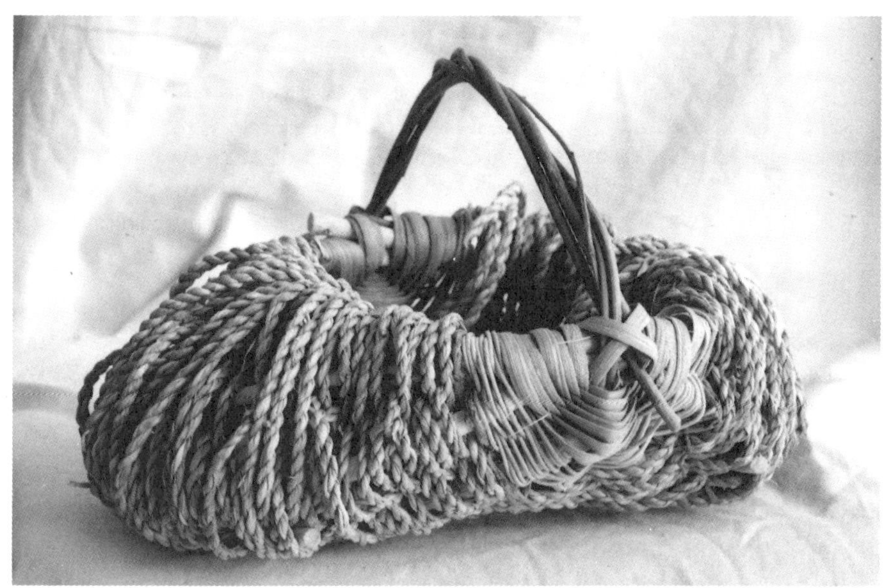

Egg basket by Jose, a patient at Napa State Hospital, Napa California. Rattan reed and Oriental sea grass, height 8 inches, length 12 inches. Courtesy of the Napa State Hospital Arts in Mental Health Program.

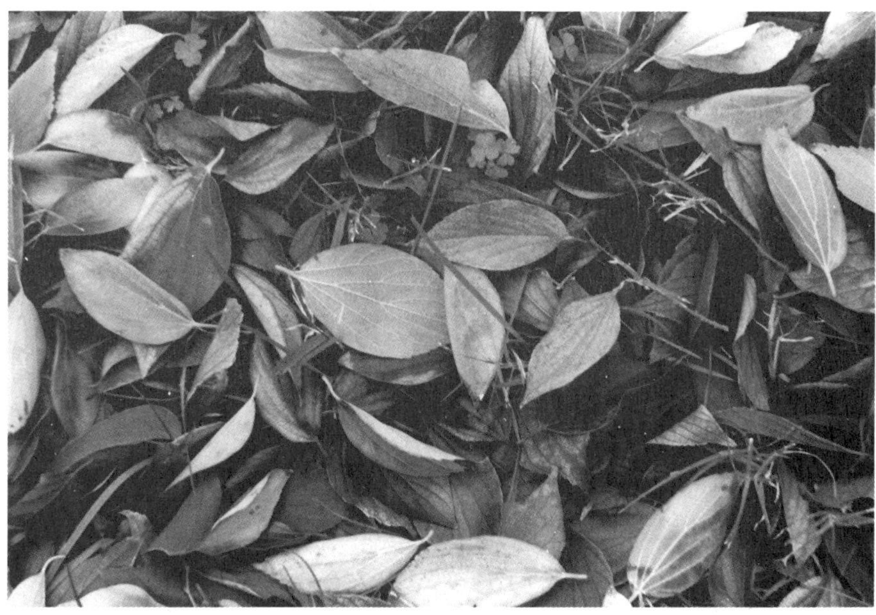

"Leaves," photographed by a patient at Napa State Hospital, Napa, California. Dimensions: 8 by 10 inches. Courtesy of the Napa State Hospital Arts in Mental Health Program.

their art. Others show their art at outside locations, but do not overtly market it. Still others only show the art on their premises and have no involvement with the outside. The great majority of institutions will make arrangements to show and sell their patients' art to interested buyers.

Art by inmates in correctional institutions. Some correctional institutions have organized arts programs where artists working on grants come into the facilities and work with all interested inmates. While many institu-

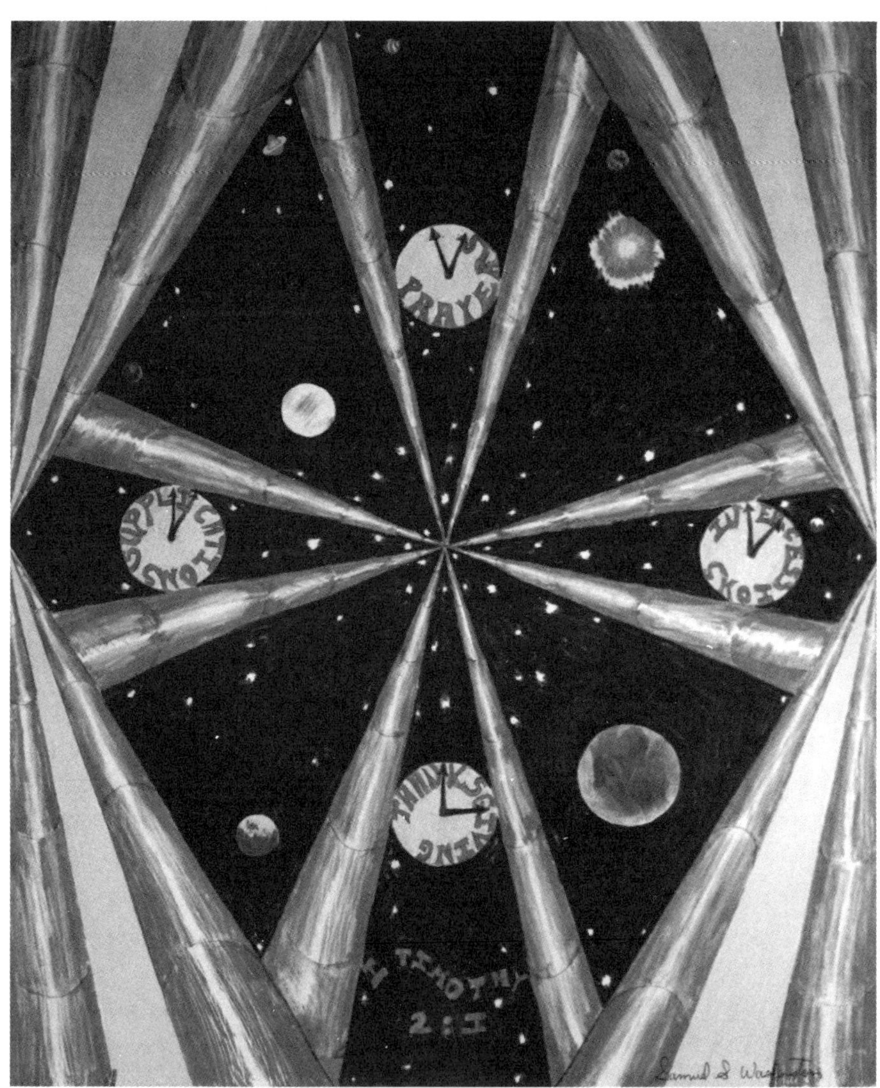

"1 Timothy 2:1" by Samuel S. Washington, inmate and artist, San Francisco County Jail. Courtesy of the Multi-Residency Arts Program at San Francisco County Jail and the Skyline College Theatre Gallery, San Bruno, California.

tions do not have such extensive programs almost all have inmates who produce art and are known to the institutional authorities. Find out about inmate art and artists by contacting prisons directly and asking whether they have prison art programs or have knowledge of inmates who produce art.

Once you establish that art does exist, ask what arrangements must be made in order to see it. The art may be available at institutional gift shops, periodically exhibited on the grounds or, in some cases, shown at outside locations. Under the appropriate circumstances, contact can usually be made with the artists either by phone, letter or in person. Art by inmates is just beginning to be appreciated by collectors and prices are still very reasonable.

Art by veterans in Veterans Administration hospitals and outpatient facilities. Locate this art by calling VA hospitals directly. Ask for either psychiatric or physical disability occupational and recreational therapy departments. Most often, the art is produced in psychiatric occupational therapy programs, but some institutions have multiple independent programs. Because VA hospitals are such complex facilities, you may have trouble working through the maze of extensions, answering machines or referrals, so be persistent and leave messages. Your calls will eventually be returned and you will find the art.

Whenever you make contact, ask for an appointment to visit the facility and see the art. Art programs vary in quality and complexity from location to location so shop around before making any commitments. In general, program directors are casual, agreeable and eager to show and sell their art.

Regarding prices, they're usually negotiable and very reasonable, occasionally you may even be asked to pay what you feel like paying. Some programs are more organized than others and have periodic art sales; some VA artists are highly talented and sell on their own as well as through programs. Incidentally, veterans' centers are also good places to acquire information about and locate individual artists.

Art by homeless, disadvantaged or low-income people. Contact homeless shelters, inner-city community service organizations or arts councils to find out where these programs are located. Some states, such as South Carolina, work with individuals in rural as well as urban areas. Comparatively speaking, a larger percentage of the artists involved in these programs are somewhat skilled, but many still fall into the category of having little or no formal training. One thing that separates the more advanced programs from other collecting options mentioned in this section is that they exist to help get some of the more talented artists off of the streets and back into acceptable living situations.

Much of the art that these artists produce can be quite dramatic and thought-provoking—reflecting difficult life situations and confronting powerful social issues. Depending on the program, the art is shown and sold either on-site, at participating outside galleries or in periodic exhibits at galleries or community centers. Prices tend to vary widely as certain more

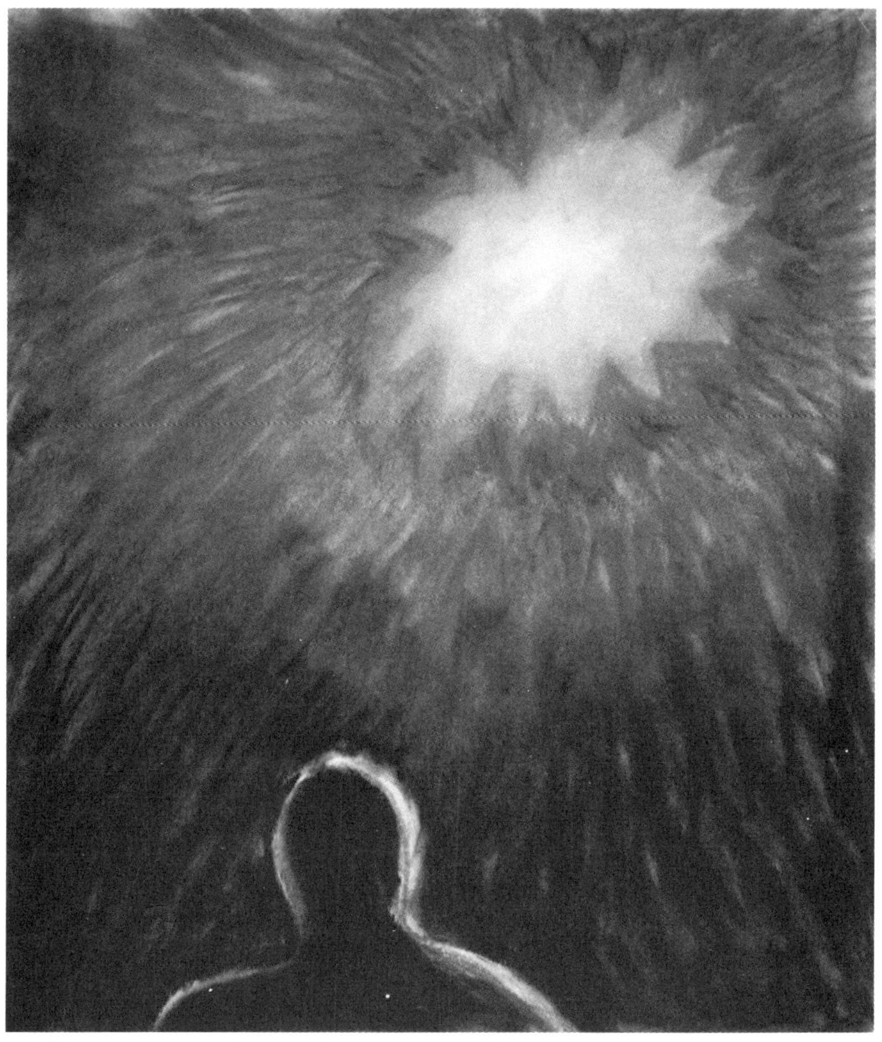

"Gulf War Impression," by Daniel Nieto, veteran and artist. Pastel on paper, 17 by 14 inches. Courtesy of Occupational Therapy, Department of Veterans Affairs, Oakland Outpatient Clinic.

high-profile programs attempt to market their artists like established galleries do. As always, shop around and get a feel for the marketplace in order to avoid overpaying.

Art by the physically, psychologically or emotionally abused. Programs serving these individuals are a relatively recent development in non-traditional art and also ones that need to be approached with a certain amount of sensitivity. They have their roots in the therapeutic values of art, but as with related programs, some participants exhibit a great deal of talent and potential and, sooner or later, showing and selling the art becomes an

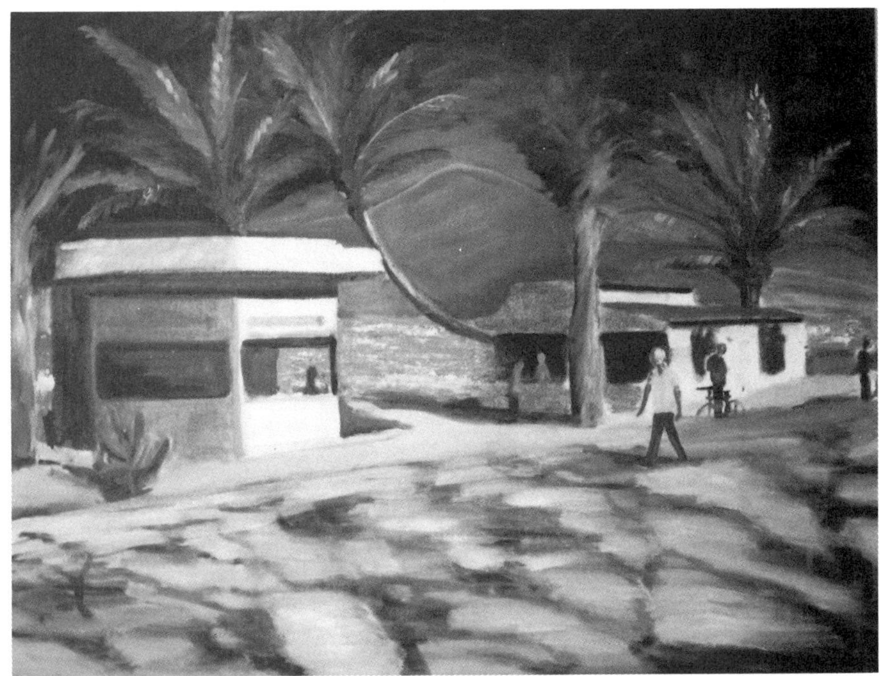

"Vun Tau, Vietnam," by Daniel Nieto, veteran and artist. Oil on canvas, 26 by 33 inches. Courtesy of Occupational Therapy, Department of Veterans Affairs, Oakland Outpatient Clinic.

issue. State arts councils and Very Special Arts are, once again, good contacts for specific program information. Be aware in advance that some programs or participants may not have facilities for showing their art or be interested in selling it. This should change, though, as programs become more established and requests from outsiders to see and buy the art increase.

Tips on Selecting Non-Traditional Art

A sentiment that is continually echoed by dealers, collectors, program directors and other lovers of non-traditional art is to trust your instincts and buy what you like. This is a wide open and steadily evolving field of collecting with huge amounts of underexplored art. When you find yourself saying things like "This is something that moves me," "This is something that I really enjoy," or "This is a type of art or artist or individual that I want to learn more about," you're on the right track. In almost no other area can you feel as comfortable with your own personal preferences as you can here.

When you're just starting out or you see art that you're unfamiliar with, speak with the people who run the programs or work with the artists to get an idea of what's being produced, which artists show the most promise, what separates the better art pieces from the rest. As with other collecting disci-

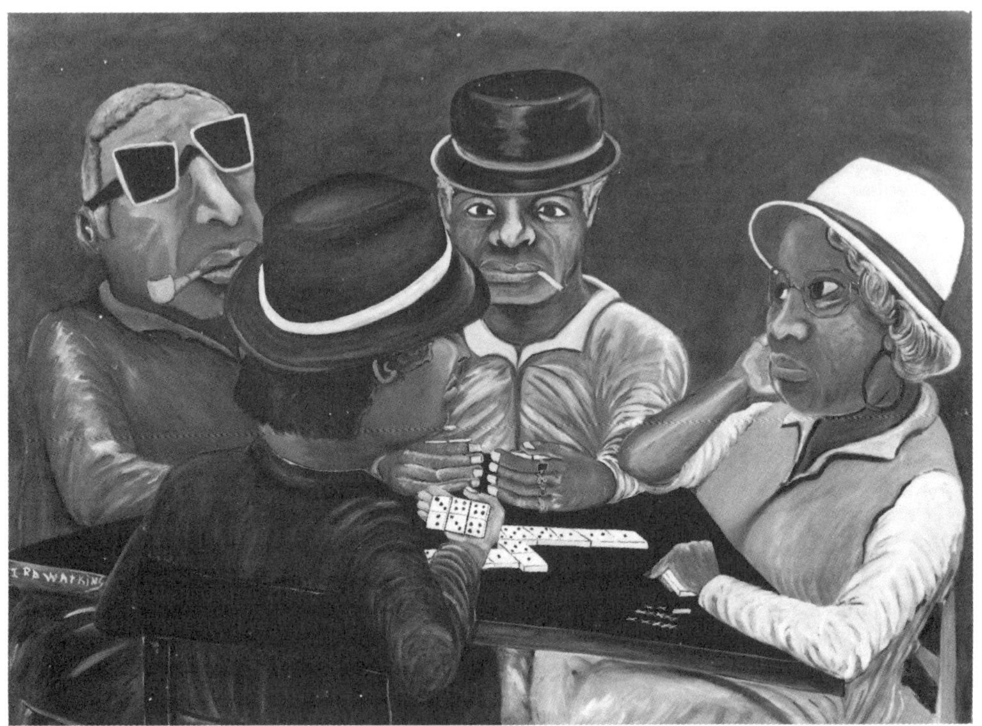

"The Domino Players," oil on canvas by Ira Watkins, a formerly homeless man. Courtesy of Central City Hospitality House, San Francisco.

plines, see a good variety of art before you buy and take every opportunity to learn from the experts. Whenever possible, ask questions, have them explain the fine points of what you're looking at. Attempt to see the art through their eyes, make price comparisons along the way, and familiarize yourself with the territory.

Depending on how adventurous you feel, either stick with established organizations that formally market their art or seek out programs or artists that few, if any, collectors patronize. Either way, the art is going to be affordable. A few of the best-known programs publish their catalogues that explain what they do and show examples of their artists' work (whenever you make contact with a new group, always ask about brochures or other printed information). The downside of better-known programs is that some of their art is beginning to get a little expensive with better-quality pieces being priced into the hundreds of dollars. In the great majority of cases, however, they'll also have good selections of interesting pieces for $100 and less.

Comparison shopping is the key. Once you know your way around, you'll be able to find this art for just about any price you want to pay, even if your budget is $10 or $15. There's far too much non-traditional art available for anyone to control supply, selling prices and public access to it at this time, except in very localized circumstances.

When evaluating art that you like, consider variables like the age of the artist, the amount of work that he's produced, his dedication to producing more, how his style is evolving, and so on. For example, younger artists with significant bodies of work that show promise are sometimes better to collect than older artists with smaller bodies of work or artists who only produce intermittently or irregularly. The younger artists have entire careers ahead of them; the others may not. Figuring out who's going to last or maintain consistent levels of quality can be difficult, though, because of the nature of the artists and the increased probabilities of rapidly changing life situations.

A significant body of interesting work is always a good sign, though, and allows experienced observers to recognize whether a certain amount of talent, definable or not, is at play. An individual cannot produce only one or two interesting pieces and instantly be dubbed a success—he could be dubbed lucky or potentially gifted, but that's about it. So stick with artists who have been at it for a while, at least when you're just starting out. Once you become more experienced, you'll be able to effectively go after isolated pieces.

This tact also applies to programs in general. The more quality work that they have to show, the longer they've been in existence, the more experienced the teachers, the more organized the classes and working conditions, the better. Individual artists may be erratic or transient, but as a group, the participants may exhibit consistently high levels of quality, ability and talent.

Artful Collections

Art by veterans with post-traumatic stress disorder. Some noteworthy work is being produced by these individuals as they explore issues like the pain and suffering of war from first-person standpoints.

Art that's related to a cause. Perhaps you are concerned about the plight of the homeless, people with physical disabilities or the economically disadvantaged. Not only does buying their art help them financially, but it's also a great boost for their confidence and self-esteem. In addition, a certain percentage of the selling prices are often put back into the programs, and you win too—you get wonderful works of art.

Art by the blind or visually impaired. This may be hard to believe, but some of these individuals are highly competent artists.

Art that reflects the lives of the artists. You might buy works where the artists picture themselves dealing with their personal situations.

■ Not all of the art worth collecting has to be in the form of original pieces produced by fine artists. Sometimes the people who reproduce the original

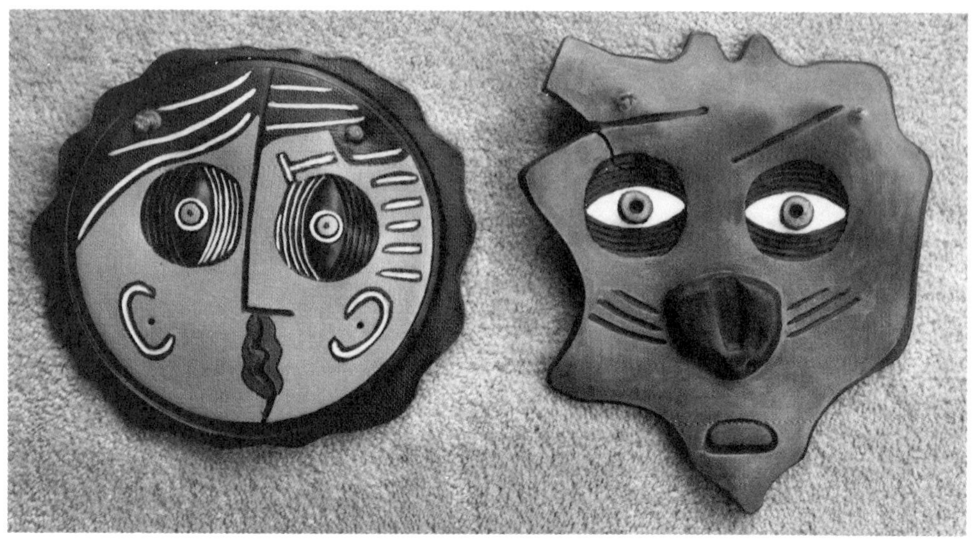

Ceramic masks by Dennis Murphy, visually impaired artist. Height: 12 inches.

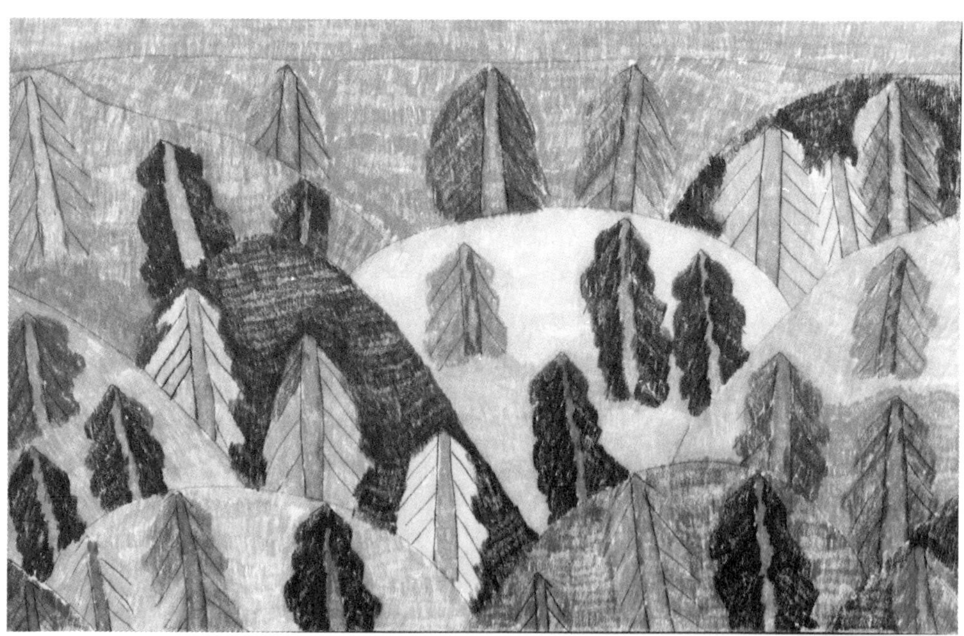

Landscape with hills and trees, by Lois Barnett, 32, developmentally disabled and visually impaired artist. Pen and pencil on paper, 26 by 30 inches. Courtesy of the National Institute of Art & Disabilities, Richmond, California.

works are themselves true artists. These people are known as fine art printers and the best among them have mastered specialized techniques capable of magnificently reproducing works of art in the form of book or magazine illustrations, prints and posters. Relatively few collectors focus on the arts of the printer, though, and as a result, a wealth of affordable material is, once again, available in the marketplace.

15 The Arts of the Printer

This chapter is about prints and it's primarily for those of you who like older art, although it does have contemporary applications. The focus is on collecting examples of those printing techniques that were used to mass-produce illustrations in the decades before and immediately after modern photographic processes were developed. During that time period, which lasted approximately throughout the 19th and into the early 20th centuries (especially the latter half of the 19th century), artists created the surfaces or plates by hand from which publishers printed many of the illustrations found in books, periodicals, posters, decorative wall hangings and other forms of printed matter. The resulting prints, though often common and commercial in nature at the time they were produced, are beginning to be appreciated and collected as original works of art.

These prints are similar to those discussed in Chapter 11, but differ in several major respects. Chapter 11 prints are collectible primarily because they are original works of art by famous artists. The prints described in this chapter are also original works of art, but the artists are not necessarily household names—some are totally unknown. Their prints are not only collectible as works of art, but depending on the print, may also be collectible as historical documents and/or examples of fine printing techniques.

As historical documents, many record the way life was in days gone by. They are visual records of how people lived, what they wore, who the most popular individuals of the times were, and what major events took place. Even when the artist or publisher is unknown or the printing technique is of only marginal quality the picture still has a certain collectible value if the subject matter has historical significance.

With respect to printing history and techniques, these prints are examples of how visual information was conveyed to people before photographic reproductive processes were developed. The finest examples of technique and production are collectible even when artists or subject matters are not all that desirable. The quality of the printing and how and when it was done become the primary considerations in forming this sort of a collection.

Another collectible aspect of these prints is their impending scarcity. Though still common and inexpensive, supplies will eventually dwindle. The techniques used to produce them are prohibitively time-consuming and expensive today, and when they are used, they are almost exclusively confined to illustrating expensive limited edition books and portfolios.

You still have time to build a quality collection because most of these prints are sold as decorative items with virtually no attention being paid to artistic, historic or technical merits. Not much in the way of reference material is available, not much structure exists in the marketplace and you pretty much have free reign in terms of what you choose to buy or how you wish to organize your collection.

The Two Most Common Types of Prints

Although a multitude of printing techniques were used in the 19th century, the great majority of prints are either engravings or lithographs. These were the most practical for purposes of mass-producing images and, therefore, the most commercially viable for publishers. Illustrating for the public was a business, and engravers and lithographers were employed by publishers, much like commercial photographers are employed today. They produced whatever images their superiors required in whatever sizes, styles and specifications were indicated. These professionals were not necessarily thought of as fine artists and did not necessarily sign their work.

The great majority of these lithographs and engravings are inexpensive and readily available for several reasons: they were often printed in large runs, lithographers and engravers are still generally viewed as commercial and not fine artists, and many collectors do not consider them original compositions. All this has begun to change, however, as many other art forms become too expensive for most collectors to afford.

Engravings. Most often, an artist or designer created an image that was then engraved by an engraver onto a hard surface and printed by a printer. Depending on the situation, these images were engraved onto copper, steel or wood plates. The plates were then inked and the images printed by placing them into direct contact with paper and applying even pressure. The great majority of engravings are black and white.

Engravings were most often used to illustrate better books and periodicals. Some were even sold in packets like postcards are sold today. A few were larger in size and created specifically to be displayed as wall decorations. Popular subject matters for engravings were topographical views, famous works of art, historical scenes, ornamental designs, scientific and technological advances, mechanical and manufacturing devices, news events of the day, and decorative genre or story pictures. Examples of more collectible engravings are illustrations for *Harper's Weekly* by Winslow

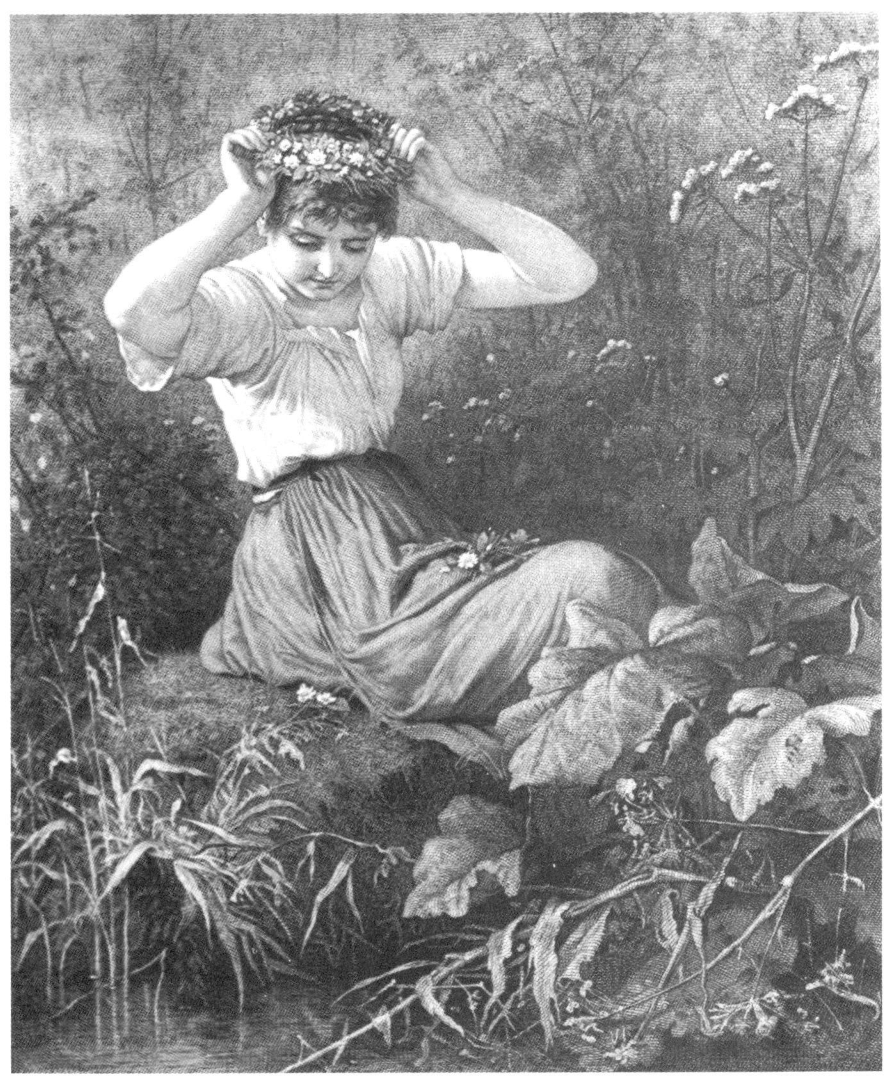

"Weaving the May Coronet" engraved by Thomas Langer after the painting by L. Pohle, circa 1870. Steel engraving, 6½ by 8¼ inches. Courtesy of Kathleen Manning, Prints Old and Rare, San Francisco.

Homer (1836–1910) and Frederic Remington (1861–1909), and topographical views painted by William Henry Bartlett (1809–1854).

Lithographs. Unlike an engraving, a lithograph is produced by drawing or printing an image directly onto a smooth flat surface such as stone, zinc or aluminum. Basically, the image is then chemically treated to make it receptive to printer's ink while the background remains resistant. The surface is then inked and the image is printed by covering it with paper and applying pressure.

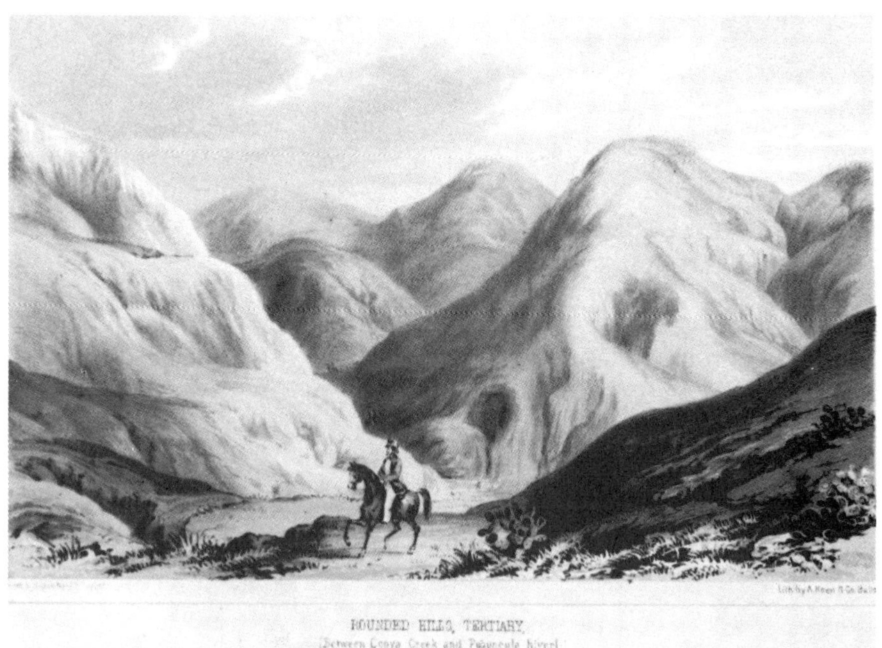

"Rounded Hills, Tertiary" sketched by Charles Koppel and lithographed by A. Hoen & Co, Baltimore, circa 1855. United States railroad survey lithograph, $8\frac{3}{4}$ by $11\frac{3}{8}$ inches. Courtesy of Argonaut Book Shop, San Francisco.

Lithography became popular as a means for illustration because of the ease with which images could be applied to the smooth printing surfaces and the rapidity with which they could be printed. The intricate and relatively complex process of engraving onto hard wood or metal plates and manually printing the images was no longer necessary.

Lithographs were far more often printed in colors than engravings were, with one stone or printing surface prepared for each color that was necessary in the final image. The finest color lithographs appeared in the most expensive books and portfolios of the day. Popular subject matters included topographical views, city scenes, plants, animals, designs and patterns, decorative compositions, and reproductions of famous places or works of art. Examples of highly collectible and relatively expensive lithographs are Currier and Ives (active 1835–1907) and Audubon (1785–1851) prints.

Lithographs were also used to illustrate less expensive publications such as popularly priced view books, some periodicals, city or county histories, and government publications like railroad surveys, geological surveys and agricultural annuals. These illustrations are still relatively common and far more affordable than those produced by famous artists or companies.

Government survey lithographs, dating back as far as the early 1800s for example, are finely executed topographical views, with interesting historic content. Likewise, a number of government agricultural annuals published

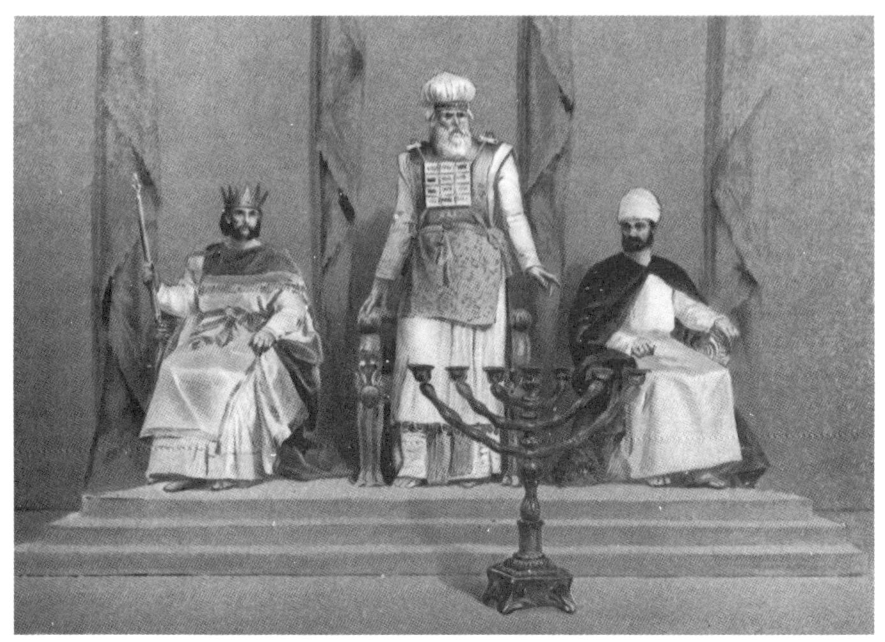

Masonic chromolithograph, circa 1890s. Officers of the Chapter, 5½ by 7¾ inches.

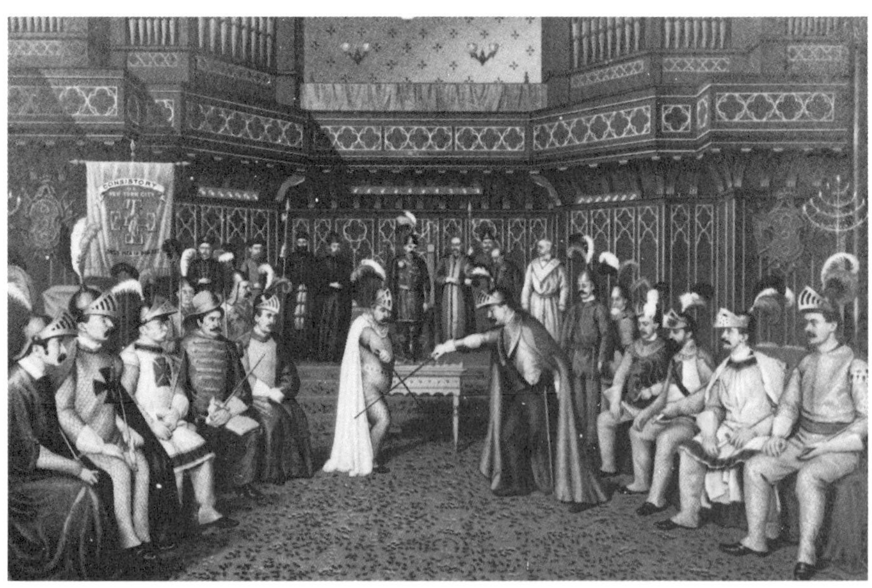

Masonic chromolithograph, circa 1890s. A Scottish Rite, 5¼ by 8 inches.

as late as the early 1900s contain quality color lithographs of fruits, vegetables, insects and other relevant subjects. These lithographs can be purchased individually for as little as $5 to $10, or you can pay even less by buying entire publications with their lithographs still intact.

Chromolithograph is simply another word for color lithograph and does not denote a special production technique. It came to describe popular commercial lithographs with decorative or illustrative subject matters that were in vogue mainly during the second half of the nineteenth century. A number of companies were well known as publishers of chromolithographs such as Louis Prang and Company in America and Raphael Tuck and Sons in Great Britain. Their best-known images have been collected for some time now, but they were both prolific and many of their prints still can be purchased at reasonable prices. Images by other companies are even more common and affordably priced.

How to Recognize Prints

Identifying what type of print you're looking at and whether it's original or not can be confusing at times, especially for the novice. A number of prints are labeled along their lower margins with references to particular engravers, lithographers, companies or other types of printmakers. Single prints that were published for decorative purposes, particularly chromolithographs, are sometimes labeled on the back. When prints are not individually labeled, but are still intact in books or periodicals, check tables of contents, lists of illustrations, title pages and sometimes the last pages of the books, particularly those published in Europe. Specific types of illustrations are often identified.

When prints are not labeled, the best identification tool available is a reference book called *How to Identify Prints* by Bamber Gascoigne (Thames & Hudson, New York, 1986). It is a complete guide to identifying virtually all print processes known to man. Gascoigne not only provides historical background information about specific print types and discusses their identifying features, but he also includes numerous illustrations of details and surface characteristics, both actual-sized and magnified, in black-and-white and color. Keep this book with you at all times, or borrow it from your local library, and use it whenever you're not sure what you're looking at.

By the way, many types of prints and printing techniques exist in addition to lithographs and engravings. If you discover that you enjoy the technical aspects of this field, you might consider collecting examples of obscure, unusual or less-popular printing techniques. *How to Identify Prints* has more than enough information to get you started and explains even the most complex processes in easy to understand language. Hardly anyone collects in this manner, which means that, once again, affordable opportunities abound.

When you're out in the field, always carry a magnifying glass, a

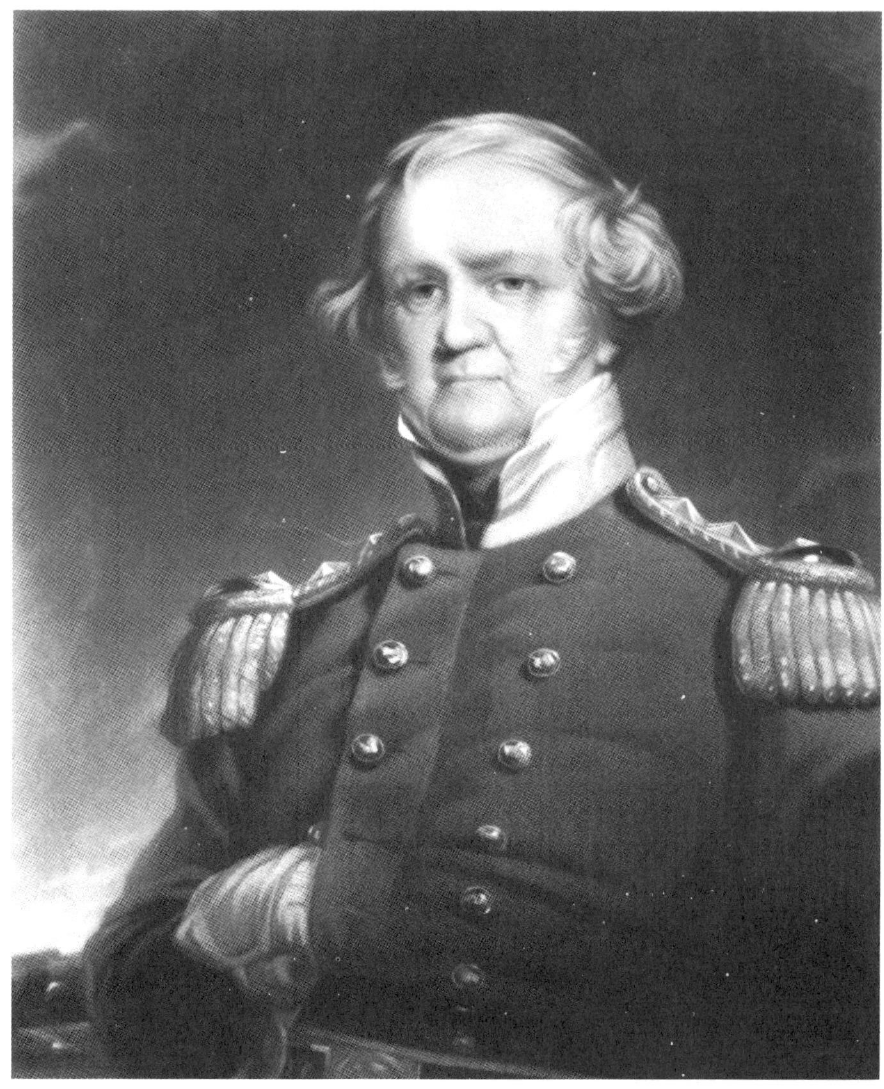

General Winfield Scott engraved by T.P. Barlow from the painting by Robert W. Weir, circa 1860. Mezzotint, 18¾ by 15 inches. Courtesy of Kathleen Manning, Prints Old and Rare, San Francisco.

jeweler's or photographer's loop and a pocket microscope (Radio Shack sells an excellent one for about $10). Almost invariably, an image must be magnified in order to conclusively identify what type of print it is. As soon as possible, learn how to recognize differences between qualities of paper that prints are printed on and whether you're looking at originals or photo-reproductions. Poor quality paper will deteriorate over time and photo-reproductions should be avoided because, as discussed in Chapter 5, they are not original works of art.

The best way to learn to recognize prints is by getting advice from an expert. Get to know either a print collector, an art teacher or professor with a knowledge of prints, a print dealer, a museum curator or curatorial assistant. You might even think about paying such an individual to take a little time and teach you basic identification techniques. There is no substitute for qualified first-hand explanations.

Where to Find Prints

You can find wonderful examples of the print arts just about anywhere, especially places where secondhand goods change hands. Likely locations are bookstores which sell used and rare books, book auctions, flea markets, library, garage and estate sales, antiques shows, and book fairs. A few dealers specialize in this field and carry better-quality prints, but if you want to save money or you enjoy the thrill of the hunt, you can be successful on your own. Either way, you should have little trouble finding good prints at reasonable prices.

Wherever you go, check what's hanging on walls and go through loose prints that are sitting in file cabinets, folders, boxes or print bins. Page through any large old books or periodicals that you see lying around (with experience, you'll learn to recognize what types of publications are likely to

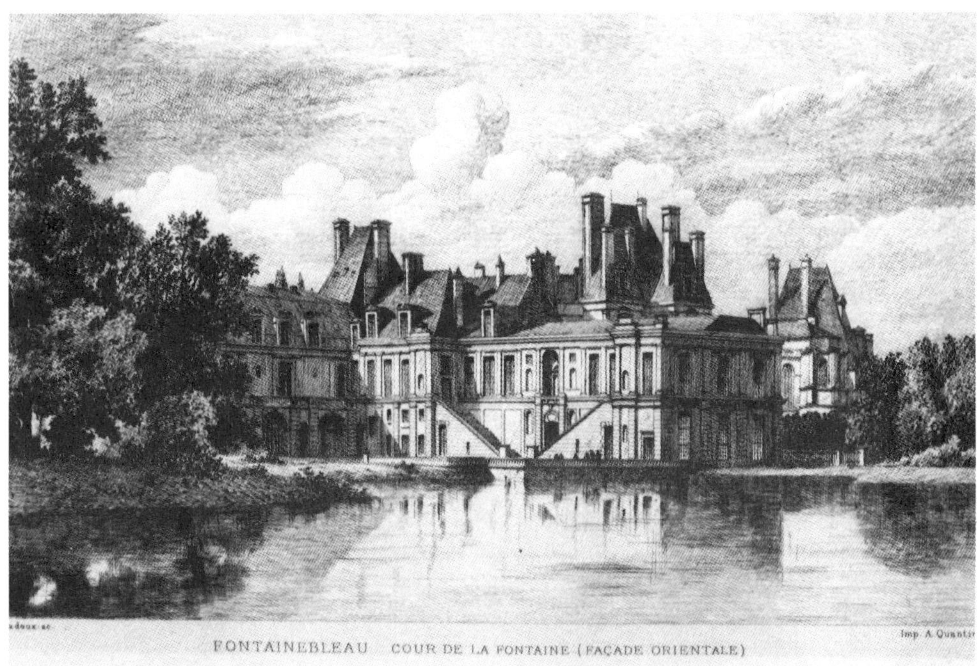

Original etching of the Fontainbleau by Eugene Sadoux taken from the three volume set La Renaissance en France *by Leon Palustre (Paris, A. Quantin, 1879). Image size:* $6\frac{1}{2}$ *by 10 inches.*

contain quality illustrations). Always tell sellers what you're looking for because they may not keep prints in plain view.

TIPS ON COLLECTING

The variety of prints that are available is so vast that you should focus on a topic as soon as possible. Choose something you're really interested in such as a particular historical event, famous person, subject matter, geographic location, or type of print. Maybe you're an Abraham Lincoln fan, you have a favorite artist, you like pictures of old buildings in your city or state that no longer exist or you're a flower, bird or animal lover. Specialization is the key to success in this field.

If price is a concern, good bargains tend to be prints with subject matters that look exactly the same today as they did at the time the prints were produced—for example, steel engravings of great art treasures in famous museums or interiors of historic buildings. The rarer or more interesting, unusual or exotic the images, the more you're going to pay.

You can also find bargains by concentrating on smaller-sized prints, works by lesser-known artists or publishers, and unsigned, untitled or unidentifiable images. In a periodical like *Harper's Weekly,* for example, some illustrations are elaborate, signed and either full or double-paged. Others are smaller, unsigned and embedded within the text. While top-quality large images can run into the hundreds of dollars per piece, smaller ones can cost as little as a dollar or two.

Another way to save money is to buy in quantity. For example, paying $200 for a book with 30 original full-page illustrations may seem expensive, but you will be paying only $7 per print. You can save the images you want and either trade or sell the others. When you're looking at loose prints, employ a similar method and ask sellers how many you have to buy in order to get a bulk discount.

Regarding signatures and other identifying features, the general rule is that the more information contained in the print, the better. A good collectible print, for instance, would be titled, dated and bear the names of the artist, engraver or lithographer, and publisher. Occasionally, prints are hand signed, usually by the engraver, sometimes by the artist and sometimes by both. These, of course, tend to sell for more money than prints with no signature, but depending on their subject matters, prices can still be reasonable.

Condition is all important when collecting these types of prints. Because they're so plentiful, you can afford to keep looking until you find the images you like in perfect condition. Avoid problem pieces unless they are rare or important in some way.

Damage seriously devalues prints and with these types of prints in particular, restoration is rarely cost-efficient—costs far exceed the values of the prints in most cases. Keep an eye out for problems like rips, tears, water

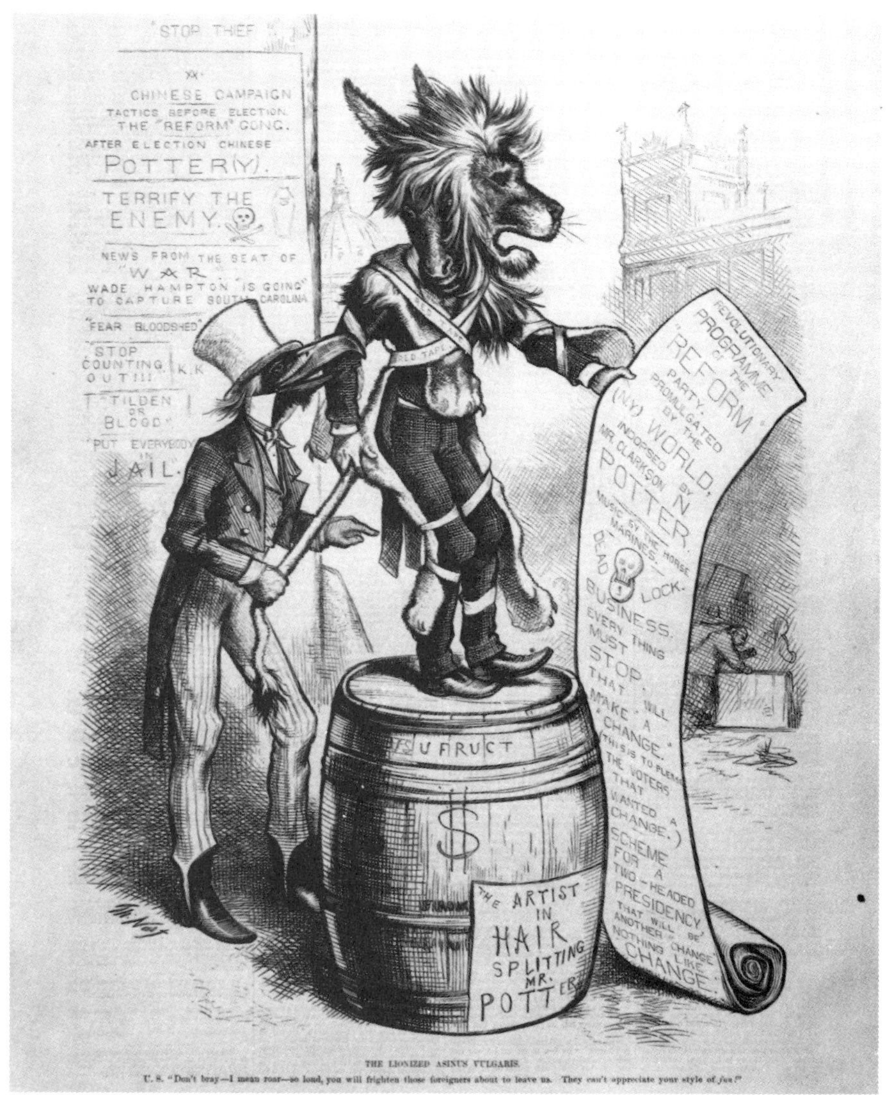

"The Lionized Asinus Vulgaris" by Thomas Nast. Wood engraving after the original, Harper's Weekly, *December 16, 1876. Dimensions: 14 by 10 inches. Courtesy of Kathleen Manning, Prints Old and Rare, San Francisco.*

stains, folds, trimmed margins, holes, fading, foxing, yellowing, and surface abrasions. Stick with clean, fresh, well-defined images. Remove any frames or mats so that you can carefully inspect the print. Frames and mats can sometimes hide serious damage or margins that have been cut down.

A somewhat controversial issue in this field of collecting is whether or not to remove prints that are contained in books, periodicals and other publications. If you find yourself confronted with this choice, think before

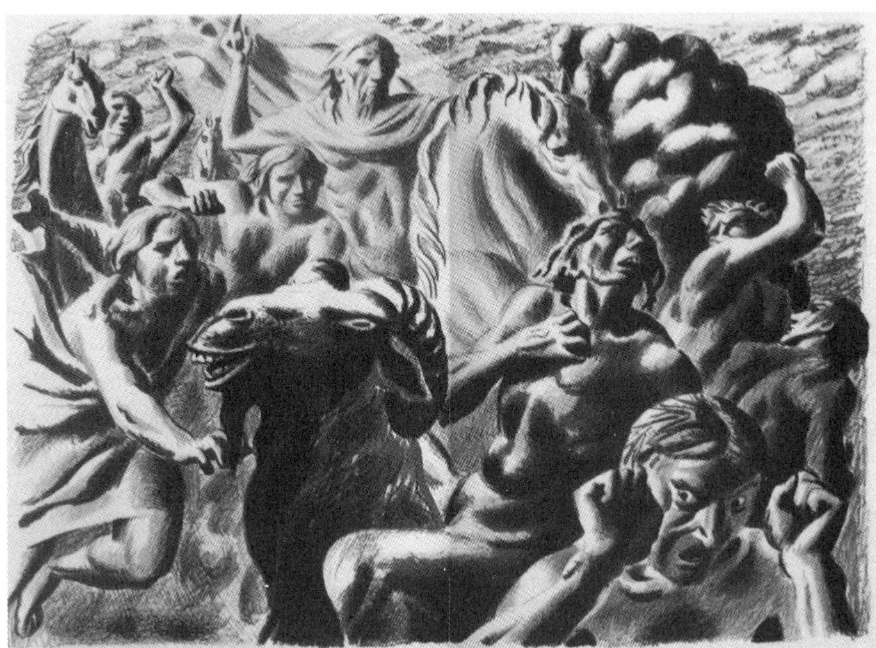

"The Battle in Heaven" by Hans Feibusch, from the book The Revelation of Saint John the Divine, *circa 1940s. Double-page lithograph in color, 14¾ by 19¾ inches.*

you cut. Depending upon the condition of the publication, the importance of the text to the prints, the quality of the binding and other related factors, you may wish to keep it whole and enjoy the prints without removing them. Value of the complete item may be greater than the combined values of the prints when separated. On the other hand, many times removing the prints will have no adverse affects on value. Check with experts when you're unsure how to proceed.

Another situation to keep in mind is that some dealers are now selling black-and-white prints that have been recently hand-colored. This detracts from their collectible value because the original images have been altered, but it enhances their decorative value because color is generally preferred over black and white. Depending on your intentions, you decide what you want to buy. If you are collecting for purposes other than pure decoration, avoid recently colored prints. They can sometimes be difficult to recognize so protect yourself by asking sellers, getting guarantees in writing and consulting with outside experts when necessary.

Artful Collections

Examples of one particular type of print. Depending on how much time, money and dedication you have, seek out examples of either common or less-common techniques. For instance, steel engravings are inexpensive and easy to find; top-quality chromoxylographs (color wood engravings) are less common and more costly.

By location. Collect prints by artists or companies that were located in your city or state.

Prints that have been hand signed.

Prints of one particular subject. The variety is endless—dogs, boats, women's hats, steam-powered machines, public squares or gathering places, kitchen scenes, cowboys, cannons, bridges, mountains, musical instruments, log cabins, or fairy tale scenes, to name just a few ideas.

Miniature prints.

Illustrations from a specific publication.

Prints from a specific year or time period.

Collecting mass-produced illustrative prints is affordable because plenty of material is available and not that many collectors are going after it. Art memorabilia is a similar commodity in that collectors basically ignore the vast amount of items that artists produce or participate in producing that are not necessarily categorized or thought of as art. This next chapter focuses on the affordable option of collecting all those things besides art that come directly from the hands of artists—and a little art to boot.

16 Art Memorabilia

One of the more overlooked and undervalued commodities in the art business is art memorabilia. These are items that relate, in varying degrees, to either the art that artists produce during their lifetimes or to the artists themselves. Artists do other things besides create art and much of it can be a source of great collecting enjoyment if you know what to look for and what your options are.

You can begin to get an idea of the nature of art memorabilia by thinking for a moment about some of the day-to-day activities that you are involved in. You sign checks, write letters, pose for occasional photographs, sign documents, pay bills, pass out your business cards, fill out forms, and perform written assignments on your job. An artist does many of these same things and, in addition, he may sign books or catalogues that include his art, scribble quick drawings for friends or acquaintances who might request them, correspond with art dealers and collectors, keep records of his work, and so on. You can image how much of this "art memorabilia" accumulates throughout an average artist's career.

Everything tangible that comes directly from an artist, no matter how insignificant, can be considered as art memorabilia. Each and every item contributes, to one extent or another, to our understanding of what that individual's life is or was all about. Even a canceled check for an artist's monthly electric bill, for example, contains his autograph and provides information about where he was living at that time.

Art memorabilia has historical and collectible value just as memorabilia does that relates to the lives of known personalities in other fields like acting, writing, politics, or sports. Its historical value centers on how informative it is. Its collectible value centers on our desire to own things that either belonged to, were produced by, or were touched in some way by individuals who we revere or respect.

The primary reason why art memorabilia is particularly attractive as a collectible is that its been somewhat ignored compared to that from other walks of life. The substantial majority of art collectors tend to focus only on art and nothing else because they consider the art the ultimate memorabilia, everything else is irrelevant. Memorabilia price comparisons bear this out. For example, signatures of the more famous American politicians cost hundreds and sometimes even thousands of dollars each while those of America's more famous artists frequently can be purchased for well under a $100 each. Signatures of moderately well-known artists cost even less.

Buying art memorabilia can be a very viable solution to collecting with a limited budget and can provide a lifetime of fun and fulfillment.

Characteristics and Types of Art Memorabilia

As has already been stated, anything that has to do with art or artists can be considered in the realm of memorabilia. Be as creative as you want in deciding where your interests lie and what you want to collect. There are no limits—you can collect greeting cards sent by artists, clothing worn by artists, checks signed by artists, paint brushes owned by artists, artists' business cards, or photographs of artists' mothers.

Several factors are generally taken into consideration and weighted in varying degrees when evaluating a piece of memorabilia. One is whether or not it has handwork or handwriting on it. For example, a gallery invitation to an artist's opening may be hand signed, signed and inscribed, signed with a small drawing, or not signed at all. Likewise, a book from an artist's library may or may not have his signature in it, underlining, margin notes or comments. The obvious advantage to having some form of handwriting present is that no question exists about the relationship of the item to the artist. Original signatures and accompanying handwork are generally viewed as collectible no matter what they're found on.

Another factor is importance. More important items provide significant information about artists, art movements, or art history. For example, a sketchbook with 20 sketches in it tells more about an artist than does a signed or inscribed gallery invitation and is, therefore, more important and more collectible.

A third factor is scarcity. In general, the less common an item is, the more desirable or collectible it is. For example, a one-of-a-kind letter sent by an artist is more valuable than a gallery newsletter printed in an edition of 500 that contains the same information.

Good places to see and familiarize yourself with art memorabilia are art museums, historical societies with art collections, artist associations, and art libraries associated with special collections. If you're a fan of American art, for instance, the Archives of American Art (Room 331, American Art–Portrait Gallery Building, Washington, DC 20560; 202-357-2781), with regional centers in New York, Detroit, Boston and San Marino, California, is probably the best source of information. Countless documents, letters and other publi-

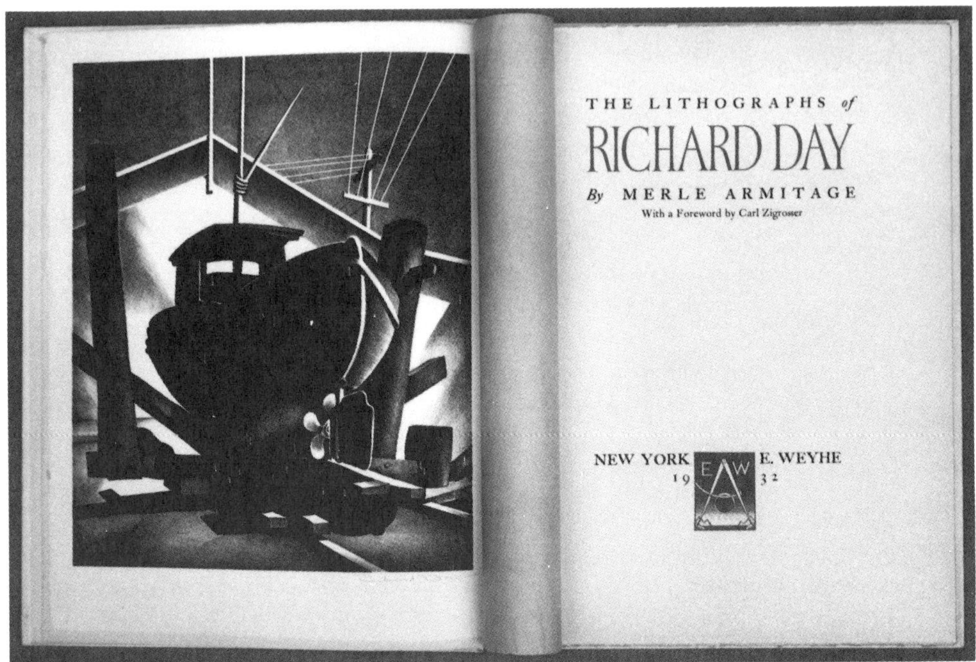

Monograph on lithographer Richard Day containing an original lithograph pencil-signed by the artist. Image size: 9⅞ by 7⅞ inches.

cations relating to American art and artists, all of which have been photographed onto microfilm, are available for public viewing. Smaller local and regional museums are also among the better locations to view this sort of material. They often have at least some of it on public display in glass showcases alongside their art.

Various terms are used to classify the different types of memorabilia that exist. A *signature* or *clipped signature* refers to a signature that is not accompanied by additional writing. *Inscribed* generally means a signature accompanied by a brief personal statement, greeting or salutation. *Manuscript material* refers to personal letters, documents, sketchbooks, diaries, journals, writings, and so on. *Ephemera* describes smaller items like business cards or gallery invitations. *Association items* are things that have little or nothing to do with an individual artist other than that they were owned by him, like art books, paint brushes, tools, or paperback books.

Where to Buy Art Memorabilia

For older memorabilia, antiquarian booksellers, autograph dealers, book fairs, book auctions, paper and ephemera shows, estate sales and sometimes antiques or secondhand stores are your best sources. Those of you who enjoy research can seek out relatives and descendents of artists by checking with local and regional museums, historical societies, art associations and older artists. Relatives and descendents often own significant amounts of memorabilia and are sometimes willing to part with a piece or two. Art galleries that specialize in older art are also good resources.

If your tastes angle more toward contemporary art or if you're on a budget, a great way to collect is to personally contact artists, either at their studios or at art openings. Ask them for publications relating to their careers like gallery or show invitations, exhibit catalogues, business cards, brochures or other printed pieces, especially those that picture their work. Tell them the nature of your collection, request that they sign and date whatever they have for you and, whenever possible, ask to have those signatures accompanied by quick statements or, better yet, by drawings or sketches. Don't be surprised if some artists charge for those additional features. You can also make these requests by mail, especially with artists who live in other states or countries. For additional ideas, reread Chapter 10 with an eye to buying memorabilia instead of art.

Galleries are probably the best places for tapping into the contemporary art scene. Anytime you visit one, ask to be put on their mailing list and request that they send you invitations to their openings. While you're there, tell them what you collect and ask whether they have any invitations or catalogues relating to shows that they've held in the past.

Tips on Collecting

Memorabilia collecting is like piecing together little bits of history, and memorabilia collectors are often more like historians than anything else. Their collections provide insight into lives, careers, events, personalities and living conditions at various points in time. Whether the material being collected is brand new or 100 years old, a good-quality assemblage always tells a story and reads like a book.

The best collecting tip is to get specific as soon as possible. That way, you'll be able to concentrate on one particular area, become an authority of sorts and put together a solid collection. Know what you're looking for, how much it costs and who sells it before you start buying seriously. The memorabilia field is far too large for you to wander around without direction and still be effective in your collecting. As soon as possible, make decisions like whether you want everything you buy to be hand signed, whether you want to collect items relating to one artist or many, what time period or geographical locations you're focusing on, etc.

If you prefer signed material, look for more than just signatures when you buy. In terms of collectibility, a signature by itself is at the low end of the desirability spectrum (the good news is that for those of you on budgets, that also means the high end of the affordability spectrum). Signatures that are accompanied by inscriptions or quick drawings are better. More complex drawings or extensive inscriptions are better yet. Complete sketchbooks, journals, diaries and important correspondence like writing that explains an artist's philosophy or relates to important events or periods in his career are the most desirable, but unfortunately, also the most expensive.

Be careful about hype, especially when entering the realm of autograph dealers, autograph collectors and autograph sales events. Keep in mind how many times you sign your name during your life, how many times you write significant documents and what a significant document is. In other words, keep whatever you're being offered in its proper perspective. Certain types of autograph collecting have become quite popular and somewhat speculative in recent years and, as a result, some dealers and collectors can tend to overemphasize the importance of some of the less significant pieces that they sell.

Remember:

- The more common or available the material, the less it should cost.
- Large attractive signatures are more collectible than small illegible ones.
- Signed is better than unsigned.
- Dated is better than undated.
- The more the material relates to the art aspects of an artist's existence, the more value it has. A receipt for art supplies, for instance, is more valuable than a receipt from the dry cleaner's.
- The more famous the artist, the more valuable the memorabilia (assuming a personal hands-on connection between the memorabilia and the artist).

There are many options for the budget-conscious. If you like more important artists, think about collecting clipped signatures, signatures on checks, or unsigned items like invitations from gallery shows and books or exhibit catalogues that have been written about the artists. If you want more for your money, collect significant material relating to less well-known, younger or local artists. Items relating to unidentified artists, such as small unsigned sketches or unsigned photographs of artists holding their pallettes or standing in front of their easels, are also possibilities.

Suggestions for Displaying Art Memorabilia

You may not be aware of the potential visual appeal of memorabilia or realize that when properly assembled and displayed, these bits and pieces can achieve a wonderful, historical, fascinating and important status.

Learn from autograph collectors—they know how to make something as minor as a clipped signature look like a major museum piece. First, they acquire the signature, which may be on a canceled check, three-by-five card or other small piece of paper. Next, they locate pictures relating to the personality. In the case of an artist, they find and remove illustrations of the artist and/or major pieces of his art from books, magazines or exhibit

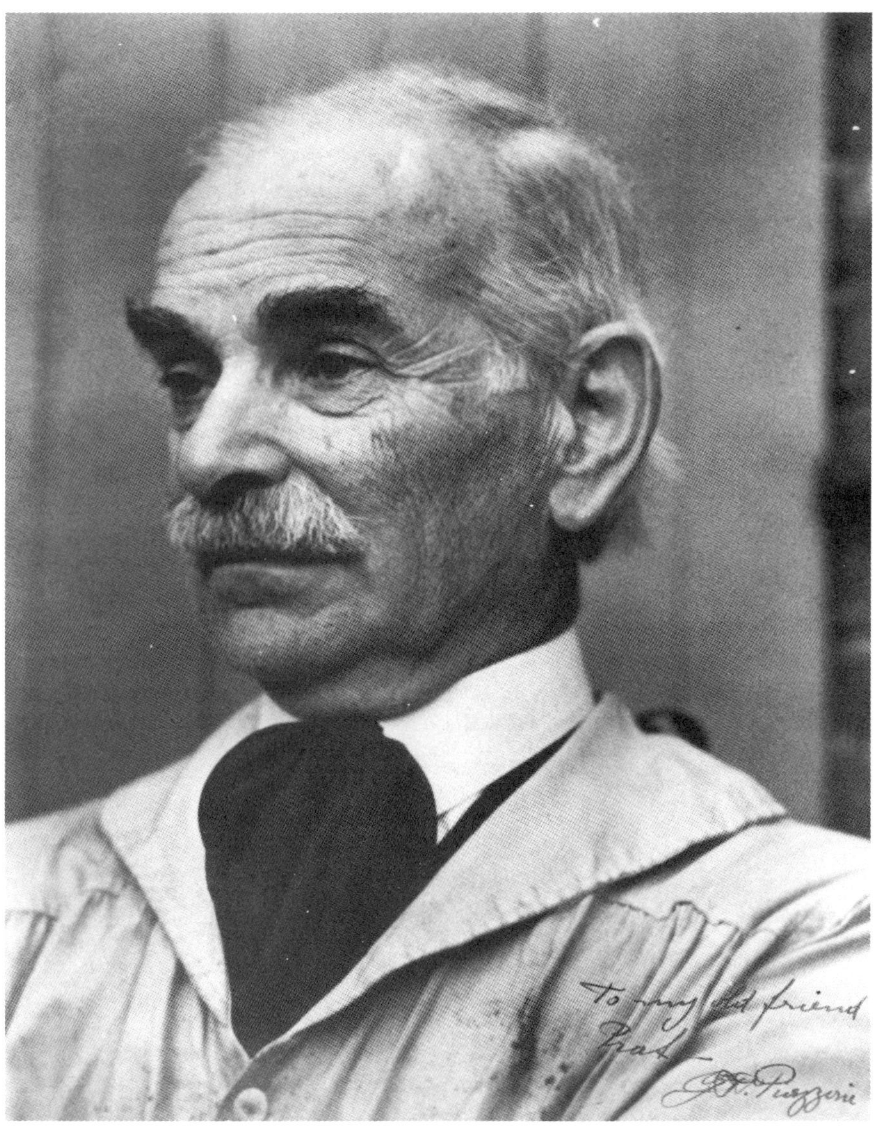

Inscribed vintage image by an unknown photographer of American artist Gottardo Piazzoni, circa 1920. Dimensions: $9^{1}/_{8}$ by $7^{1}/_{4}$ inches.

catalogues. Then they combine the signature with a picture or two into a single presentation piece by placing them all together in one mat, a separate opening cut for each piece, and under one frame. What started out as a small signed piece of paper ends up a substantial and dramatic arrangement under glass that's appropriate for hanging in any normal-sized room.

This format is particularly adaptive to art—single signatures can be framed alongside or directly underneath single illustrations of works of art by their respective artists to create the illusion of a collection of signed originals. Ansel Adams, for example, signed his name so many times during his life that single or clipped signatures can be purchased relatively inexpensively. Add to that the fact that illustrations of his most famous photographs are available everywhere—in books as well as in poster shops. You can assemble an entirely original presentation by having an actual photographic print of his work made from a negative (see Chapter 12) and framing it above the signature.

Not all memorabilia collectors are interested in framing and hanging, though. A collection can also be displayed in good-quality albums or portfolios. They're available at art supply stores in a wide variety of sizes, styles and price ranges. Group related pieces together in the same album or portfolio according to your collecting objectives. For instance, arrange material relating to a particular artist by date, small sketches by subject matter, gallery invitations by location, and letters or documents by topic.

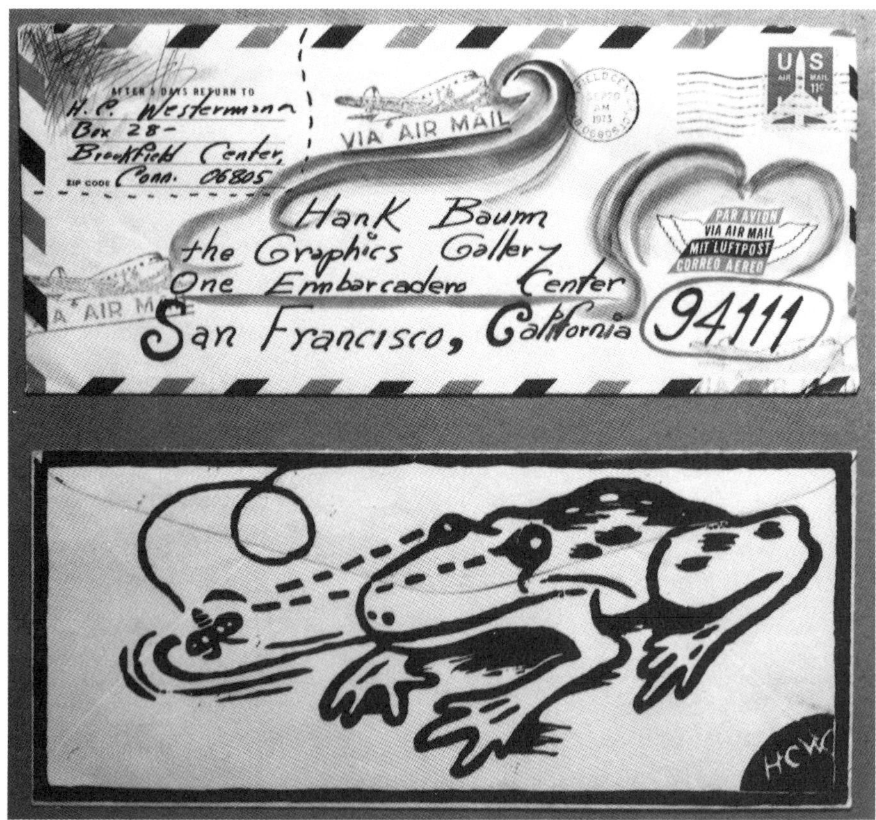

Envelope art by Horace Clifford Westermann, circa 1973. Top: Ink, watercolor and rubber stamp. Bottom: Block print initialed in the plate. Dimensions: 4¼ by 9½ inches.

Additional suggestions:

- Find yourself a good framer who's reasonably priced and can come up with creative solutions to suit your display needs.
- Small sketches, drawings, signed gallery invitations, or letters can be framed inside wide mats and be made to look larger and more dramatic.
- Frame several related items together under a single frame. For example, place half a dozen signatures with small drawings in a specially cut mat.
- Display related items together on the same wall. Six separately framed small pieces can be artistically arranged to fill a substantial amount of wall space.
- Whenever you buy a piece of art, remember to get as much in the way of memorabilia as possible. Not only does it contribute to the value and meaning of the art, but it also takes on a value and a collectibility of its own. With living artists, ask for written or printed statements explaining the art, signed exhibit catalogues that discuss the art, signed gallery invitations, and so on. For art by deceased artists, collect related gallery catalogues, invitations, books, or periodical articles.

Artful Collections

Art by nonartists. If you like sports, for example, collect signatures of athletes that are accompanied by small drawings or sketches. Write to athletes and ask for their signatures accompanied by small drawings or make those requests in person at sports collectibles events. Many personalities in a variety of fields will do this for you at little or no added charge.

Photographs of artists. You can either search for older photographs or collect images of contemporary artists. Personally photographing artists in their studios or at art-related events and having them sign or inscribe your photographs is a fun and inexpensive way to build a collection.

Collect firsts for artists. For example, collect invitations or catalogues from artists' first one-person shows, first mentions in books or exhibit catalogues, and so on.

Signatures of nineteenth-century American artists.

Items relating to the art scene in your city, region or state.

Signatures of artists accompanied by a quick drawing or inscription. Decide what you would like each artist to say or draw, make the same exact request to every artist you meet and see how they choose to fulfill it.

Throughout this book, periodic references have been made to the extra affordability of art by younger artists. Generally, the younger the artist, the more affordable the art. Great collecting opportunities exist in the world of art students, artists who are still in training and artists who have not yet formally showed or exhibited their work. You're about to learn how to effectively acquire their art.

17

Art by Students

Under normal circumstances, art by students is the most inexpensive of all original art. As in any walk of life, art students, apprentices, and trainees are at the very beginnings of their careers. The more time they spend as artists, the more they learn and the better they get. Their reputations grow, demand for their work becomes greater, and their prices rise accordingly. Before all that happens, however, affordability prevails.

Art-student art is lower in price than art by established artists for several significant reasons. One is the risk factor involved. All art students want to become artists, but they do not all realize that ambition. They stop producing, move on to other things and pretty much leave behind art that has minimal value or collectibility. In other words, buy student art because you like it and are supportive of their efforts to complete their educations and graduate—not because you think you're going to get in on the ground floor and retire on your discoveries of the Picassos and Monets of the future.

Two additional reasons for the affordability of this type of art is that students tend to have little or no overhead and little or no spending money. Most survive primarily on whatever parental or other outside support they can muster and live modestly. So not only can they afford to charge low prices, but they can really use every penny of outside income that they get. Although this puts them in a somewhat vulnerable position, if you want to do well in this collecting realm, don't take advantage.

Art students dearly want to sell their art. At such early stages in their careers, making sales means a huge amount to them, not only in terms of income, but also in terms of self-esteem, confidence and validating their accomplishments and chosen life paths. Remember that as a collector, you'll be giving them far more than just money.

Where to Find Student Art

The best places to find student art are, of course, art schools, college and university art departments, art institutes and sometimes museum-sponsored art programs. Virtually all such establishments provide regular opportunities for the general public to visit, view and purchase student art. Many have their own galleries, some have multiple galleries, most offer a variety of student shows annually, some conduct special major sales events or art fairs that are held several times per year. Depending on the establishment and the makeup of the student body, art-buying events may be all-school, senior class only, graduate students only, inter-department, solo or small group, juried or open invitation. The quantity of pieces available for purchase at any given show can range from several dozen to several thousand. The great majority of buying opportunities are held on-campus; a few take place at outside locations.

Unlike events in the established art world, those in the student art world are rarely publicized. Find out about the educational scene in your area or the area of your choice by checking the *American Art Directory* under the heading "Art Schools" or the appropriate *Yellow Pages* under the heading "Art Instruction & Schools." You'll need to make contact with each individual facility in order to learn what their arrangements are. Call, state your interests in seeing and possibly purchasing student art and, depending on the establishment, you'll be referred to student affairs offices, student galleries, gallery directors or exhibit coordinators.

During the course of every contact you make, ask for a copy of the institution's catalogue. These are normally sent out to prospective students and contain not only detailed information about admissions policies, departmental programs, courses of study and faculty members, but are also illustrated with numerous examples of student art. Catalogues are great resources and provide excellent overviews of the range, variety and quality of art produced at their respective institutions.

Also obtain information about what kinds of shows and events are held and when they take place. Sometimes you can receive exhibit schedules or an issue or two of student newspapers or bulletins, but usually, exhibit dates and related details are only dispensed verbally. If you live in the area, find out about campus visiting policies and make arrangements to visit and look around. Whether or not any shows are currently in progress, plenty of art is always on display in public areas as well as in classrooms.

Visiting serves another important purpose. When you like what you see as you walk around the halls, classrooms and common areas, you can advertise for it right then and there. Fill out the appropriate request forms at departments of student affairs or job placement offices and also post notices of your specific wants on campus bulletin boards and at other places frequented by students. Students will then contact you.

In addition to seeing the work of current students, you can also get in touch with recent graduates and older alumni. Just as employers can file job

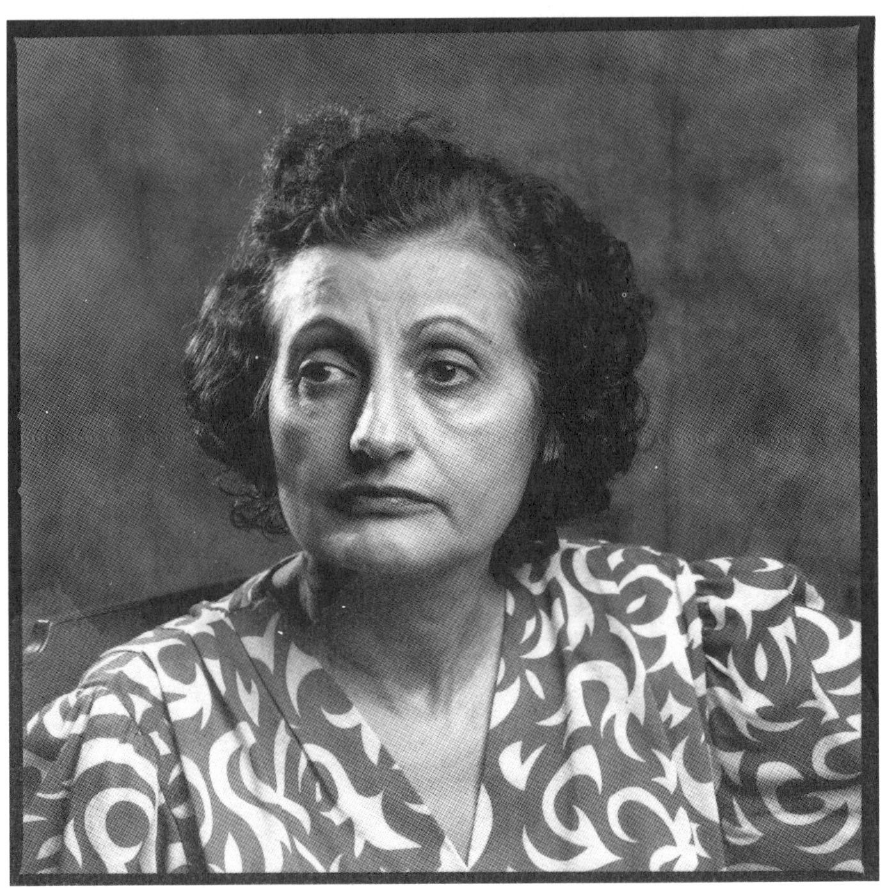

"Portrait of a Woman" by professional photographer Tullio Deorsola. Dimensions: 8 by 10 inches. Taken while he was a student at the Academy of Art College, San Francisco.

descriptions for available positions, you as a collector can list your collecting requirements (including your budget) with job placement offices or departments of student affairs.

Private art teachers and local art studios can also be good resources for locating art-student art. These are listed along with art schools in the Yellow Pages under "Art Instruction & Schools." As with other establishments, call first and ask how you can see and possibly purchase student work. These are often one-person operations and you'll most likely end up speaking with the artists or teachers in charge.

Depending on the classes and the settings, you'll be able to visit studios, sit in on classes, have coffee or snacks with the students, watch teachers teach or maybe even take a free lesson or two. Private classes are generally less formal, atmospheres are more relaxed and friendly, artists are more often adults (as opposed to college-aged), and your special requests or requirements may be more readily and comfortably dealt with. Private classes tend also to be better resources for more traditional styles of art than for abstract or avant-garde work.

How to Access Student Art

The range and variety of student-art is pretty much limitless. The student art world is a microcosm of the established art world in virtually all respects and can be especially interesting when more experimental or progressive work is involved. No matter what your personal tastes are, you'll be able to find what you're looking for.

Don't think that you have to confine your search to fine art only. Students train in all fields. These include painting, sculpture, drawing, printmaking, fashion design, commercial art, illustration, advertising layout, computer art, graphic design, architecture, interior design, crafts, jewelry, industrial design, furniture making, textiles, and photography. If you like architectural drawings, for example, contact colleges and university graduate and undergraduate architecture departments and schools.

When you want to collect particular types of student art that are not available in your area, locate the best resources for that art by visiting the art

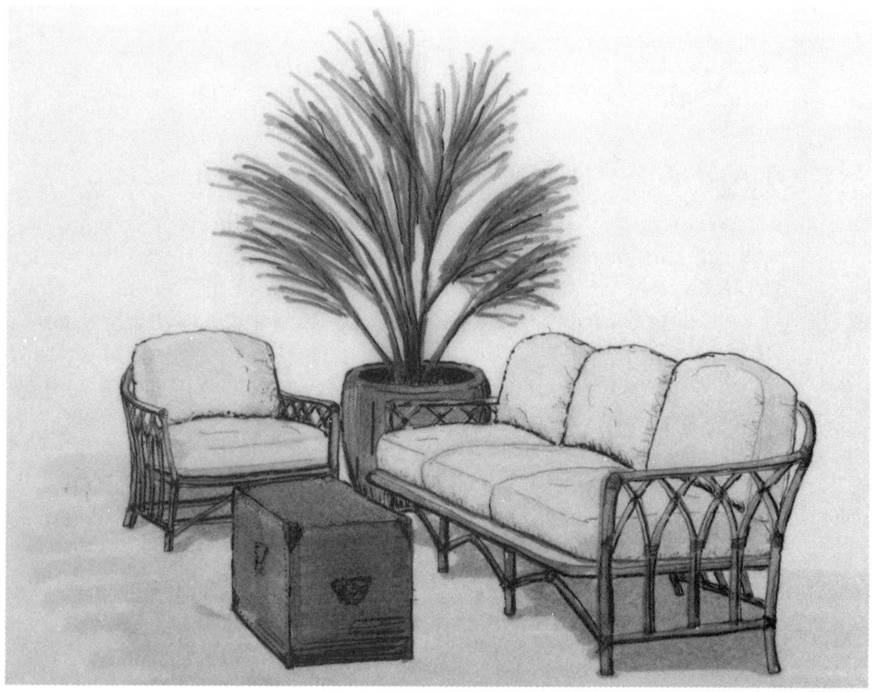

Furniture study by Audrey Tse, interior design student, Academy of Art College, San Francisco. Ink and marker on vellum, 8⁵⁄₈ by 11⁷⁄₈ inches.

department at the main branch of the local public library. They have reference books and catalogues, such as the *American Art Directory,* that list hundreds of art schools nationwide along with brief information about their specialized course offerings. You can then contact those schools that are appropriate to your needs and find out what your options are for seeing their art.

When you're unable to visit in person, ask people in student affairs or job placement offices to place notices of your collecting interests on campus bulletin boards, in job files and, if possible, take out small classified ads in student events calendars or newspapers. In addition, you can also contact specific professors or department heads, have them announce your wants to students and ask that interested individuals call or write to you. Students will be happy to send you photographs or slides of their work and, if you're really interested, the work itself.

Establishments with more sophisticated on-site gallery operations can also send your photographs or slides of student work according to your specifications. Gallery directors or exhibit coordinators can then put you directly in touch with the artists whose work you like the most. Depending on the circumstances, this may be easier than direct transactions with students.

Another way to shop for art is to use school catalogues to get in touch with students whose illustrated work you find attractive. Illustrations are almost always credited so all you have to do is give the names to departments of student affairs. Those students will then be notified and requested to get in touch with you.

Negotiating with and Buying from Students

For starters, be aware that art school galleries and sales events rarely charge commissions. This immediately reduces art prices by as much as 50% to 60% over what costs would be at for-profit galleries.

General procedure for buying student art is that when you see something you like in a studio, exhibit, catalogue, classroom or other display situation, mention it to the person in charge. For privacy reasons, they usually won't give out names and addresses of students. You'll be asked to leave your name, address, phone number and the descriptions of the art pieces you're interested in. This information is then passed on to the students and they make arrangements to see you.

Meeting with students before buying their art is a good idea—you get to know who you're patronizing and find out what their aspirations are: Have them show you the full spectrum of their art—they may have pieces that you like even better than those that attracted you initially. Discuss selling prices in general and get an idea of how and why various pieces are priced as they are before moving on to specifics.

Always treat art students with respect. Resist tendencies to make lowball

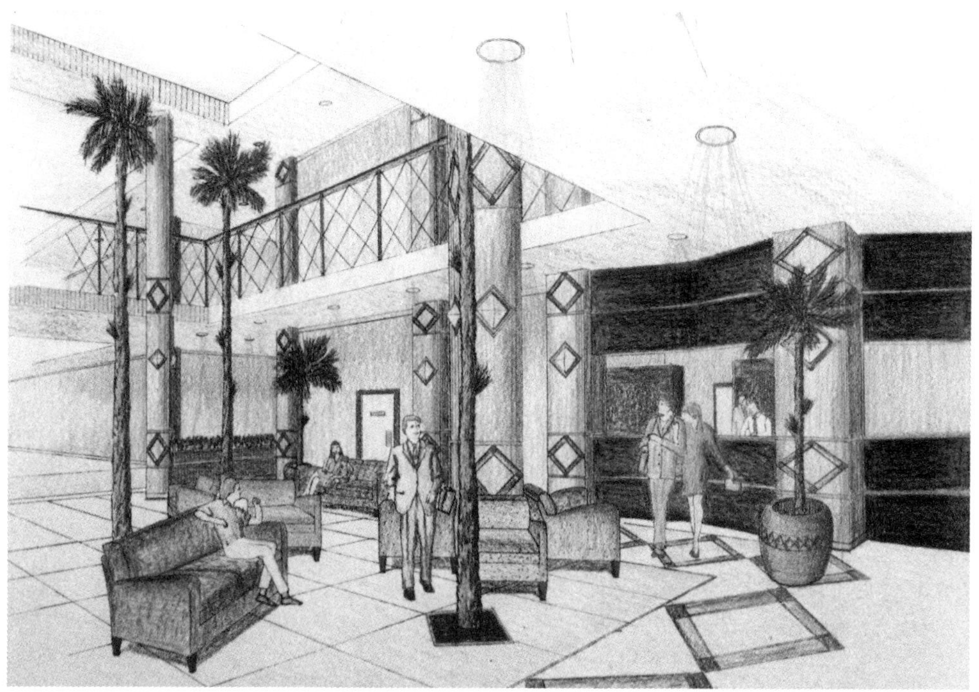

Interior scene by Audrey Tse, interior design student, Academy of Art College, San Francisco. Colored pencil on art paper, 9¾ by 11½ inches.

offers or denigrate their art as being only student work. Keep in mind that what you are looking at is probably the best work these individuals have produced to this point in their lives and that they're proud of it. In a sense, everything you say and do in negotiations with students is magnified in terms of emotional impact because their ideas and self-images are still in the process of being formed.

Regarding dollars and cents, the students set their own asking prices. Those can range anywhere from $10 to thousands of dollars for large scale sculptures or paintings that take a great deal of time, effort or materials to produce. Be aware that student-set prices are not always accurate. These artists are learning how to price and sell their work just as they are learning all of the aspects involved in creating it. Be patient and allow for the possibility that you may occasionally become involved in philosophical discussions about the relationship between art and money or the value of art. Students are often testing their beliefs, even though they may sound firm.

Whenever you have price questions, consult with faculty members. They usually have a pretty good handle on what should be selling for how much, as well as a familiarity with the students in question. As always, the best way to accurately assess price is to speak with experts and see as much art as you can.

One final note about negotiating with students: A significant number tend to overvalue their art primarily because they haven't had enough experience in the real world to understand how competitive and difficult the road to success can be. Youthful optimism and the ideas that sacrifices, compromises or open exchanges of thoughts are unnecessary or irrelevant may also be at play. If you find yourself up against this sort of a mind-set, the best procedure is to move on to the next artist. There is no shortage of quality art from students who are willing to work with you.

TIPS ON COLLECTING

Begin your collecting adventures by visiting a variety of educational facilities, shopping around and seeing what they have to offer. You won't necessarily be able to minimize your chances of buying art by students who will eventually drop out of the art world or maximize your chances of patronizing those individuals who will go on to become famous. The future of student art is more uncertain than just about other type of art and not even the experts can predict outcomes with any degree of accuracy. You can, however, learn how to get the best available art at the fairest possible prices.

Focus on the type of art that you want to collect and get a feel for what the going prices are. As in any other field, you'll find that prices vary widely from institution to institution and artist to artist. Find out which places have the best selections and which schools, departments or professors have the best reputations for producing quality work and quality graduates.

Learn how your type of art is assessed and evaluated. Faculty members and department heads are happy to give you an overview of what you need to know. Also speak with students. Find out about what they're doing, why they've done it, what directions they're headed in, what their art represents, and so on. One great advantage to collecting in the student realm is that everyone is far more relaxed about dispensing information than they are in the established art world.

It is beneficial to visit competitive or juried shows and exhibitions whenever possible. First of all, they separate out the best art for you. Secondly, you can find out who the judges are, meet with them and learn how they make their decisions. Competitive events are also the best places to get good solid collecting advice because they are the closest thing in the student art world to the established art world. Lastly, of course, these shows are the best places to buy quality art.

When you reach the point of considering specific pieces for purchase, check students' track records just as you would those of professional artists. Find out how faculty members view their work and how they're doing as students. Have the students themselves tell you what their accomplishments are both inside and outside of their learning environments. In circumstances where you like several pieces equally well and are having difficulty deciding which one to buy, comparing student accomplishments could become the determining factor.

By the way, not all art students are starting out fresh in the world of art. A fair number have already completed undergraduate courses of study or had outside gallery or sales experience, especially graduate students who have returned to acquire advanced degrees. Don't expect their art to be nearly as affordable as that of artists with little or no outside experience.

You can find good quality student art no matter how little you have to spend. Significant pieces are usually priced in the low to mid hundreds of dollars, but prices start as low as $10 to $20 and sometimes even less. If you're on a budget, focus on younger students and those with no outside gallery experience. Their paintings and drawings start at around $50 and can range into the low hundreds for larger pieces. Smaller works of art by more advanced students is another affordable option. Prints are especially good for price-conscious buyers, so don't forget to call or visit print departments and speak with faculty members to get details on buying opportunities.

Artful Collections

By student. Patronize students whose work you like by buying one piece per school year.

By teacher. Buy from students of one professor, one department, one class year, or one school. This is an especially good idea if you strongly support a particular philosophy or teaching style.

Award winners. Buy pieces that win awards at school competitions or were created by students who were given special honors.

Commissions. Request students to produce specific pieces for you such as portraits of you or your family, pictures of your house, or sculptures of your dog.

By school. Buy only from students who attend the best art schools.

If, at this point, you're still not satisfied with the range of affordable options that have been presented, don't give up. There's more—much more. Take a look around and you'll see that art is being produced just about everywhere you can think of. Art isn't scarce and expensive like the established art business would like you to believe. It's everywhere and anyone can own it! These next five affordable options will bear this out.

18

Five More Affordable Options

One of the cornerstones of affordable art collecting is to keep an eye out for what's being ignored, overlooked or is otherwise not in demand. The fact that no one currently collects it does not automatically mean that is has no redeeming value. It could just as easily mean that no art dealer or business person has yet been able to figure out how to make money selling it. Remember also that virtually all art, no matter how much it may be worth now, started out selling for very little. With that in mind, here are five more affordable options.

Commercial Signs and Posters

Many vintage signs and posters that were originally produced for commercial purposes have come to be recognized as works of art in and of themselves. This has been a small but active field of collecting for quite some time and is currently increasing in popularity because of its relative affordability as compared to one-of-a-kind art. Rare and important images by famous artists are already heavily in demand and expensive, but there's plenty of room left to get started at affordable prices.

The most reasonably priced pieces are usually grouped together according to subject matter. For example, posters relating to World War I, World War II and wars in general can be had for as little as $30 or $40 each.

Other areas of affordability are post-World War II travel posters and 1940s through 1970s B-movie advertisements in either poster or show-card sizes. Entertainment event advertisements in general are fun to collect with lots of opportunities, especially on the local or regional levels, and in the areas of theater productions, modern dance, ballet, music concerts, sporting events, and special occasions at restaurants or night clubs. Notices of protests or rallies, county fairs, appearances by political candidates or other celebrities, and openings and closings of department stores, movie houses

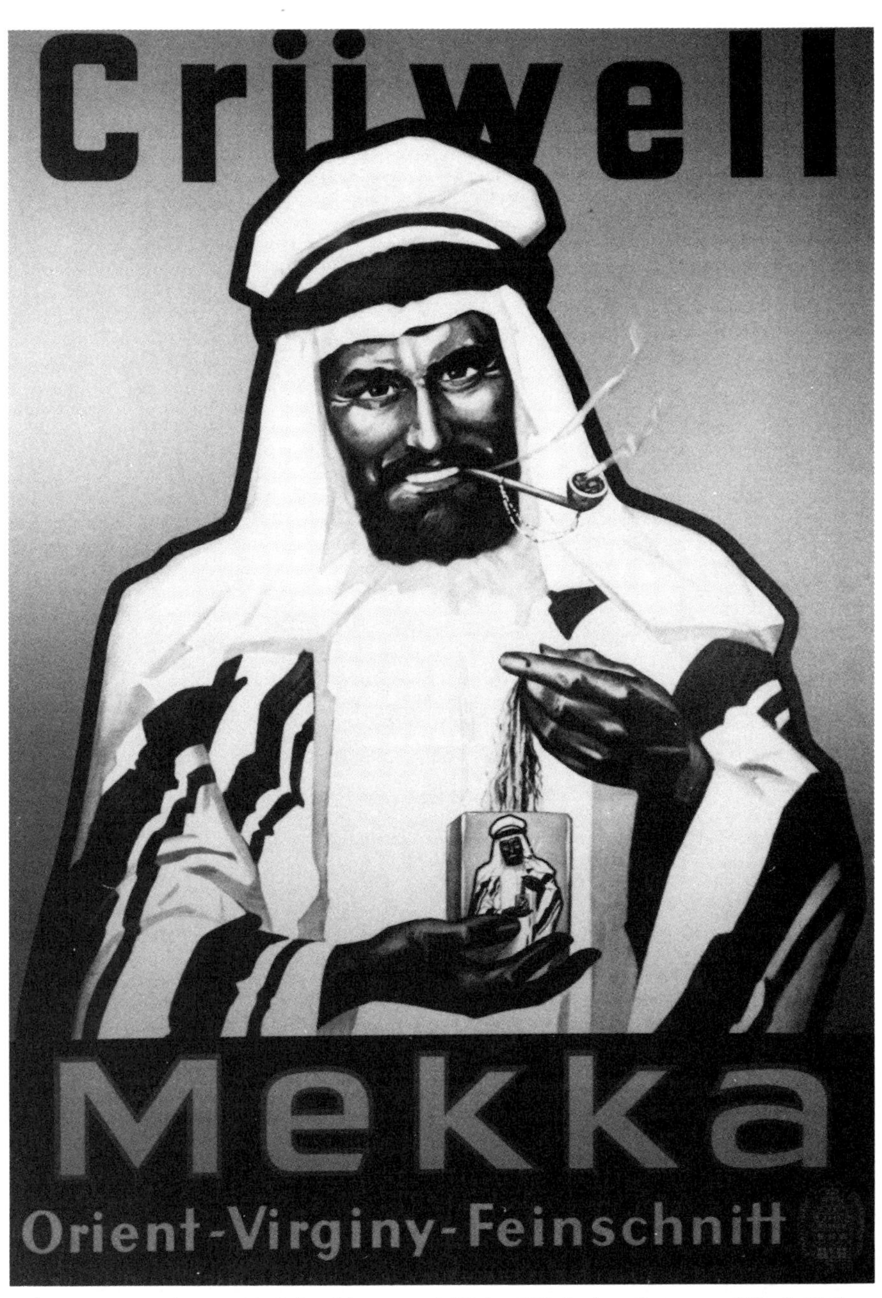

Tobacco poster, circa 1950. Color lithograph, 35⅝ by 23¼ inches. Courtesy of Harris Gallery, Berkeley, California.

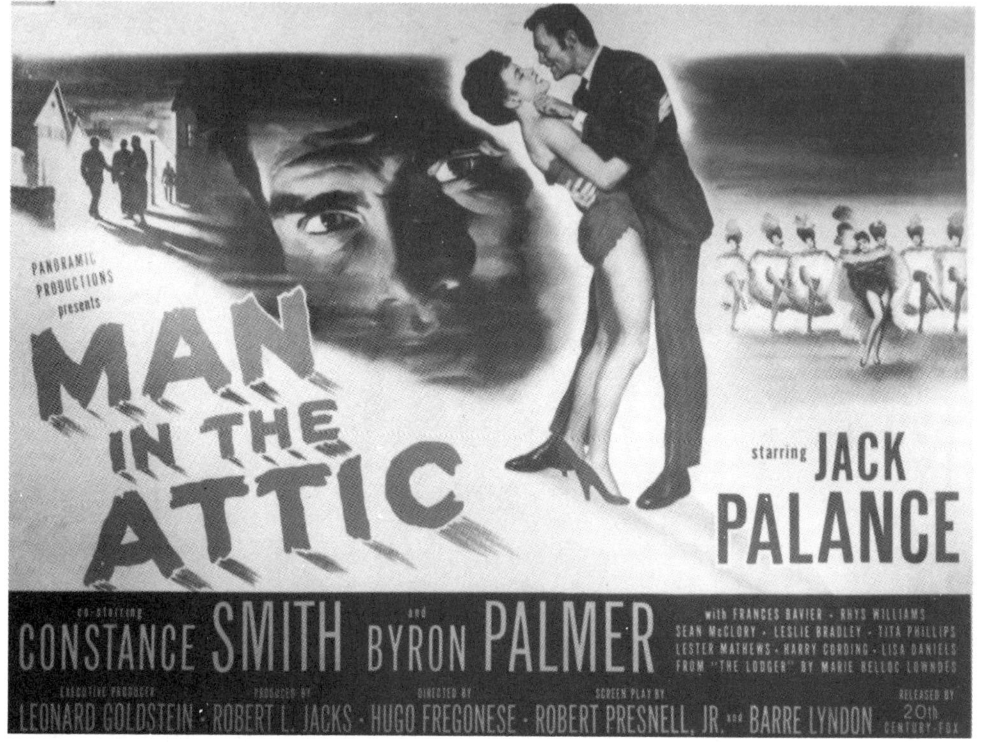

B-movie poster, 1953. Color lithograph, 22 by 28 inches. Courtesy of Harris Gallery, Berkeley, California.

and other local businesses or landmarks can also be visually appealing as well as historically significant.

Broadside collecting is another possibility. These posterlike announcements are composed almost entirely of words with little or no illustrations. Particularly good examples are those advertising demonstrations, strikes, boycotts or unusual or radical gatherings. Broadsides are often more historical than aesthetic and are a great way to document events of whatever time periods, groups, organizations or localities intrigue you.

If history or specialized subject matters don't excite you, think about collecting by artist, designer, printing company, advertising agency, poster style or geographical area. Perhaps you like the work of one particular artist or posters with a 1930s look or images created by artists who lived or are living in your state. The field is limited only by your imagination.

Good places to find posters are at antiques and collectibles shows, ephemera shows, used and rare bookstores, estate sales, local auctions, book fairs and antiques or secondhand shops. Commercial liquidations and going-

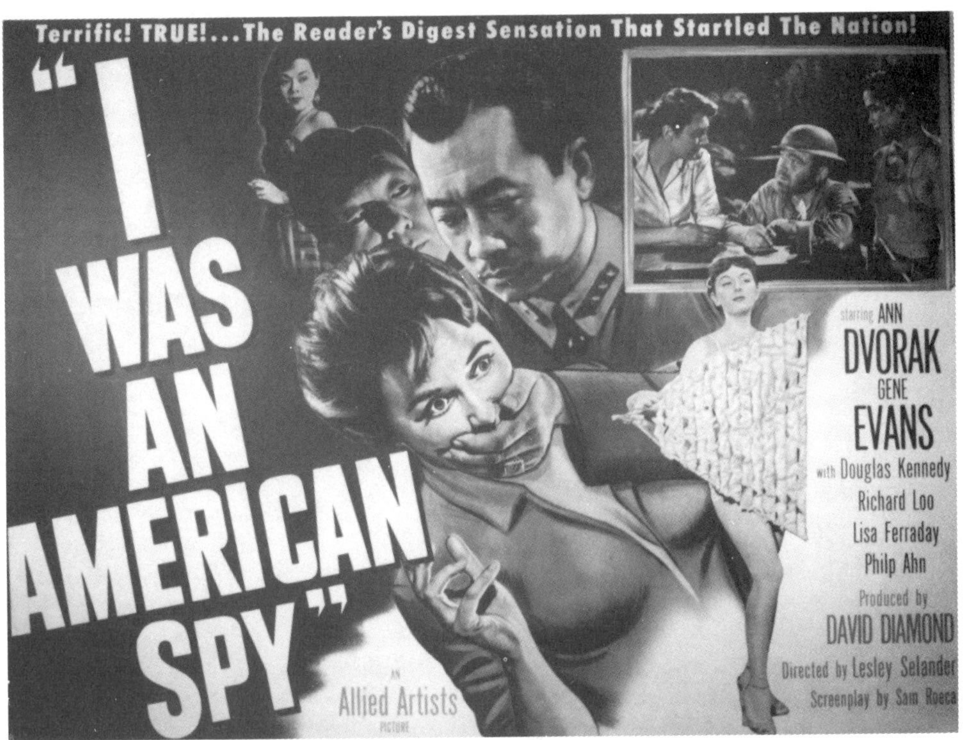

B-movie poster, 1951. Color lithograph, 22 by 28 inches. Courtesy of Harris Gallery, Berkeley, California.

out-of-business sales are also good resources, as are businesses that have been around for awhile and may have saved old signs and posters. Travel agencies, department stores, theaters, and advertising agencies are especially good sources.

When shopping for posters, keep an eye out for lithographic or serigraphic images as opposed to offset ones. These tend to be more collectible. Recent posters are usually offset, but the farther back you go, the more variety you'll find in printing techniques. See Chapters 5 and 15 or check the book *How to Identify Prints* by Bamber Gascoigne whenever you have questions about how particular posters were printed.

If you prefer modern offset examples, try to avoid images produced by poster publishers specifically to be mass-marketed as collectibles or decorations in and of themselves (these are the types of posters you see for sale at frame shops and poster galleries). Stick with pieces that are published for the commercial purposes of advertising and communicating information and are not initially intended to be used as wall hangings in private homes. You'll

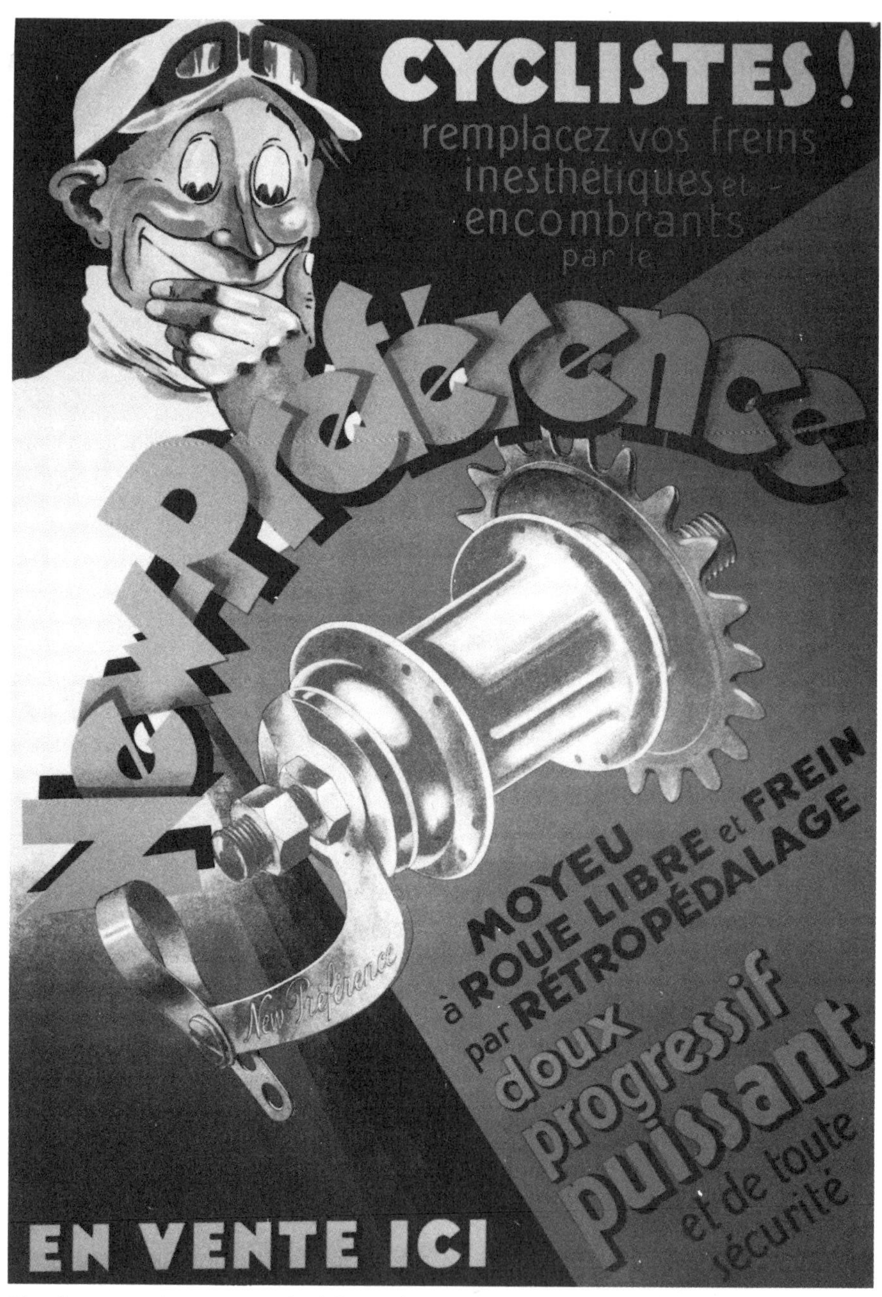

Bicycle poster, circa 1925. Color lithograph, $21^{1}/_{2}$ by $14^{1}/_{2}$ inches. Courtesy of Harris Gallery, Berkeley, California.

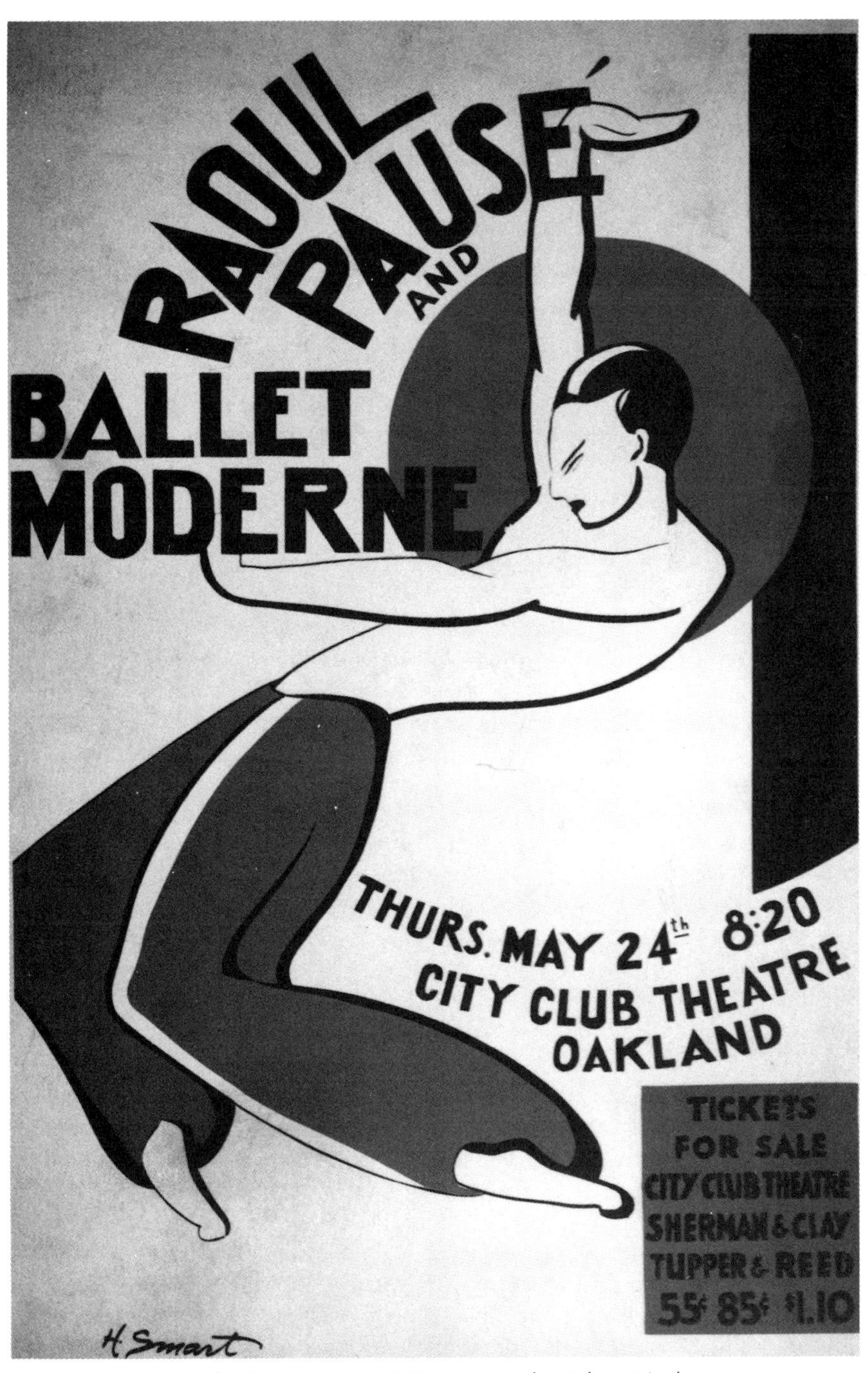

Modern dance poster by H. Smart, circa 1930s. Serigraph, 22 by 14 inches.

find them at places like travel agencies, movie theaters, grocery stores, video rental stores, new car dealerships, department or specialty stores, and other businesses that regularly use signs, posters or standing displays to advertise current offerings. Many of these places will save old pieces for you that they would otherwise throw away.

Contacting manufacturers, corporations or companies directly is another way to obtain good-quality examples of contemporary advertising art. Ask for either advertising or promotions departments, explain what you're collecting, and find out what they have available in the way of large-format posters or display items. Suppose, for example, that you're in a department store and see an advertisement for a brand of clothing that you're particularly fond of. If the department store is unwilling to part with the piece once it's served its purpose, call or write the clothing company, describe the item and ask whether they'll send you one. Policies on these sorts of requests vary from business to business so be prepared to pay for certain items (costs should be nominal) and don't be surprised if your requests are occasionally denied altogether.

Related to poster art is art by signmakers. People don't often think of signmakers as artists, but that's what they are. Find the names of individuals and companies in the Yellow Pages under the heading "Signs." See whether they've kept older inventory around or, in the case of individuals, ask whether they'll sketch or make small inexpensive pieces that are suitable for framing. For older signs, check commercial businesses that have been around for awhile to see whether they've saved anything. Also keep an eye out at flea markets, liquidation sales, antiques shops or shows, and secondhand stores.

Regarding condition of less expensive posters or signs, look for images in perfect or near-perfect condition. So much material is available in the lower price ranges that you can afford to wait. Most collectors will agree that a minor image in excellent condition is preferable to a somewhat more-desirable one in poor condition.

Computer Art

Computer art is truly in its infancy. In the 1960s, several books were published on the subject, but they dealt primarily with geometric patterns generated by computer programs and had little in the way of widespread appeal. Today, just about any type of art can be produced, reproduced or manipulated by computers, and the art form is rapidly becoming an increasingly significant part of our daily lives.

For the first time, art and technology have blended together to yield results that everyone can see and appreciate. An entire generation has been raised in a world where computers are relied upon for just about everything. Computer-generated art is a natural consequence of this, and advances in the field are being made on a daily basis.

Much of today's computer art is photography based and commercial in nature. Images, usually photographs, are scanned into computers and then manipulated into unique original works of art by a process called digital retouching. The results can take the form of graphics or images, video art, animation art, and totally new concepts like virtual reality where participants are literally surrounded by imaginary environments. Affordable art collectors should focus on ways of seeing and buying graphics and images that can be printed out (or outputed), framed and displayed.

Talented computer artists are continually creating images that will one day be shown in specialized galleries of computer art. At the present time, however, a working and easily accessible marketplace for computer art has not yet developed. Locating computer artists or seeing shows of their art is not nearly as straightforward as locating and seeing other types of art. Best procedure is to seek out computer artists by tapping into the computer world in general.

Familiarizing yourself with computer magazines and newspapers on national, regional and local levels is one way to go. Individuals and businesses everywhere search constantly for new and talented artists and interesting images, so most computer publications encourage submissions, illustrate work, and contain regular features on art and artists. In particular, a

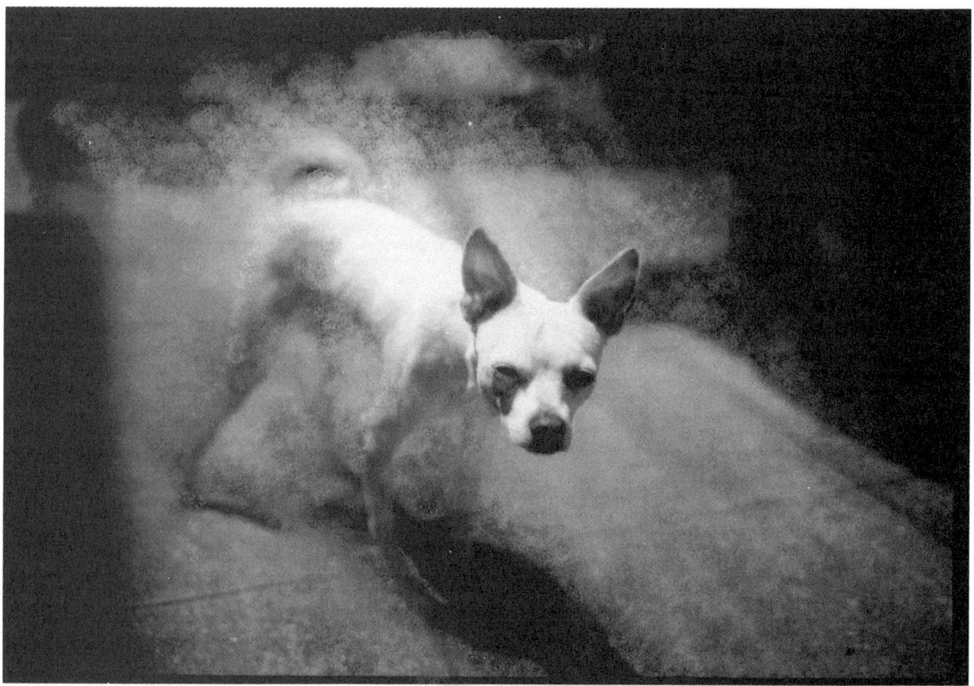

"Little Dog #1" by computer artist Andrew J. Hathaway. Digitally manipulated photograph, 6¾ by 9½ inches.

magazine called *Verbum* is entirely dedicated to computer art (for subscription information, write Verbum, P.O. Box 12564, San Diego, CA 92112; or call 619-944-9977).

Don't stop there, though. Check as many computer magazines as possible and either contact them for addresses of artists when you see examples of images that you like or take out classified ads explaining what you're looking for and request that artists contact you. You might also check ads placed by firms that produce computer-generated image equipment or firms that do imaging and write them with your requests. In addition, high-tech trade shows that are either partially or entirely dedicated to showcasing new computer developments are regularly advertised and you can often obtain lists of the exhibitors or catalogues of the shows (or even attend them when they're in your area).

Another good way to locate artists, especially local ones, is to check your Yellow Pages under the headings "Computer Graphics," "Graphic Designers," "Photo Retouchers" and "Photographic Color Prints" and note advertisers who use words like digital imaging, digital retouching, computer imaging, computer graphics and digital illustration. Call these places, state your interests and find out how you can either see art or meet artists. Whenever possible, ask whether you can come in and look through com-

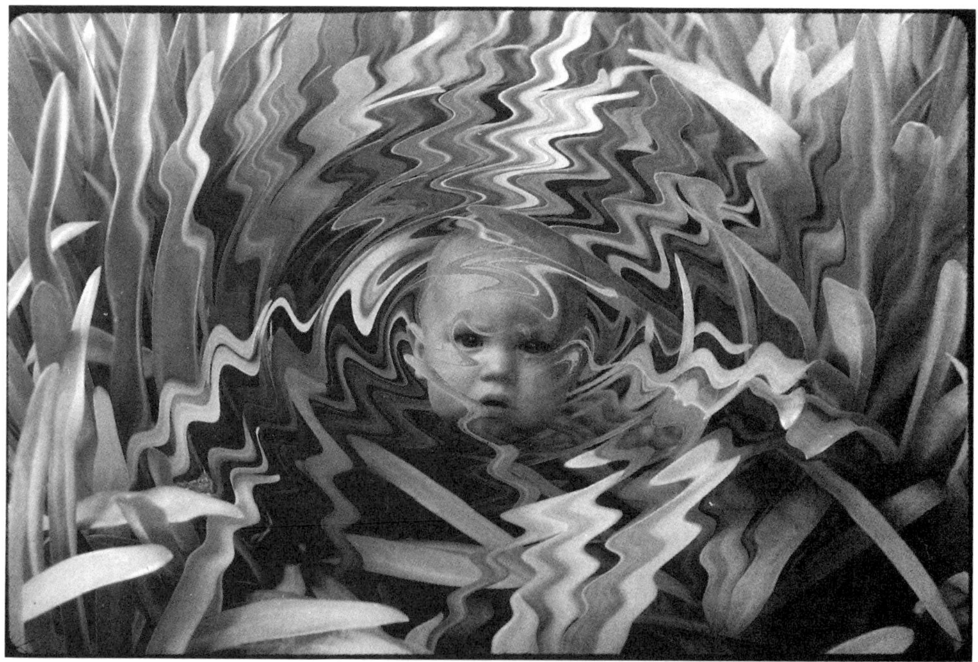

"Psychograph" by computer artist Andrew J. Hathaway. Digitally manipulated photograph, 5¾ by 8½ inches.

mercial artist and photographer sourcebooks, directories and annuals to get an idea of who's producing what types of work.

And don't forget art schools and universities with computer sciences, commercial graphics or computer graphics departments. In a field so young, plenty of fascinating work is being done by students in academic settings. Use the procedure outlined in Chapter 17 to locate art and artists in these sorts of circumstances.

A minor drawback to collecting computer art is that much of the newest and most advanced imaging and generating equipment is extremely expensive which increases the costs of the art. This means that you may have to shop around a bit before you find artists who produce their art through less costly processes or offer a variety of cost options in terms of outputting techniques. Prices of advanced equipment will eventually come down, though, as they do in all high-technology areas, so if you wait a few years, prices of computer-generated art will likely decrease accordingly.

Another argument against paying high prices now is that much computer art is printed in vegetable-based inks. These may have a tendency to fade over time. The early examples will always have historical significance, but if they deteriorate visually, values will be adversely affected. One possible way to get around this problem is to have images outputted as photographs rather than prints (always check with artists to see what your options are).

Plenty of computer art remains affordable in spite of cutting-edge developments, however. Under a variety of circumstances, costs of outputting works of art into visual formats have remained nominal and prices for quality pieces range from $10 to the low hundreds. As always, shop around and get an overview of the artists and the marketplace before you begin buying.

Every time you buy a work of art, have the artist sign, date and title it. Whenever possible, get additional information like written or printed explanations of what the art is about and how it was produced or created. Since computer art can be outputted from data bases over and over again with precisely the same results, you need enough accompanying documentation to make your pieces unique and separate from all others. The more information you get, especially of the handwritten variety, the better. To conclusively date your art, have each piece notarized.

The Art of the Framer

People tend to focus on art and ignore frames and framers. Frames are frequently viewed as little more than the devices necessary to hold pictures up on walls, but far more often than not, a well-chosen frame can have an immensely positive impact on the way a picture looks. For affordable art collectors, this means that good frame choices can greatly enhance the appearance of minor or less significant works of art.

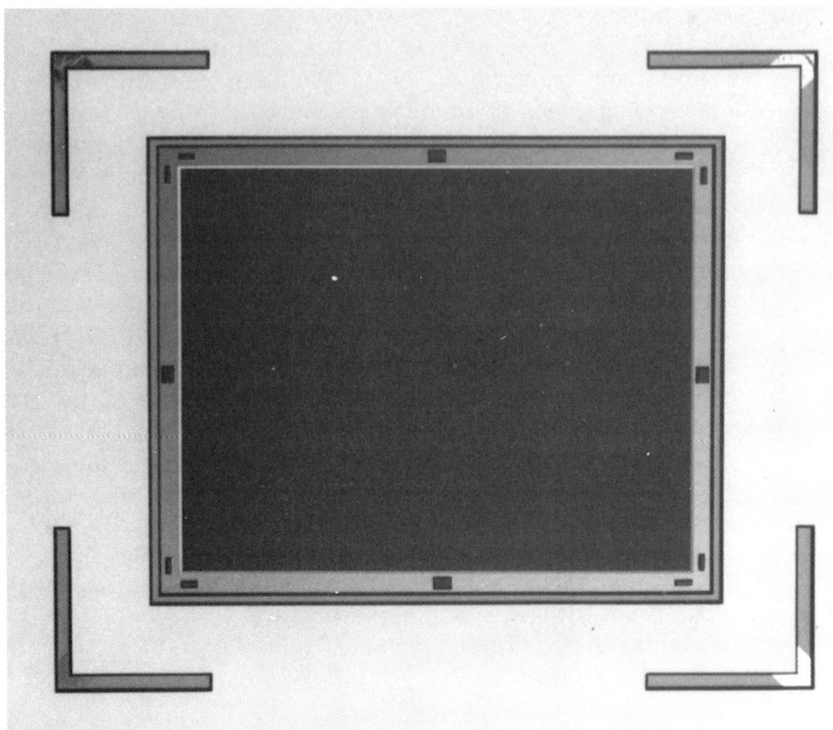

Custom-made decorative mat with a layered design by Ed Martinez of Piedmont Lane Gallery, Oakland, California. Dimensions: 14 by 16¼ inches.

Framers and framemakers are in business to make art look as beautiful and important as possible. To get an idea of the range of their talents, visit frame shops and art galleries not to look at art, but only to study how it is framed. Pay special attention to ways that galleries and framers make minor works of art look important.

When works of art are small, for example, galleries sometimes cut exceptionally wide mats for them. A 3-by-5-inch original can be transformed into a 12-by-16-inch presentation by cutting a 4-inch wide mat for it and surrounding it with a 1-inch-wide frame. Rich, elegant looking frames, such as those with real or imitation antiqued, polished, gilded or lacquered wood finishes, also enhance pictures.

Once you've seen what good framers can do and begin to define your style preferences, take a piece or two of your art to different frame shops and get some framing suggestions. Speak with framers, state your budget, point out what types of frames you find appealing and let them do the rest, including proposing framing options that you might not have thought of. Hold off on picking a framer until you've comparison shopped. As always,

Custom-made decorative mat with a freeform floral design by Ed Martinez of Piedmont Lane Gallery, Oakland, California. Dimensions: 18 by 14 inches.

quality of materials, workmanship and prices can vary substantially from framer to framer.

You can sometimes save additional dollars by purchasing odd-lot, slightly irregular and leftover moldings or frames that are almost out of stock or were ordered by clients but never picked up. Ask specifically whether any of these items are available. Another way to save is by combining elaborately cut mats with simple, inexpensive moldings—mats cost significantly less than moldings. For example, placing a simple black wood frame around a double or triple mat with a fancily cut interior border can produce a visual effect comparable to that of a plain mat surrounded by an expensive gold leaf frame.

You can also minimize costs by buying art that fits standard-sized frames and mats or having it matted to fit standard-sized frames. Pieces that measure (in inches) 3 × 5, 4 × 6, 5 × 7, 8 × 10, 10 × 12, 12 × 16, 14 × 18, 16 × 20, 20 × 24, or 24 × 30 are much easier to measure and frame than odd-sized pieces. In addition, many frame shops and frame outlets stock very reasonably priced pre-assembled frames and mats that are cut to these standard sizes, some of which look far better than their prices would indicate.

Those of you on really tight budgets should think about looking for used or older frames. These can be purchased for very little money and sometimes acquired for no money at all. For instance, almost all framers who reframe older pictures on a regular basis have no use for the old frames. Ordinarily they throw them out, but are often willing hold them for you if they know you are interested. Secondhand, thrift and charity stores are also great resources. They usually have decent selections of low-cost frames. Incidentally, collecting standard-sized art greatly increases your chances of finding older frames that fit without alterations. Or work the other way around—find the frame first and then look for the art.

If you go the used-frame route and do a little studying ahead of time, you could eventually profit. Find out what frame styles were most in demand

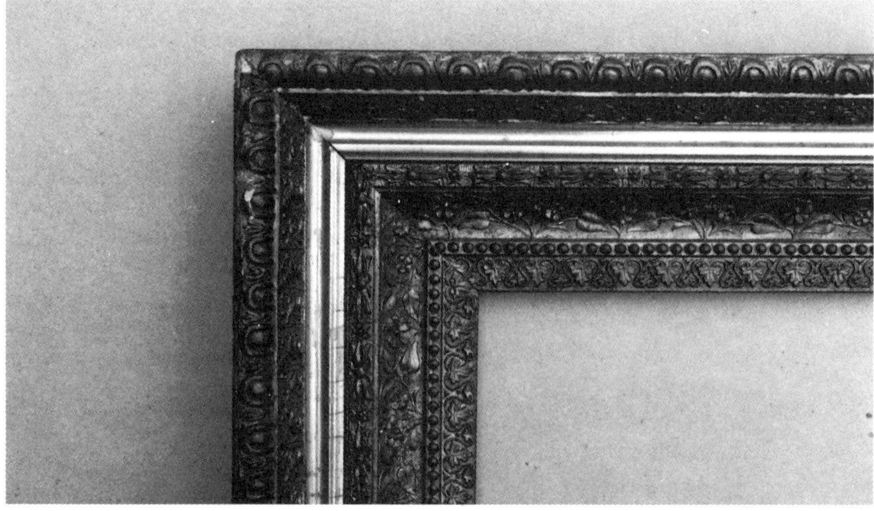

Victorian frames, circa mid to late 1800s can still be bought for reasonable prices at auctions, antiques shops and flea markets. Width: 5 inches.

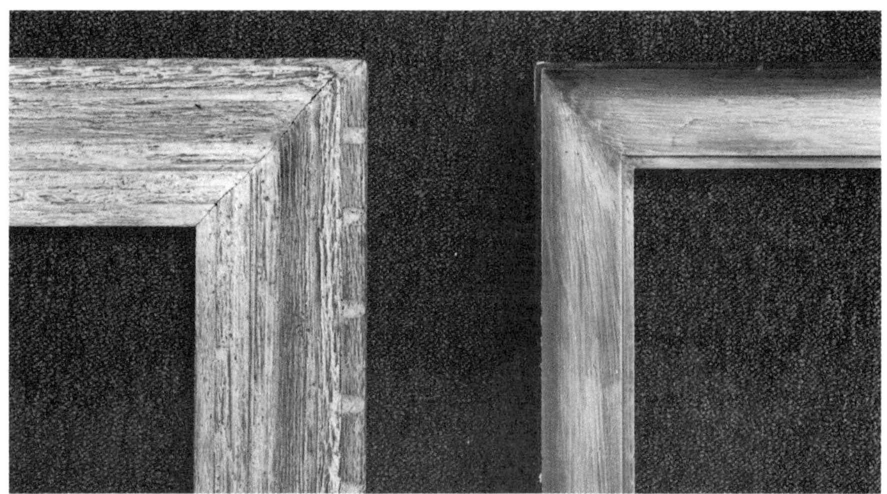

Once fashionable but currently out-of-style frames, circa 1940s, that can be purchased for very little money at flea markets, secondhand stores, thift shops, yard sales and so on. Molding at left is 4 inches wide, molding at right is 2⅜ inches wide.

during the past forty years or so and learn how to recognize quality moldings as well as expert workmanship. All popular frame styles eventually come back, and when they do, the better examples tend to increase in value. Currently, good-quality antique frames are at a premium and heavily in demand by collectors and framers who want period originals to go with their old art pieces that either needed reframing or have no frames at all.

Or forget about art—collect only frames and mats. Framers and framemakers are artists in their own right. Add to that the many artists who make their own frames and you've got a wide variety of choices. Hang your frames with nothing in them, with mirrored glass, blank paper, inexpensive prints or illustrations cut out of newspapers or magazines.

Think about commissioning framers or artists to make special frames for you. If you can't afford large elaborate pieces, have them create small ones that don't use much molding. Also keep an eye out for unique, unusual or special older frames if you enjoy frequenting secondhand stores or going after frame shop throwaways.

Two additional tips: Make sure that any framers you choose are able to cut and join frames cleanly. Avoid thin, inexpensive-looking metal or wood frames, especially low-end pre-cut versions. Problems in either of these areas can usually detract from the art.

Art by Children

How many times have you overheard someone remark "My seven year old could have done that" when referring to a particular piece of art? As offensive as such statements may sound, to the more elitist art world inhabitants, many have probably had to confess, at one time or another and in hushed tones, of course, that what they were looking at could well have been done by a seven year old. Nevertheless some seven year olds are pretty good artists—and six year olds and twelve year olds and children of all ages.

Talented young artists are everywhere and they create oceans of quality work. A substantial number of books have been published on the subject of children's art; experts and authorities study and analyze it all the time. Interscholastic art competitions for all grade levels are held on local, regional, national and international levels. Major corporations like Pentel and Chesebrough-Pond's Q-Tips have sponsored exhibitions of art by children. Yet with all this attention, collectors of children's art are virtually nonexistent. Supply is huge and demand is low, which means that you can get an awful lot for your money.

Begin your search for art by children by contacting the art departments at public or private schools in your area. When you speak with teachers, have them tell you about their classes, but also ask for information about independently run outside art programs and about any student contests, competitions or exhibits that are held in your area. Contact local or regional arts commissions, art museums, art institutes and community centers too. Many either sponsor or are aware of children's art programs.

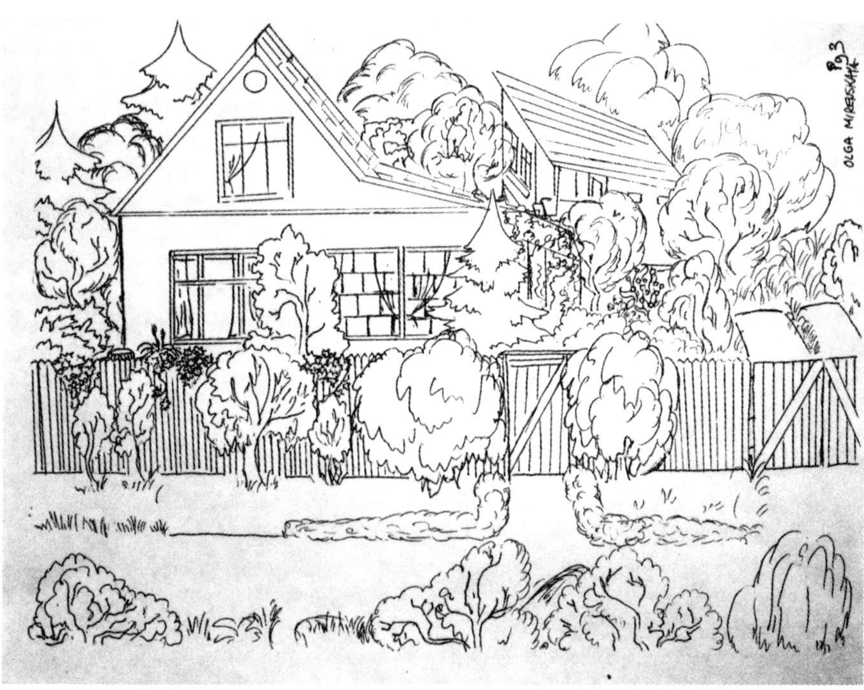

Outdoor scene by Olga Mirenskaya, 13, student of Kendra Langer at Presidio Middle School, San Francisco. Pen and ink, 8½ by 11 inches.

Inform whoever you speak with about what you're looking for and ask how you can see and possibly buy the art. Be prepared for a variety of responses—requests of this sort are highly unusual. You'll probably have to convince more than a few teachers or program directors that you're serious about collecting and then feel your way around and work out the details on a school-by-school or program-by-program basis.

Whenever you can, make appointments to visit art programs while classes are in session. This gives you a chance to see the young artists at work, see the variety of their work and find out from them as well as from their teachers about what they do and why they do it. As usual, don't buy anything until you've seen plenty of classes, plenty of art and can really zero in on your preferences.

Spotting better-quality pieces is just as possible with children's art as it is with any other type of art. By attending shows, competitions and contests, for instance, you can see top-notch, award-winning art, speak with judges and learn what to look for. Many teachers are also willing to tell you who their best students are and explain why certain pieces of art are considered superior to others. Here are several additional tips:

- Students who take regular classes with full-time teachers generally produce the best art.
- The greater an effort a teacher makes to involve children in art-related activities outside of the school as well as in it, the better.
- The more a teacher enters student work in outside competitions and exhibits, the better.
- The more awards that students have won, the better.
- The more interested a student is in becoming an artist, the better.
- The more time and energy a student puts into a work of art, the better.
- By the middle school grades (sixth through eighth), students begin to come into their own as artists and produce some surprisingly fine work. Great art is created at all grade levels, though, so don't restrict your searchers.

When you see art you like, point it out to teachers or program directors and speak with them as well as with the artists. Find out from everyone involved how motivated the artists are, what the stories are behind their art, what points they're trying to get across, how much time they've spent on the art, and so on. Also ask to see other works by these artists—you may see pieces you like even more.

If you have a specific collecting interest and teachers are amenable to working with you, have them present it to their classes as an assignment and you, in turn, offer prizes for the top two or three pieces that are produced. Teachers will help you evaluate the results in much the same ways that they do when the students create art for corporate or publicly sponsored art exhibits.

Regarding buying a work of art, begin by asking the student whether he is interested in selling it and, if so, how much he is interested in selling it for.

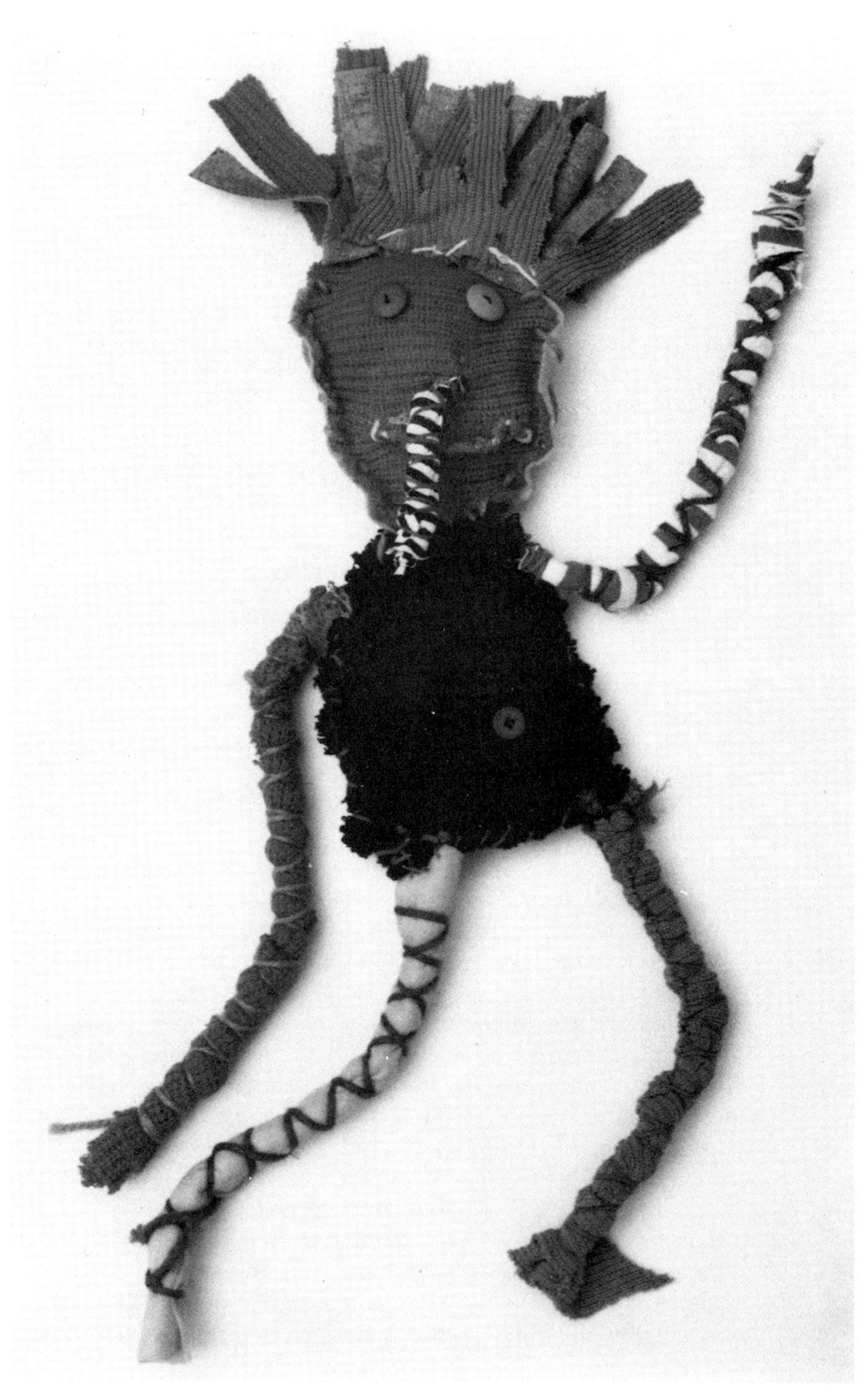

Rag doll by Kelli Williams, 11, student of Karen Klimak at the San Francisco School. Fabric remnants and discards, height, 30 inches.

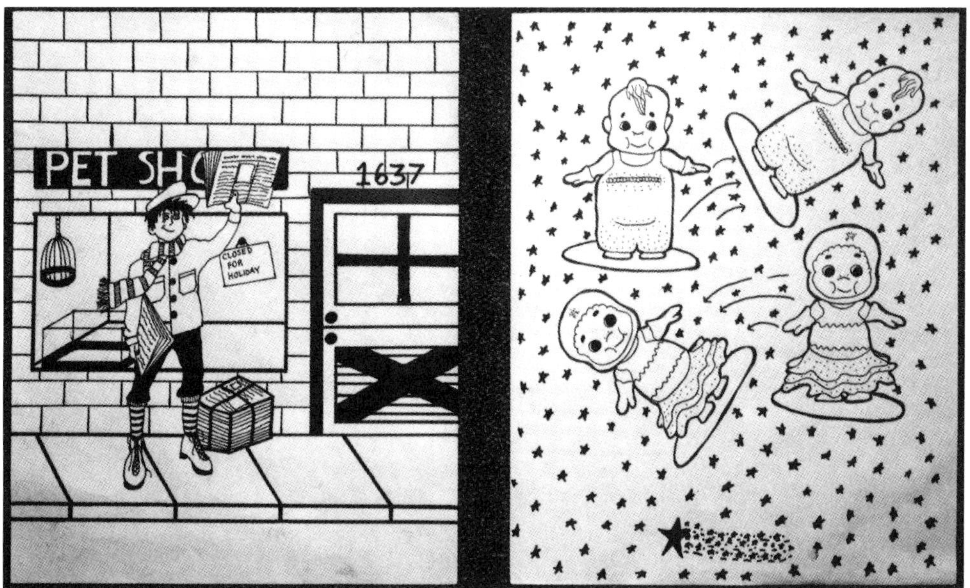

Illustrations created expressly for this book as a classroom assignment by, left to right, Nina Serrano, 14, and Irene Hung, 13, students of Kendra Langer at Presidio Middle School, San Francisco. Pen and inks, 8½ by 11 inches.

When you reach an instant agreement, go ahead and complete your transaction. Occasionally, an asking price will be unrealistic, however, and you'll either have to help the student figure out a reasonable price or work along with the teacher to settle on a sensible amount. Always take into consideration how much time and effort is invested in the art as well as the artist's attachment to it. In actual dollars and cents and unless you're negotiating with top-quality high school artists, anywhere from $1 to $25 are generally acceptable prices to pay, with $50 or so being the absolute upper limit for the best and most labor-intensive pieces.

One final point—parental permission is often necessary before you can buy a student's art. How you go about getting it depends on the teacher and the school system or program, so don't be surprised when you're asked to make formal requests. In the great majority of cases, parents are proud and honored when their children are asked to sell their art.

Art by Senior Citizens

Other than Grandma Moses and a small handful of contemporaries, collectors almost totally ignore art by individuals who begin producing late in life. Prevailing beliefs are that seniors with little or no art experience can't possibly have innate talents, they won't live long enough to produce very much, or they're too old to learn. The truth is that thousands of seniors take up art as a regular hobby or pastime after they retire and quite a number of them turn out to be talented as well as productive.

The great majority of seniors who take up art are highly motivated to do well. They seek out art programs, both public and private, and take their educations seriously. The phenomenon is much more than one of people with too much time on their hands doing something just to keep busy. Seniors are dedicated, they pay close attention to what they are taught and they take the time to practice and improve.

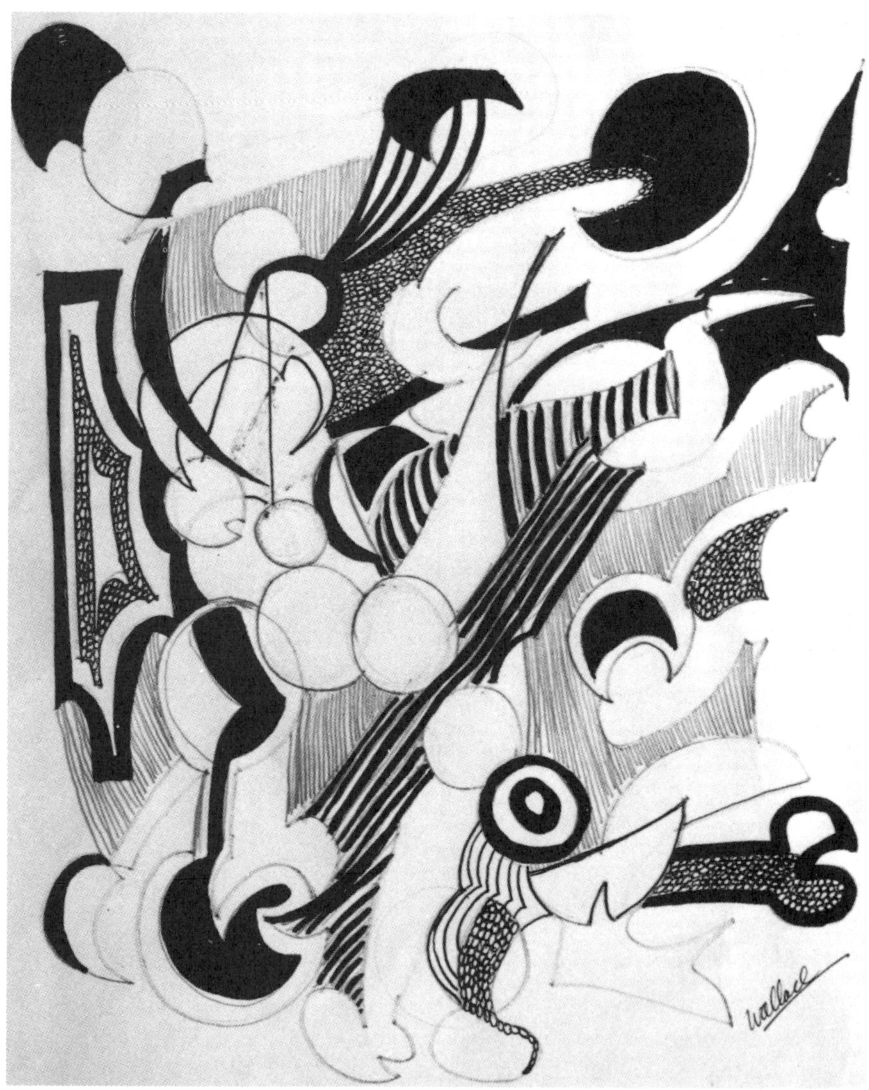

Abstract drawing by William Wallace, senior artist. Pen and ink, 16¾ by 14 inches. Courtesy of Sixth Avenue Senior Center, San Francisco.

The best way to see and buy senior art is to locate senior art programs. Start by checking the Yellow Pages under the heading "Senior Citizens' Services and Organizations." Note the numbers of day programs, residential care homes, senior centers and general information services. Places that cater to active seniors, like organized retirement communities, community centers that have programs for seniors, and some religious institutions, are also good resources. Local and regional arts commissions can often be helpful too, so give them a call.

Not every place you contact will have an art program. When one doesn't, find out whether any seniors independently produce art on a regular basis and, if so, whether you can be put in touch with them. Also ask whether they are aware of any other programs. You'll probably have to call around a bit, but you'll be able to gather plenty of numbers without too much effort.

When you contact places with programs, ask to speak with the program directors or persons in charge. Describe what you collect, find out whether they sell it (just about all do), and make appointments to visit the facilities. A few programs display their art in gallery or sales-type settings, but not that many do, so whenever possible, visit when classes are in progress. This way, you can see the art, watch the artists at work and speak with them as well as with the teachers.

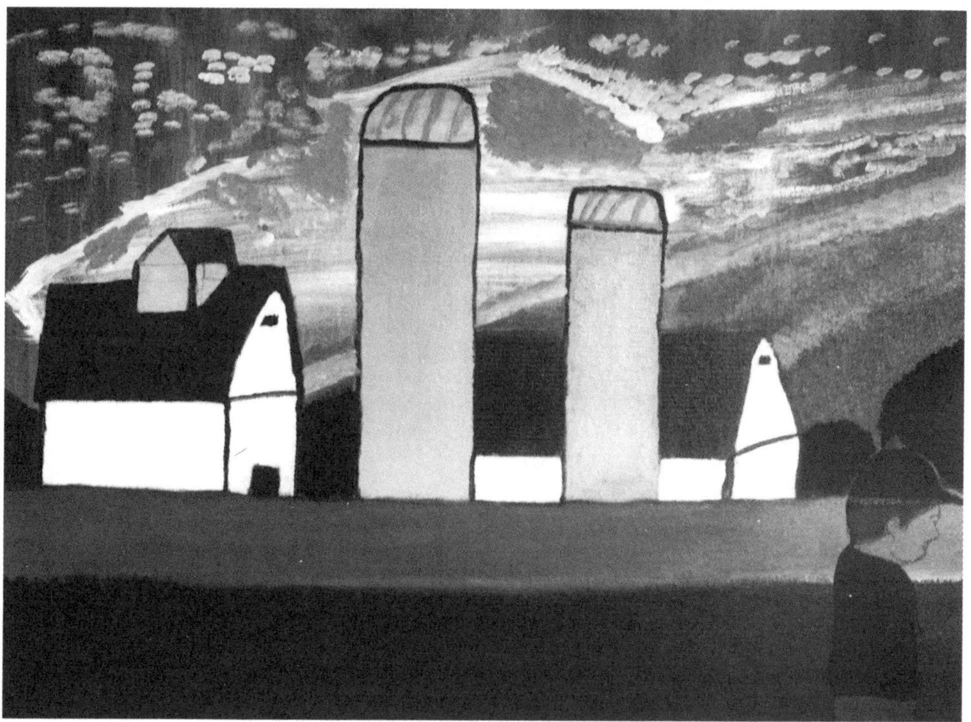

Farm scene by John Acree, senior artist. Oil on canvas, 18 by 24 inches. Courtesy of Sixth Avenue Senior Center, San Francisco.

Some programs are more sophisticated than others, so pay extra attention to those that are staffed by professional artists, skilled art teachers and visiting artists who teach on grants. Interview artists and program directors about the successes of their programs just as you would interview any other artists about their past accomplishments. Find out whether the artists exhibit regularly, whether they've won any awards, whether their programs have received special recognition, who the most respected artists are, and so on.

When you meet an artist or visit a program that has art you like, see the full spectrum of what they have to offer. Artists tend to have accumulations of work so ask whether you can sit down with them and look through it—artists enjoy nothing more than showing their work. When artists are not available, request that teachers or directors show you the art. More extensive art programs have hundreds of pieces for sale at any given moment.

Shop around and see plenty of art at a variety of locations before you buy. Art by seniors is among the most affordable art available no matter where you look, but reasonable prices should not be your only consideration. Trends and talents emerge from the senior art world just as they do from anywhere else and, with experience, you can learn how to recognize them.

Artful Collections

By age or grade. Collect children's art or art from the elderly by age or grade. For example, collect art by eight year olds or eighty year olds exclusively.

Alphabets. Have a variety of signmakers draw or paint single letters for you. Each signmaker can make you a different letter, all can make you the same letter in different sizes and colors, or all can print your initials.

Complex movie displays from video rental stores. These cannot be considered original works of art by artists because they are photo-reproduced, but rather works of art by printing companies and design firms. They're definitely collectibles of the future.

Signs advertising particular types of products or sales events. For instance, collect food and beverage advertisements from restaurants and grocery stores.

Unusual frames. Perhaps they are hand carved, hand painted, multicolored, asymmetrical, or oddly shaped.

New senior students. Buy art by seniors who never studied art when they were young, have been at it for less than a year, but show special talent.

Create your own contest. Have school art teachers ask students to show through art how they would make the world a better place, help preserve our environment, or solve a problem of your choice. Your cause or concern can become the students' cause or concern as they confront the issue and present possible solutions with their art.

If you're still not taken with any of these dozens of affordable art collecting options or perhaps you have your own ideas that have not been covered, this final chapter is for you. It's equally important for those of you who know exactly what you want. You'll find out how to collect and how do it right. The chapter also summarizes and reviews statements and techniques that have been mentioned repeatedly throughout this book, but only within specific collecting contexts. No matter what you're after, general procedures for building a quality collection are always the same.

19 Building Your Collection

Everybody collects something and that includes you. Perhaps you clip coupons, keep a jar full of pennies, save rubber bands, hold on to your children's report cards, have shelves full of old paint cans in the basement or save ticket stubs from concerts. Whether or not you're aware of it, anytime you accumulate a group of items that share a common bond, what you own is a collection and what you are is a collector.

Your collection, whatever it happens to be, may be great, good, average or awful. Unfortunately, most collections fall into the average-to-awful category for one simple reason—the people who assemble them are not conscious that what they are doing is collecting. They acquire randomly, haphazardly, arbitrarily and with little purpose other than that they find the individual pieces in some way attractive at the moments that they are acquired. Anyone who goes this route ends up with more of a jumble than a collection.

With respect to affordable art, this means that if you intend to buy any more than one or two pieces, you should approach what you are doing as a collector and follow certain principles in order to maximize your success. Admitting to yourself that you are a collector is the first and most important step in either transforming a mediocre collection into a great one or creating a great collection from scratch. Understand at the outset that this in no way involves compromising your tastes; you still buy only what you like, but now you do it with forethought and purpose.

Acquiring in this manner has many benefits:

- The whole becomes greater than the sum of the parts.
- You increase the resale value of what you own, should you ever decide to sell.
- You and anyone else who views your collection is able to understand and appreciate it on many levels in addition to the visual.

- You become the expert, you learn the dollar values better than others, you learn how to buy the best art at the right prices.
- If you really do a great job, you set the standards and determine trends and patterns for your fellow collectors.

These are goals that every collector can set and accomplish. Not a lot of effort is involved and what's more, once you learn the principles, collecting becomes fun, easy and rewarding. In fact, you'll have difficulty understanding how anyone can do their buying in any other way.

What you're about to read is a recipe for successful collecting that you can go as far with as you feel comfortable going. Keep in mind that you don't have to become one of the world's great collectors or spend all your time obsessing about details. Remember that you're the boss and that when something doesn't feel right, you don't have to do it.

Pose the Problem and Map Out the Solution

A good art collection usually begins as little more than a curiosity. You see either a piece of art or a type of art that you like, something about it strikes you in a favorable manner and you decide that you want to know more. The key, at this early stage, is being able to generalize that curiosity and formulate it as a problem, the solution of which will be revealed through the art that you buy.

For example, you attend an art show and see a painting of a coastal scene that you really like. On the one hand, you can find out the price, decide that you can afford it, buy it, take it home, hang it and forget about it—this is the arbitrary, random, haphazard way to buy art. On the other hand, you can study the painting, reflect on how it impacts you and ask yourself questions such as the following:

- What about this painting attracts me?
- Does it depict an actual or a compositional coastline?
- Who is the artist and what is he like?
- Why did the artist paint this picture?
- What is the artist trying to accomplish?
- How does this painting make me feel?
- Would I like to own other paintings by this artist or would I rather own paintings that are similar in style, pallette, setting, size, subject matter or some other consideration?

Questions such as these help provide insight into what your preferences are, what attracts you to the art and what collecting direction you may wish follow. On the basis of your answers, for instance, you might find yourself leaning toward collecting the following types of art:

- New England coastal scenes.
- Landscapes and coastal scenes that show either sunrises or sunsets.

- Paintings by the artist who painted the coastal scene that you like.
- Landscapes and coastal scenes by artists who seek to preserve undeveloped areas or raise our awareness about the environment.
- Scenes with boats, people, buildings, animals and activities in them.
- Paintings that make you feel as though you're in wonderful faraway places.

As you continue to explore your situation and look at more and more pieces of art, you get a better and better idea of what goals you would like to accomplish for yourself through your buying. In an even broader sense, you may wish to expand that mission to include others as well by using your collection to make a point or teach a lesson. This is the moment at which you formulate and pose for yourself the specific problem that you will set out to answer, solve or satisfy through the art that you buy. For example:

- I want to own pictures that show how various artists paint sunrises over bodies of water.
- I love a particular artist's work and I want my collection to show how his style develops and evolves over time. I'll do this by buying one of his paintings per year.
- I love Cape Cod and want to own art that shows how various artists paint Cape Cod area landmarks.
- I am an environmentalist. I want to own paintings by artists who believe that we should be sensitive to our natural resources and who are able to convey those beliefs through their art.
- I want to buy seascapes that either cost less than $300 or are no larger than 10 by 12 inches.
- I want to own paintings that relax me and remind me of places that I've visited in my travels. I also want those paintings to relax friends, relatives and guests who visit me at my home.

The more precisely you state your problem, the more focused you become in your collecting. You define what you want your art to look like, who produces it, where you want to buy it, how much you want to pay for it, what underlying ideas or philosophies will either control your buying or be expressed through your buying, and so on. Once that's taken care of, the search is on.

Specialize

One of the keys to successful collecting is specialization. With all the millions upon millions of pieces of art available, trying to see and learn something about everything is a hopeless task. Stating your interests up front and precisely, as discussed above, is the first step; making a commitment to stay within those guidelines is the next.

Many people hesitate a little at this point due to a concern that they'll be missing out on something. This is entirely unfounded. Even with the most stringent set of constraints, the amount of art you'll have to choose from will astonish you. This may not seem true at the outset, but any experienced collector will tell you that once you begin to explore and get a feel for the territory, you'll be inundated with choices.

The way to miss out is exactly the opposite—by not specializing. With no in-depth understanding of what you're looking at, you can never hope to develop the abilities to make qualitative judgments, enjoy the full spectrum of what the art has to offer, determine which asking prices are fair and which aren't, keep track of the latest developments within the field, get to know the artists or their representatives in any meaningful sort of way, or learn from the experts.

Research

Many people who hear the word research immediately think of being imprisoned within a library cubicle, surrounded by stacks of books and endlessly seeking out obscure data bits that have little or nothing to do with the real world. This may be the definition of research for some, but it's far from the one that applies to the field of affordable art collecting. In fact, it's not even close. This kind of research is fun, exciting and you're the one in charge.

In many ways, research makes collecting a treasure hunt with art as the treasure—the closer you get to what you're looking for, the more motivated you become. Start with a work of art that you find visually appealing, add a little research, and you begin to understand and appreciate it on levels that may have little or nothing to do with the initial visual impact, but that can be equally as gratifying and engaging, if not more so. The phenomenon is like peeling the successive layers away from an onion until you finally reach the center.

The two basic types of research that you engage in in art collecting are "background" and "specific." Background research provides the foundation and the framework from which you operate. In other words, once you know the history behind the art you like, what types of artists produce it, how to locate it, who sells it, under what circumstances it is sold, what the average costs are and who the experts are, you can maximize the amount of art that you have to choose from.

Specific research comes into play after you have used background research to see a variety of art and have reached the point of seriously considering which individual pieces you want to own. Especially when you find yourself liking more than you can afford to buy or liking several pieces equally well but only wanting to buy one, specific research becomes the most effective way to narrow the field and select the finalists. By taking each piece and evaluating it in terms of who the artist is, what he has accomplished, what he stands for, what the art represents, how well it satisfies your collecting criteria, how much it costs, why it is priced the way it is, and so on, you are able to make informed final selections rather than random ones.

Here are several tips on how to perform effective research:

- Find out which are the best books, catalogues, videos and other materials to use to learn about the art that you like.
- Find out how experts assemble and evaluate data in your chosen area and what the most important characteristics of any work of art are.
- Whenever you have an opportunity to learn, take advantage of it.
- In a new field or one with little or no formal collecting or research structure, get your information from personal interviews with knowledgeable people and, whenever possible, either write down, video tape, or record what you learn. This type of information can become the raw material for future collectors as well as for any books, catalogues and other materials that may eventually be published.

Document

Every time you buy a work of art, the best procedure is to assemble complete information about it as soon as possible. In addition to getting a receipt that fully describes the art, ask the seller about books, catalogues, newspapers or magazines that contain relevant articles or entries. Written statements from the artist and other informed experts are especially good to have, so ask for them whenever possible. When all you can get is verbal information, write it down yourself and save it. Also include a good clear photograph of the art (you can do this yourself) and, when necessary, a condition report and a guarantee of authenticity from either the seller or a qualified expert. Save everything in file folders or notebooks and never alter any documents or throw them away.

Good documentation serves several purposes. On the personal level, you can use it to educate yourself as well as others about your art. The more you know about what you're looking at, the more you're able to appreciate it beyond the visual. On the business level, you can always look back and see when you bought a particular piece, who you bought it from and how much you paid for it. The larger your collection becomes and the more time passes, the more important this information becomes as a ready reference resource.

Good documentation also informs your descendents about the value and significance of what you've assembled. All too many times, inheritors have no idea what they've inherited because collectors have mistakenly assumed that family members know as much as they. This often becomes highly problematic, especially in dollars and cents terms, if or when descendents decide or are forced to sell.

What repeatedly happens is that uninformed family members sell whatever they don't want to outside dealers or at garage or yard sales for pennies on the dollar—and that's assuming they don't simply give or throw it away. One important thing to remember whenever significant amounts of money are involved is to have your collection appraised every two or three years, both for insurance and estate purposes. And don't forget to include full instructions on what to do and who to contact should anything happen to you and the art has to be sold.

Get Involved

Research, document and save what's necessary to save. Do a good comprehensive job and you'll find yourself immersed in your chosen area of collecting to a degree that few casual buyers ever experience. By getting involved, your art world adventures can become as satisfying as a love affair. You learn more and more about the objects of your desire all the time and each new experience allows you a deeper and more profound connection with the art and the artists who create it.

Investment considerations fade into the background. Fame of the artists or trendiness of the art have no meaning anymore. What your boss or your friends think makes no difference. You are in the process of surrounding yourself with the things you really love and that's what counts. All accomplished collectors will tell you that this is what happens to them as their collecting progresses.

Here are some activities that dedicated, thorough and involved collectors find themselves participating in:

- Trying their own hands at creating the art that they collect.
- Getting to know the artists, experts, program heads and other art people that they come into contact with on a less formal basis.
- Supporting the charities, philosophies, organizations and causes that the artists whose work they collect either support or are part of.
- Doing community service work related to their collecting.
- Sharing their collections with members of their communities, both young and old.
- Watching the artists create their art and learning about how they do it.
- Helping artists whose work they believe in so that more time can be spent creating art and less time has to be spent trying to survive from one day to the next.

When you find yourself doing these sorts of things, you can consider yourself a total collector. Owning fine art is far more than a money, status, fashion or trend issue. It is allowing these objects to become a part of your life and an essential aspect of your existence.

Be Complete

A superior collection explores every aspect of the problem that the collector has initially proposed. Not only is his curiosity satisfied, but so is the curiosity of others who attempt to understand what his collection is all about. Each piece of art becomes like a piece of a puzzle—when taken as a whole, they represent an entity that is something more than the sum of the parts. Together, they illustrate or prove what the collector has set out to accomplish.

Suppose, for example, that a collector is interested in seeing how various mentally, psychologically and physically challenged individuals portray themselves in their art. He decides to confine his selection to either self-portraits or works of art in which the artists place themselves within the compositions. He also decides to accompany each piece of art with some sort of explanation, preferably from the artist, of what that portrayal represents.

In order for this collection to work as the collector has outlined it, the art must emanate from all segments of the mentally, physically and psychologically challenged communities. If he purchases art from all but the visually impaired, for instance, he will have a hole in his collection—it will not be complete.

Here are the types of questions that serious collectors continually ask themselves in the course of assembling their collections:

- Can anyone question any aspect of my collection?
- Do I adequately solve the problem that I've posed for myself?
- Is my collection missing anything?
- Am I weak in a certain area?
- Do I have too much of one thing and not enough of another?

Keep considerations such as these in mind as you collect and you'll maintain the evenness and balance characteristic of any quality collection. You may find yourself selling off certain pieces along the way or buying more in areas that you thought you had adequately covered. You might even modify your goals, but that's all part of the process. A collection is a continually evolving entity.

Organize

Organizing your collection is important for several reasons. First, it allows others to understand what you're doing. Second, you can keep track of what you've purchased and solve any problems or fill any holes with minimal effort. Third, it provides you with continual insight into how and why you buy what you do. No set rules for organizing exist; you are the one who decides how you want to present what you've collected.

Before you begin organizing, look around and see how other collections are organized. Visit museums and note how they present their permanent collections as well as their temporary exhibits and traveling shows. The latter two are especially good to study because they often contain fewer pieces, and the text, explanations and order of the individual pieces are easier to understand. Historical societies, local museums, libraries and corporations that have historical or business-related displays are also good places to get ideas for organizing.

Here are some of the more common ways that collectors organize their collections:

- By time period.
- By subject matter.
- By region.
- By artist.
- By style.
- By nationality or ethnic group.

Ask yourself questions such as the following in order to best organize what you collect:

- What similarities or differences are apparent in my art?
- Can I arrange pieces in a way that tells a story?
- Is any sort of evolutionary process apparent in my art?
- What types of changes are consistently evident from one piece to the next?
- How can I use my organization to teach other people about me or my collection?

Play around with different ways of looking at and arranging your art. Many times, the final way you chose to present it does not become apparent until you're well along in your collecting. Keeping organizational considerations at the forefront of your buying, however, prevents you from losing your focus and lapsing into random, arbitrary and haphazard accumulating.

Believe in Yourself

No matter what anybody says, buy what you want to buy and collect what you want to collect. Far too many people deny their own preferences, compromise their tastes, follow the crowd and end up with dull, boring collections. One person's art looks just like the next's as they try far harder to be correct than they do to collect. This type of buying behavior is all too often based on fear—fear of being rejected, ridiculed, or wasting money.

In a way, these fears are justified. By being true to yourself and following your own inner urges, you lay yourself out for all to see, through the art that you end up owning. That art tells outsiders revealing things about you like what you believe in, what your philosophies are, who you like, and how your mind works. And revealing yourself like this can be scary.

But the positive consequences of honest collecting far outweigh the negatives. For one thing, you end up owning what you really love and not art that you feel lukewarm about just because someone else told you to buy it.

You call the shots, you direct the show, you have total freedom and control over your actions—conditions that are not easy to come by in this day and age. The ultimate secret to forming a gratifying and successful collection is this: Be true to yourself and never be afraid. Now get out there and have some fun!

Artful Collections

Items carved or painted with initials, drawings, sayings or messages. These might include pieces of old sidewalk, tree bark, old hardened fungus, or public signs or advertisements covered with graffiti.

Your own art. The above directives apply to your art as well as to anyone else's. Maybe you've always had a secret desire to become an artist. Even if you've never created a single piece of art in your life, give it a serious try and don't give up. You could be surprised at the results and, moneywise, nothing's more affordable.

Things that you think look like art. Perhaps you've seen an old bent piece of metal by the side of a road or a driftwood branch washed up on a beach that looked as though artists could have created them. Put enough of these items together and people will understand how you see beauty in the discards of others.

Rejects. Your collection would consist of artists' mistakes, ideas that didn't work, or art that got damaged. You might have a bit of trouble saving some of these disasters from the trash pile, but then again, make a good case for yourself and you could also experience a great deal of success.

Art by non-artists. Have your friends, co-workers, relatives, and anyone else whose acquaintanceship means something to you contribute their creative efforts—however modest those may be.

Appendices

1

General Art Trade Publications

Art Calendar
25638 Frenchtown Road
Westover, MD 21871
410-651-9150

Artweek
12 South First St., Suite 520
San Jose, CA 95113
408-279-2293

American Artist
1515 Broadway
New York, NY 10036
212-764-7300

Artnews
48 West 38th Street
New York, NY 10018
212-398-1690

Dialogue: Arts in the Midwest
9 Buttles Avenue, #318
Columbus, OH 43215
614-621-3704

Art in America
980 Madison Avenue
New York, NY 10021
212-734-9797

Artist's Magazine
1507 Dana Avenue
Cincinnati, OH 45207
513-531-2222

Art New England
353 Washington Street
Brighton, MA 02135
617-782-3008

Art Papers
1083 Austin Avenue, Room 206
Atlanta, GA 30307
404-588-1837

New Art Examiner
20 West Hubbard, Suite 2W
Chicago, IL 60610
312-836-0330

This list is by no means complete, but it's more than enough to get you started. Numerous smaller local and regional newspapers and magazines also exist. One good way to find out about them is to phone the publications listed above and ask who serves the specific geographical areas that you're concerned about. Most will tell you, but some may be too busy or not have the information right at their fingertips. They all exchange publications with each other, however, and are well informed about who's doing what.

2

State and Regional Arts Agencies and Organizations

If you want the absolute most up-to-date listings, the National Endowment for the Arts updates this list several times per year and will send it to you at no charge. Write them at 1100 Pennsylvania Ave. NW, Washington, DC 20506-0001, or call 202-682-5400.

If you want information about art-related activities within specific counties, cities, regions of states or other smaller geographical areas, contact the appropriate state organizations and ask for the names, addresses and phone numbers of arts councils or commissions within those areas.

State Organizations

Alabama State Council on the Arts
One Dexter Avenue
Montgomery, Alabama 36130
(205) 242-4076
FAX: (205) 240-3269

Alaska State Council on the Arts
411 West 4th Avenue, Suite 1E
Anchorage, Alaska 99501-2343
(907) 279-1558
FAX: (907) 279-4330

Arizona Commission on the Arts
417 West Roosevelt
Phoenix, Arizona 85003
(602) 255-5882 or 255-5884
FAX: (602) 256-0282

Arkansas Arts Council
1500 Tower Building
323 Center Street
Little Rock, Arkansas 72201
(501) 324-9766
FAX: (501) 324-9154

California Arts Council
2411 Alhambra Boulevard
Sacramento, California 95817
(916) 227-2550
FAX: (916) 227-2628

Colorado Council on the Arts
750 Pennsylvania Street
Denver, Colorado 80203-3699
(303) 894-2617
FAX: (303) 894-2615

Connecticut Commission on the Arts
227 Lawrence Street
Hartford, Connecticut 06106
(203) 566-4770
FAX: (203) 566-6462

Delaware Division of the Arts
State Office Building
820 North French Street
Wilmington, Delaware 19899-8911
(302) 577-3540
FAX: (302) 577-3862

District of Columbia Commission on the Arts & Humanities
410 8th Street, NW
Washington, DC 20004
(202) 724-5613 or 727-9332
FAX: (202) 727-4135

Division of Cultural Affairs Florida Department of State
The Capitol
Tallahassee, Florida 32399-0250
(904) 487-2980
FAX: (904) 922-5259

Georgia Council for the Arts
530 Means Street, NW, Suite 115
Atlanta, Georgia 30318
(404) 651-7920
FAX: (404) 651-7922

(Hawaii) State Foundation on Culture & the Arts
335 Merchant Street, Room 202
Honolulu, Hawaii 96813
(808) 586-0300
FAX: (808) 586-0308

Idaho Commission on the Arts
304 West State Street
Boise, Idaho 83720
(208) 334-2119
FAX: (208) 334-2488

Illinois Arts Council
State of Illinois Center
100 West Randolph, Suite 10-500
Chicago, Illinois 60601
(312) 814-6750
FAX: (312) 814-1471

Indiana Arts Commission
402 West Washington Street, Room 72
Indianapolis, Indiana 46204-2741
(317) 232-1268
FAX: (317) 232-5595

Iowa Arts Council
600 East Locust
State Capitol Complex
Des Moines, Iowa 50319
(515) 281-4013
(515) 281-7471
FAX: (515) 242-6498

Kansas Arts Commission
Jayhawk Towers
700 Jackson, Suite 1004
Topeka, Kansas 66603
(913) 296-3335
FAX: (913) 296-4989

Kentucky Arts Council
31 Fountain Place
Frankfort, Kentucky 40601
(502) 564-3757
FAX: (502) 564-2839

Division of the Arts
Louisiana Department of Culture, Recreation, & Tourism
1051 North 3rd Street, P.O. Box 44247
Baton Rouge, Louisiana 70804
(504) 342-8180
FAX: (504) 342-3207

Maine Arts Commission
55 Capitol Street
State House Station 25
Augusta, Maine 04333
(207) 287-2724
FAX: (207) 287-2335

Maryland State Arts Council
601 North Howard Street, 1st Floor
Baltimore, Maryland 21201
(410) 333-8232
FAX: (410) 333-1062

Massachusetts Cultural Council
80 Boylston Street
The Little Building, 10th Floor
Boston, Massachusetts 02116
(617) 727-3668
FAX: (617) 727-0044

Michigan Council for Arts and Cultural Affairs
1200 6th Street, Executive Plaza
Detroit, Michigan 48226
(313) 256-2692
FAX: (313) 256-3781

Minnesota State Arts Board
432 Summit Avenue
St. Paul, Minnesota 55102
(612) 297-2603
(800) 652-9747—Toll Free Within MN
FAX: (612) 297-4304

Mississippi Arts Commission
239 North Lamar Street, Second Floor
Jackson, Mississippi 39201
(601) 359-6030 or 359-6040
FAX: (601) 359-6008

Missouri State Council on the Arts
Wainwright Office Complex
111 North Seventh Street, Suite 105
St. Louis, Missouri 63101
(314) 340-6845
FAX: (314) 340-7215

Montana Arts Council
316 North Park Avenue
Room 252
Helena, Montana 59620
(406) 444-6430
FAX: (406) 444-6548

Nebraska Arts Council
The Joslyn Castle Carriage House
3838 Davenport Street
Omaha, Nebraska 68131-2329
(402) 595-2122
FAX: (402) 595-2334

Nevada State Council on the Arts
329 Flint Street
Reno, Nevada 89501
(702) 688-1225
FAX: (702) 688-1110

New Hampshire State Council on the Arts
Phenix Hall
40 North Main Street
Concord, New Hampshire 03301
(603) 271-2789
FAX: (603) 271-2361

New Jersey State Council on the Arts
4 North Broad Street
Trenton, New Jersey 08625
(609) 292-6130
FAX: (609) 989-1440

New Mexico Arts Division
228 East Palace Avenue
Santa Fe, New Mexico 87501
(505) 827-6490
FAX: (505) 827-7308

New York State Council on the Arts
915 Broadway
New York, New York 10010
(212) 387-7000
FAX: (212) 387-7164

North Carolina Arts Council
Department of Cultural Resources
Raleigh, North Carolina 27601-2807
(919) 733-2821
FAX: (919) 733-4834

North Dakota Council on the Arts
Black Building, Suite 606
118 Broadway
Fargo, North Dakota 58102
(701) 239-7150
FAX: (701) 239-7153

Ohio Arts Council
727 East Main Street
Columbus, Ohio 43205
(614) 466-2613
FAX: (614) 466-4494

State Arts Council of Oklahoma
Jim Thorpe Building, Room 640
2101 North Lincoln Boulevard
Oklahoma City, Oklahoma 73105
(405) 521-2931
FAX: (405) 521-6418

Oregon Arts Commission
550 Airport Road, SE
Salem, Oregon 97310
(503) 378-3625
FAX: (503) 373-7789

Commonwealth of Pennsylvania Council on the Arts
Finance Building, Room 216
Harrisburg, Pennsylvania 17120
(717) 787-6883
FAX: (717) 783-2538

Rhode Island State Council on the Arts
95 Cedar Street, Suite 103
Providence, Rhode Island 02903
(401) 277-3880
FAX: (401) 521-1351

South Carolina Arts Commission
1800 Gervais Street
Columbia, South Carolina 29201
(803) 734-8696
FAX: (803) 734-8526

South Dakota Arts Council
230 South Phillips Avenue, Suite 204
Sioux Falls, South Dakota 57102-0720
(605) 339-6646
FAX: (605) 332-7965

Tennessee Arts Commission
320 Sixth Avenue, North, Suite 100
Nashville, Tennessee 37243-0780
(615) 741-1701 (Switchboard)
(615) 741-6395 (Office)
FAX: (615) 741-8559

Texas Commission on the Arts
P.O. Box 13406, Capitol Station
Austin, Texas 78711
(512) 463-5535
FAX: (512) 475-2699

Utah Arts Council
617 East South Temple Street
Salt Lake City, Utah 84102
(801) 533-5895 or 533-5896
FAX: (801) 533-6196

Vermont Council on the Arts
136 State Street
Montpelier, Vermont 05633-6001
(802) 828-3291
FAX: (802) 828-3233

Virginia Commission for the Arts
223 Governor Street
Richmond, Virginia 23219
(804) 225-3132
FAX: (804) 225-4327

Washington State Arts Commission
234 East 8th Avenue
P.O. Box 42675
Olympia, Washington 98504-2675
(206) 753-3860
FAX: (206) 586-5351

Arts & Humanities Section
West Virginia Division of Culture & History
Capitol Complex
Charleston, West Virginia 25305
(304) 558-0220
FAX: (304) 558-2779

Wisconsin Arts Board
101 East Wilson Street, 1st floor
Madison, Wisconsin 53702
(608) 266-0190
FAX: (608) 267-0380

Wyoming Arts Council
2320 Capitol Avenue
Cheyenne, Wyoming 82002
(307) 777-7742
FAX: (307) 777-5499

Regional Organizations

Arts Midwest
Hennepin Center for the Arts
528 Hennepin Avenue, Suite 310
Minneapolis, Minnesota 55403
(612) 341-0755
FAX: (612) 341-0902
(Illinois, Indiana, Iowa, Michigan, Minnesota, North Dakota, Ohio, South Dakota, Wisconsin)

Mid-America Arts Alliance
912 Baltimore Avenue, Suite 700
Kansas City, Missouri 64105
(816) 421-1388
FAX: (816) 421-3918
(Arkansas, Kansas, Missouri, Nebraska, Oklahoma, Texas)

Mid Atlantic Arts Foundation
11 East Chase Street, Suite 2-A
Baltimore, Maryland 21202
(410) 539-6659
FAX: (410) 837-5517
(Delaware, District of Columbia, Maryland, New Jersey, New York, Pennsylvania, Virginia, Virgin Islands, West Virginia)

New England Foundation for the Arts
678 Massachusetts Avenue
Cambridge, Massachusetts 02139
(617) 492-2914
FAX: (617) 876-0702
(Connecticut, Maine, Massachusetts, New Hampshire, Rhode Island, Vermont)

Southern Arts Federation
181 14th Street, NE, Suite 400
Atlanta, Georgia 30309
(404) 874-7244
FAX: (404) 873-2148
(Alabama, Florida, Georgia, Kentucky, Louisiana, Mississippi, North Carolina, South Carolina, Tennessee)

Western States Arts Federation
236 Montezuma Avenue
Santa Fe, New Mexico 87501
(505) 988-1166
FAX: (505) 982-9307
(Alaska, Arizona, California, Colorado, Idaho, Montana, Nevada, New Mexico, Oregon, Utah, Washington, Wyoming)

3

Commercial Art Trade Publications & Organizations

Architectural Drawings

American Institute of Architects
1735 York Avenue NW
Washington, DC 20006
202-626-7300

Architectural Digest
5900 Wilshire Boulevard
Los Angeles, CA 90036
213-965-3700

Unique Homes
801 Second Avenue
New York, NY 10017
212-503-3430

Commercial Illustration

Society of Illustrators
128 East 63rd Street
New York, NY 10021
212-838-2560

Industrial Design

Industrial Designers Society of America
1142 Walker Road, Suite E
Great Falls, VA 22066
703-759-0100

ID: Industrial Design Magazine
250 West 57th Street
New York, NY 10107
212-956-0535

Graphic Design

American Institute of Graphic Arts
1059 Third Avenue
New York, NY 10021
212-752-0813

Communication Arts
410 Sherman Avenue
Palo Alto, CA 94306
415-326-6040

Graphic Design
120 East 56th Street
New York, NY 10022
212-759-8813

Cartoon Art

Association of American Editorial Cartoonists
4101 Lake Boone Trail, Suite 201
Raleigh, NC 27607
919-787-5181

National Cartoonists Society
157 West 57th Street, Suite 904
New York, NY 10019
212-333-7606

Fashion Illustration

Women's Wear Daily
7 West 34th Street
New York, NY 10001
212-630-3520

Information about these and numerous other organizations and publications related to commercial as well as fine art can be found in *The American Art Directory*. College, university and public library art departments often shelve it in their reference section.

Index